# Romantic Revisions in Novels from the Americas

## Comparative Cultural Studies
## Steven Tötösy de Zepetnek, Series Editor

The Purdue University Press monograph series of Books in Comparative Cultural Studies publishes single-authored and thematic collected volumes of new scholarship. Manuscripts are invited for publication in the series in fields of the study of culture, literature, the arts, media studies, communication studies, the history of ideas, etc., and related disciplines of the humanities and social sciences to the series editor via e-mail at <clcweb@purdue.edu>. Comparative cultural studies is a contextual approach in the study of culture in a global and intercultural context and work with a plurality of methods and approaches; the theoretical and methodological framework of comparative cultural studies is built on tenets borrowed from the disciplines of cultural studies and comparative literature and from a range of thought including literary and culture theory, (radical) constructivism, communication theories, and systems theories; in comparative cultural studies focus is on theory and method as well as application. For a detailed description of the aims and scope of the series including the style guide of the series link to <http://docs.lib.purdue.edu/clcweblibrary/seriespurdueccs>. Manuscripts submitted to the series are peer reviewed followed by the usual standards of editing, copy editing, marketing, and distribution. The series is affiliated with *CLCWeb: Comparative Literature and Culture* (ISSN 1481-4374), the peer-reviewed, full-text, and open-access quarterly published by Purdue University Press at <http://docs.lib.purdue.edu/clcweb>.

### Volumes in the Purdue series of Books in Comparative Cultural Studies include <http://www.thepress.purdue.edu/series/comparative-cultural-studies>

Lauren Rule Maxwell, *Romantic Revisions in Novels from the Americas*
Liisa Steinby, *Kundera and Modernity*
*Text and Image in Modern European Culture*, Ed. Natasha Grigorian, Thomas Baldwin, and Margaret Rigaud-Drayton
Sheng-mei Ma, *Asian Diaspora and East-West Modernity*
Irene Marques, *Transnational Discourses on Class, Gender, and Cultural Identity*
*Comparative Hungarian Cultural Studies*, Ed. Steven Tötösy de Zepetnek and Louise O. Vasvári
Hui Zou, *A Jesuit Garden in Beijing and Early Modern Chinese Culture*
Yi Zheng, *From Burke and Wordsworth to the Modern Sublime in Chinese Literature*
Agata Anna Lisiak, *Urban Cultures in (Post)Colonial Central Europe*
*Representing Humanity in an Age of Terror*, Ed. Sophia A. McClennen and Henry James Morello
Michael Goddard, *Gombrowicz, Polish Modernism, and the Subversion of Form*
*Shakespeare in Hollywood, Asia, and Cyberspace,* Ed. Alexander C.Y. Huang and Charles S. Ross
*Gustav Shpet's Contribution to Philosophy and Cultural Theory*, Ed. Galin Tihanov
*Comparative Central European Holocaust Studies*, Ed. Louise O. Vasvári and Steven Tötösy de Zepetnek
Marko Juvan, *History and Poetics of Intertextuality*
Thomas O. Beebee, *Nation and Region in Modern American and European Fiction*
Paolo Bartoloni, *On the Cultures of Exile, Translation, and Writing*
Justyna Sempruch, *Fantasies of Gender and the Witch in Feminist Theory and Literature*
Kimberly Chabot Davis, *Postmodern Texts and Emotional Audiences*
Philippe Codde, *The Jewish American Novel*
Deborah Streifford Reisinger, *Crime and Media in Contemporary France*
*Imre Kertész and Holocaust Literature,* Ed. Louise O. Vasvári and Steven Tötösy de Zepetnek
Camilla Fojas, *Cosmopolitanism in the Americas*

# Romantic Revisions in Novels from the Americas

Lauren Rule Maxwell

Purdue University Press
West Lafayette, Indiana

Printed in the United States of America.

Library of Congress Cataloging-in-Publication Data

Maxwell, Lauren Rule.

Romantic Revisions in Novels from the Americas / by Lauren Rule Maxwell.

p. cm. -- (Comparative cultural studies; 30)

Includes bibliographical references and index.

ISBN 978-1-55753-641-9 (pbk. : alk. paper) -- ISBN 978-1-61249-261-2 (epdf) -- ISBN 978-1-61249-262-9 (epub) 1. American fiction--20th century--History and criticism. 2. Romanticism--Influence. I. Title.

PS379.M317 2013

813'.509--dc23

2012039049

*For MJ, my faithful reader,*
*and in loving memory of my dad, who taught me so much*

# Contents

## Acknowledgments

While writing this book, I have been inspired by and supported by many people. I would like to thank those who challenged and guided me as I began developing this project: Deborah Elise White, Deepika Bahri, Walter Kalaidjian, Mark McWatt, and Martine Watson Brownley. I am especially indebted to my mentor and advisor, Martine Watson Brownley, who has given so much to me and to this project. I am a better scholar, a better writer, and a better teacher because she took me under her wing. I would also like to thank all of the fellows and staff members at the Bill and Carol Fox Center for Humanistic Inquiry, the Emory University Department of English faculty and staff members, those who assisted me at the Robert W. Woodruff Library and the Daniel Library, and the graduate students who helped me make my work better. My colleagues in the English Department at The Citadel deserve many thanks for providing me with advice and encouragement as I made final revisions. I also thank the editor of the Purdue University Press monograph series of Books in Comparative Cultural Studies, Steven Tötösy de Zepetnek, for making this book a reality. Last but not least, my family and friends have been incredibly supportive of this project; I thank them for their enthusiasm and love.

I also want to thank the departments, centers, and societies that have supported my research: the Emory University Department of English, the Emory Bill and Carol Fox Center for Humanistic Inquiry, the Emory Department of Women's Studies, the University of the West Indies at Cave Hill, the Harry Ransom Humanities Research Center, the Hemingway Society, the F. Scott Fitzgerald Society, the Margaret Atwood Society, and The Citadel Foundation.

Parts of chapter 2 and chapter 4 were published in different forms in the journals *Modern Fiction Studies* and *The F. Scott Fitzgerald Review*, respectively. I am grateful to the editors of both of them for the permission to reprint those essays here.

# Introduction

This study developed from my desire to understand why twentieth-century American novels display a preoccupation with British Romantic poetry and its legacy. In my examination of a diverse group of such novels from former British colonies across the Americas, I have found that each work has crucial scenes that invoke Romantic poetry for a sociopolitical critique of burgeoning US empire. *Romantic Revisions* traces a transatlantic circulation of Romantic poetics, suggesting that its conceptualization of landscape allows authors to negotiate imperial politics of location by investigating the relationship between a subject's place and his or her position of power. Many postcolonial critics have dismissed Romantic poetry as a mode of resistance, but this study suggests that, on the contrary, it has provided contemporary writers with a means of more clearly charting the literary and cultural legacies of British imperialism in the New World.

In *Romantic Revisions* I examine five twentieth-century novels from former British colonies across the Americas and consider why these novels demonstrate a significant engagement with British Romantic poetry. These novels are Jamaica Kincaid's *Lucy* (1990), Margaret Atwood's *The Handmaid's Tale* (1985), Cormac McCarthy's *Blood Meridian* (1985), F. Scott Fitzgerald's *The Great Gatsby* (1925), and Wilson Harris's *Palace of the Peacock* (1960)—novels written by a diverse range of novelists in very different geographical, historical, and social contexts. Nevertheless, these novels all return to Romantic poetry as they grapple with the legacy of British colonialism within their respective American frames of reference. Although these novels are set in a variety of locations and timeframes, they all share a preoccupation with British colonial influence that becomes manifest in their Romantic intertexts. As Ian Smith has argued, "literature . . . particularly by way of intertextuality, creates opportunities for the *de-scribing* of empire, [for] the . . . dismantling [of] colonial regimes of power in language" (803). I argue that novelists from different locations in the Americas participate in this project by using intertexts with British Romantic poetry to critique and highlight the ways in which British imperialism has taken root in the American colonies. The term "de-scribing" not only represents the act of conveying to a reader what empire is like in terms that describe it, but also focuses on the use of language itself to draw attention to the ways that literature, in this case Romantic poetry, has served to inscribe colonial subjects within their proper "places" in imperial landscapes. In a sense, the de-scription process aims to undo this inscription by bringing the impression these texts make on colonial societies into greater relief.

In *De-Scribing Empire: Post-Colonialism and Textuality*, Chris Tiffin and Alan Lawson assert that considering how language has underwritten the colonial enterprise is a necessary task, because colonialism is essentially "an operation of discourse, and as an operation of discourse it interpellates colonial subjects by incorporating them into a system of representation." Although "imperial relations may have been established initially by guns, guile, and disease," they explain, these relations "were maintained in their interpellative phase largely by textuality, both institutionally . . . and informally" (3). Recent studies have supported the claim that language indeed shapes our thoughts—that the words we use affect our "private mental lives" (Begley 31). By tracing the circulation of Romantic poetics, I hope to show that the language of Romantic poetry has shaped and continues to shape how Americans see themselves in relation to the world around them.

The intertexts I analyze in the following chapters show how the words of the British Romantic poets have shaped the worldview of readers and encouraged them to see the British Empire and the colonies themselves from a particular point of view. As Tiffin and Lawson write, the "first stage of de-scribing empire is to analyse where and how our view of things is inflected (or infected) by colonialism and its constituent elements of racism, over-categorization, and deferral to the centre" (9). Some of the poems, like the daffodil lyric that Kincaid refers to throughout *Lucy*, are related conceptually to colonization and were used by colonial educators to reinforce the authority (and superiority) of the British mainland. But others, such as Keats's "The Eve of St. Agnes," have led generations of readers to question imperial dominion and the materialism of its capital enterprise. As one might suspect, the novelists' engagements with British Romanticism vary with the relationships of the poems themselves to the British Empire. What I investigate is why all of these different novels return at key moments to British Romantic poetry in order to depict distinctly postcolonial worldviews.

Building on the work of postcolonial critics, *Romantic Revisions* provides new insight into the poetics and politics of revision by focusing on the geographical region of the Americas. Scholars who specialize in Caribbean literature have noted the particular importance of the figure of Caliban seen, for example, in Aime Césaire's *A Tempest,* for Caribbean revisions. This study, whose broad range spans from the US to Canada to the Caribbean to South America, demonstrates that British Romantic poetry that has become central to another counterdiscourse operating across the Americas. Helen Gilbert and Joanne Tompkins have described canonical counterdiscourse as "a process whereby the post-colonial writer unveils and dismantles the basic assumptions of a specific canonical text by developing a 'counter' text that preserves many of the identifying signifiers of the original while altering, often allegorically, its structures of power" (16). I locate where these novels invoke counterdiscourse and examine those intertexts. By analyzing American writers' Romantic intertexts, I make the claim that British Romantic poetry—with its revolution of poetic form and remapping of landscape as a site of political reflection—provides these authors with a common language with which they can scrutinize institutions of power that were inscribed during British colonialism. As David Damrosch has pointed out, "the 'Big Six' British Romantic poets" have provided a starting point for authors to reshape the canon, "both within national literatures and across them," through a "*countercanon*" and even a "*shadow canon*" (46, 45). American writers' engagement with Romantic poetry expands our conception of the traditional literary canon and creates what Caribbean author and theorist Edouard Glissant calls "cross-cultural poetics" or a "poetics of relation," which reflects shifting politics of location in transatlantic frames of reference.

In *Romantic Revisions* I trace these shifting politics of location through the lens of comparative cultural studies, which fosters an investigation of related texts through a variety of disciplines—including literature, sociology, psychology, history, economics, and political science—across both time and geographical space. The comparative cultural studies framework highlights instances of intertextuality as opportunities for examining what types of knowledge are exchanged during colonialism and how those exchanges inflect the worldviews of both colonizers and those who are colonized. In such a framework, intertexts reveal how words themselves influence the realities of colonialism and why those words remain important as definitive markers of the colonial legacies that shape postcolonial societies. This study suggests that those effects are lasting—that even in former colonies, the force of those words remains. As I show in the epilogue, these effects are seen not only in literature, but also in other artistic media, such as film and music. *Romantic Revisions* asks why these disparate American artists return to Romantic poetry and how their reframing of it affects postcolonial identity and representation.

Because of the comparative nature of this study—comparative in terms of historical periods, physical location, genre, and dialects of the English language—*Romantic Revisions* provides a meaningful addition to the Purdue University Press monograph series of Books in Comparative Cultural Studies. The comparative cultural study in *Romantic Revisions* complements existing titles in the series, such as Yi Zheng's *From Burke and Wordsworth to the Modern Sublime in Chinese Literature*, which examines analogous transformations of aesthetics of the sublime in English Romanticism and the New Poetry Movement in twentieth-century China. *Romantic Revisions* also returns to the British Romantics, but it does so in order to trace their influence in a very different part of the world—the Americas. In focusing on the correspondences between British Romantic poetry and twentieth-century novels from across the Americas, *Romantic Revisions* shows how a wide range of American writers use Romantic poetics to highlight the continued legacy of British imperialism. These intertexts reveal what can be gained from reading not only the literature but also the postcolonial condition from a comparative cultural studies framework (on comparative cultural studies see Tötösy de Zepetnek).

To illustrate how colonial heritage affects the ways in which Americans imagine themselves and the world around them, the novels examined in this study include crucial scenes that invoke Romantic poetics of landscape. These poetics allow the writers to explore how British colonial history inflects politics relating to place. In my readings of these novels, I discuss how their authors revisit British Romantic poetry to conceptualize and negotiate postcolonial identities set in new American landscapes. Depending on the author's specific historical and social location, this engagement with Romantic poetry varies. For example, while Kincaid responds to Wordsworth's oeuvre to show how poetic genius grows out of—and in spite of—a colonial education, Fitzgerald evokes the feast scene of "The Eve of St. Agnes" to critique the excesses of US materialism fashioned on British models. By analyzing the ways in which such a diverse range of American novelists has adapted Romantic poetics for their own sociopolitical commentaries, I argue that this body of transnational fiction writing offers a decisive critique of the legacy of British colonialism in postcolonial America and more generally reconceptualizes our understanding of America itself.

Some scholars have balked at including the United States under the rubric of "postcolonial" nations despite its status as a former colony. Gilbert and Tompkins are typical: "We do not consider the United States, also once a British colony, as post-colonial because the political and military might that the United States wields in its role as global 'superpower' has long since severed its connections with the historical and cultural marginality that other former colonies share" (7). This study, however, shows what can be gained from conceptualizing the US as a postcolonial nation—especially if the US wields, as many postcolonial thinkers suggest, neoimperialistic power. Frantz Fanon, for example, claims that "two centuries ago, a former European colony decided to catch up with Europe. It succeeded so well that the United States of America became a monster, in which the taints, the sickness, and the inhumanity of Europe have grown to appalling dimensions" (*Wretched* 313). If the US has, in fact, modeled itself after its imperial parent, its literatures should evidence the reapplication of hegemonic discourses from its colonial legacy as well as the figures of resistance that accompany them. Deepika Bahri has noted that "the conflation of postcoloniality with marginality has . . . led to a reluctance to envisage American . . . cultures as postcolonial, thus blinding us to the potential for illuminating lessons from the experience and cultural productions of these sites through scrupulous comparative analysis" (39). *Romantic Revisions* reveals that comparative analyses of US literature can illuminate the genealogy of language use that responds to and, in some cases, even contributes to imperial cultural production now associated with the US.

## Why British Romanticism?

Many postcolonial novels (within and outside the Americas) which deal with imperial legacy contain intertexts with British Romanticism. British Romantic poetry—because of its revolution of poetic theory and practice; its preoccupation with individualism, the ordinary, and the outcast; and its mappings of landscape as a site of reflection—has a complicated relationship to empire that postcolonial novelists explore and exploit with Romantic intertexts. Many would argue that all writers after the Romantics are influenced by them to some degree—after all, the Romantics were "the first artist-figures in the modern understanding of the word" (Middeke 6). The Romantic period's "improved printing and distribution methods [and] rapid increase in literacy," Atwood explains, "suddenly [made it] possible for writers to become instantly popular on a scale never before imagined, to become enormously celebrated for their work: to become larger than life" (*Negotiating* 51-52). The British Romantics' influence, however, carries even greater import for postcolonial novels from the Americas: Romantic poetics figure prominently in their overall work of de-scribing empire—of critiquing the ways in which the language of Romantic poetry was used to inscribe Americans within colonial landscapes. Why do postcolonial novels from the Americas demonstrate such a preoccupation with their Romantic legacy, and what is the importance of the Romantic intertexts to these novels? Looking at the historical, political, and cultural contexts of the Romantic period provides a starting point for addressing the first of these complicated questions.

The Romantic period, generally speaking, is important to postcolonial novelists who write in English in part because it gave rise to social and political transformations that indelibly marked modern civilization, such as the propagation of modern capitalism and modern imperialism. During the Romantic period, Britain underwent massive economic development and physical expansion through capitalist industrialization that accompanied the continuing acquisition and expansion of its free-trade empire. While Britain's economy transitioned from a basis in agriculture and commerce to that of large-scale industrial production, its imperial focus intensified and turned increasingly to the eastern hemisphere. As Tim Fulford and Peter Kitson explain in *Romanticism and Colonialism*, this "move from a protectionist colonial system, based upon mercantilist economic principles, to a free-trade empire with a political and moral agenda, proverbially described, after Kipling's poem, as 'the white man's burden'" made the Romantic period "a watershed in colonial history" (3). Alan Richardson and Sonia Hofkosh discuss the importance of the Romantic period to the Americas more specifically by detailing the extent of Britain's imperialist expansion in the region during this period:

> The half-century from 1780-1830, roughly corresponding with literary Romanticism as conventionally delimited, began in a mood of imperial crisis following the loss of the thirteen American colonies, the mismanagement of Bengal, and slave rebellions in the West Indies, but went on to witness the "massive expansion of British dominion, of techniques of governance and exploitation": by 1820 200 million people—over a quarter of the world population—would come under British domination. During this period . . . Canada was aggressively developed . . . and the Caribbean possessions (or "sugar islands") were augmented with the seizure of Trinidad and Tobago, St. Lucia, and British Guyana. These years were also marked by a wrenching national debate over slavery, the abolition of British involvement in the

> slave trade (1807) and the ending of slavery in the British colonies (1834), the development of imperialist and anti-imperialist ideologies on the part of British writers, and the emergence of "modern racist categories." (3-4)

Because this unprecedented expansion of the British Empire became associated with political, moralizing discourse, it is no surprise that the writers of the Romantic period were affected by this critical cultural debate and inflected their works with imperialist and anti-imperialist ideologies. Produced during the period when the British Empire underwent massive expansion and consolidation, the work of British Romantic poets and other writers of the time engaged in the "modern discourses tied to racism, evolution, progressivism, and industrial capitalism" that arose alongside and in response to this transitional moment (Makdisi, *Romantic Imperialism* 101). Richardson and Hofkosh argue that even poems such as those in the 1798 *Lyrical Ballads,* which may seem far removed from questions of imperialism, contain "lines on the Spanish 'discovery' and penetration of the Americas in 'The Foster-Mother's Tale,' the depictions of British colonial wars and their consequences in 'The Female Vagrant' and 'The Mad Mother,' [and] ethnographic exoticism [in] 'The Complaint of a Forsaken Indian Woman'"(1). As these examples suggest, present-day readers and writers who are interested in revisiting the histories of the British Empire in the Americas must return to Romantic writings as they trace the development of these discourses and their significance for today's society.

Contemporary literary critics and scholars from a variety of theoretical standpoints draw out the poems' contributions to these modern discourses as they characterize the imperialist or anti-imperialist leanings of the poets. For example, Richardson and Hofkosh suggest that British Romantic poetry is complicit with Britain's imperial project: "such mainstays of English Romantic tradition as the imagination, the sublime, the self-possessed individual, the notion of Englishness itself, are linked to the material and ideological operation of a burgeoning empire" (8). Marlon B. Ross concurs with this estimation, explaining that "romanticism grows out of the peculiar historical situation of Britain at the end of the eighteenth century: a situation in which the power of poetry, representing all forms of *belles letters*, is being questioned on so many fronts that poets are forced self-consciously to redefine the meaning of poetry and its relation to those who write or read it" (*Contours* 22). He notes that by "help[ing] teach the English to universalize the experience of 'I,'" in a "very real sense the romantics, some of them unwittingly, help to prepare England for its imperial destiny" (25).

Alternately, Saree Makdisi argues "that the romantic period in Britain marks the earliest sustained (though largely doomed) attempt to articulate a form of opposition to the culture of modernization—included but not limited to imperialism—from its very beginnings" (*Romantic Imperialism* 9). Timothy Morton, approaching the Romantic period from a Marxist framework, suggests that Romantic poetry—in particular that of John Keats—undermines the British Empire with a "brilliant, camp reworking of a language underpinning [its] capitalist ideology" by "parody[ing] the advertising language of luxury culture, blowing it up hyperbolically rather than simply opposing it" (*Poetics* 9). Leela Gandhi highlights Romanticism's particular importance for postcolonial theory: "it is within Romanticism, I would like to argue, that postcolonial literary theory finds its particular textual provenance . . . the Romantics, as Eagleton puts it, discover in literature, 'one of the few enclaves in which the creative values expunged from the face of English society by industrial capitalism can be celebrated and affirmed.' So also, if literature compensates for the inadequacies of the world, the poetic 'imagination' and 'creative faculty' are now endowed with the political energies necessary for social transformation. The poet/writer, in other words, is fashioned as a revolutionary *par excellence*" (160).

As is evident from the brief critical discussion here, much disagreement has proliferated as to if—and how—Romantic poetry works to resist or to justify discourses of cultural imperialism. The critical ambivalence to the relationship between British Romantic poetry and empire compounds the ambivalence inscribed in the Romantics' own response to imperialism. This redoubled ambivalence highlights the heightened import of the present-day Romantic legacy. Further complicating the Romantic legacy for many American writers is the fact that they first encountered British Romantic poetry through instruction during a colonial (or colonially derived) education. As Peter Hulme asserts, "almost all intellectuals and writers educated in colonial countries before independence were introduced to metropolitan values through reading the classics of European literature and have then spent most of their subsequent careers negotiating a relationship to this inheritance" (121). This assertion applies to those educated in postcolonial countries as well, because even after these countries became officially independent of Britain, they continued to structure "English" courses around those texts taught under British colonial rule that were considered the heart of the canon, like the most popular Romantic poems. Further, Romantic poetry "with its evocation of the beauty of nature" can be used as "a perfect tool for empire": "If the colonized people can be made to celebrate nature in a totally de-contextualized way, rapt in poetry's rhythmic cadences, treasuring its signs as free-floating signifiers waiting to be assigned content through colonial replacement therapy, they can be distracted from seeing the history of nature as conquered, appropriated and made the site of forced labor" (I. Smith 817).

Perhaps, as Ian Smith suggests, colonial authorities used Romantic poetry to abstract their imperial purpose and disorient those under their control. A distancing of colonized people from their own language and cultures follows unconsciously from activities—such as repeated memorization and recitation of poems—that perpetuate colonial power structures. "The reciting of poetry," as Tiffin concludes, "was not just a practice of literary teaching throughout the empire . . . it was also an effective mode of moral, spiritual, and political inculcation" ("Cold Hearts" 913). This inculcation resulted from memorizing the texts by heart and performing an identification with them through public recitations; significantly, the "English tongue" was not only a language learned through books, but also a state of consciousness and mode of behavior taught "through memorizing the English script, that is, taking it into the body and re-producing before audiences of fellow colonials that which had been absorbed by the heart/mind" (913). In the novels analyzed here, the implication of the physical body in colonial modes of inculcation appears most directly in Kincaid's *Lucy*, whose title character recalls the "two-facedness" she experienced when reciting Wordsworth's poetry in her Caribbean school (18).

## Modeling after the Romantics

Describing her Canadian school where "the curriculum was determinedly British, and just as determinedly pre-modern," Atwood testifies to inculcation similar to that which Tiffin discusses (*Negotiating* 13): "Teaching focused more on the texts, and on the texts alone [and] we learned to memorize these texts, analyze their structure and style, and make précis of them, but none of them were placed in a historical or biographical context" (*Negotiating* 13-14). When writers like Atwood draw on such educational experiences, they frequently revisit these memorized texts in an attempt not only to go back and resituate them in their appropriate historical contexts, but also to interrogate their personal contexts: Why were these works central to their schooling? How do they contribute to their development as writers? How can they use the texts in their own work? As Atwood suggests, these kinds of educational experiences—in which Romantic poetry played a crucial role—contribute to "preconceptions about what we are or ought to be like, what constitutes good writing, and what social functions writing fulfills, or ought to fulfill" (*Negotiating* 5). "All of us develop our own ideas about what we are writing in relation to these preconceptions," she adds, and "whether we attempt to live up to them, rebel against them, or find others using them to judge us, they affect our lives as writers" (5). Atwood suggests that we can trace our conceptualizations of writing directly to the Romantics, claiming that "post-Romantic" writers "are still living in the shadow cast by the Romantic movement, or in the fragments of that shadow" (xxvi).

Giving credence to Atwood's claim, Kincaid has discussed the importance of her experiences with Romantic poetry as a student in Antigua to her development as a writer, saying that "one of the things that inspired me to write was English poets, even though I had never seen England . . . I memorized Wordsworth when I was a child, Keats, all sorts of things . . . I got stuck with a lot of things, so I ended up using them" (qtd. in Bonetti 130). More than sixty years before Kincaid, Fitzgerald also modeled his writing after the Romantic Poets, in particular John Keats, Fitzgerald's favorite writer and "model of creative sensibility" (Bruccoli 73). When trying to teach his daughter, Scottie, how to write well, he guided her to a course, "English Poetry—Blake to Keats," insisting that "a real grasp of Blake, Keats, etc., will bring you something you haven't dreamed of. And it should come now" (*A Life in Letters* 457). Despite the differences in the time and place of their educations—Canada in the 1950s, Antigua in the 1960s, and the US in the 1910s—Atwood, Kincaid, and Fitzgerald all assert that their study of Romantic poetry has had a profound impact on their own writing and their conceptions of what writing is or should do. Through readings of their novels, this study discusses what Romantic poetry has to offer these writers and identifies what, exactly, the impact of their collective Romantic revision is.

As the following chapters make clear, my readings of the novels show that these novelists' engagement with Romantic poetry is more complicated than mere counterdiscourse. Critics and scholars like Ian Smith maintain that "postcolonial subjects can reinvent substantial identities for those lost, travestied and revoked, can misuse the cultural texts of colonial history that, in effect, only ever really promised 'absent things'" (818). Here, by invoking the "absent things" promised by colonial texts, Smith points toward "the 1802 Preface to *Lyrical Ballads* [in which] Wordsworth describes the poet as that man who is 'affected more than other men by absent things as if they were present'" (806). Smith goes on to discuss the "salient irony that attends the adoption of such advice in relation to the reception of Wordsworth's own poem ["I wandered lonely as a Cloud"] in the West Indies. The 'daffodils' are truly 'absent things' that have no material, botanical referents, a fact which complicates the process of making them 'present' to the poet's, or the novelist's, mind's eye" (806). Although the ironies and misuse Ian Smith points out are true, I contend that the cultural texts themselves remain active within postcolonial contexts. These Romantic texts, I argue, provide postcolonial novelists with historically relevant and politically charged poetic traditions that they can and do use to enrich their reflections upon their colonial legacies. Rather than being "absent" from present-day postcolonial discourse, the Romantics—and what they offer American novelists—are very close to home, wherever home may be. This presence continues in postcolonial contexts not simply because literary Romanticism arose alongside and responded to imperialism or because British authorities incorporated Romantic poetry into a larger mode of colonial instruction, but also because Romantic poetry itself allows for the very possibility of resistance to empire by reframing one's relationship to one's physical and social location and to the literary tradition more broadly. I postulate that invoking a Romantic poetics of landscape that considers subjectivity, place, and power has proven to be a particularly useful strategy for American novelists who reconsider the relationship of language to empire.

## Poetics of landscape and the politics of location

While many facets of Romantic poetics mark postcolonial writing, the specific mode this book traces involves poetics that landscape their engagement with the politics of location. Building on the work of W. J. T. Mitchell, who asserts that landscape is not "an object to be seen or text to be read" but "a process by which social and subjective entities are formed" (*Landscape* 1), I argue that landscaping is a process by which one places him- or herself within geographical, historical, social, and political frames of reference and that this use of landscape as a reflective medium has implications for either inscribing or de-scribing empire. Because "landscape *circulates* as a medium of exchange, a site of visual appropriation, [and] a focus for the formation of identity," Mitchell explains, "the representation of landscape is not only a matter of internal politics and national or class ideology but also an international, global phenomenon, intimately bound up with the discourses of imperialism" (*Landscape* 2, 9). He elaborates:

> semiotic features of landscape, and the historical narratives they generate, are tailor-made for the discourse of imperialism, which conceives itself precisely (and simultaneously) as an expansion of landscape understood as an inevitable, progressive development in history, an expansion of "culture" and "civilization" into a "natural" space in progress that is itself narrated as "natural." Empires move outward in space as a way of moving forward in time, the "prospect" that opens up is not just a spatial scene but a projected future of the "development" and exploitation. And this movement is not confined to the external, foreign fields toward which empire directs itself; it is typically accompanied by a renewed interest in the re-presentation of the home landscape, the "nature" of the imperial center. The development of English landscape conventions in the eighteenth century illustrates this double movement perfectly . . . The Enclosure movement and the accompanying dispossession of the English peasantry are an internal colonization of the home country, its transformation from what Blake called "a green & pleasant land" into a landscape, an emblem of national and imperial identity. (*Landscape* 17)

Tracing the representations of landscape that circulate between Romantic poetry and these novels unravels crucial ties between literary works and imperialist discourse that ultimately reveal how this group of works collectively landscapes British colonial legacy. It is worthwhile to note here that when applying Romantic landscape poetics, many postcolonial novels foreground issues of gender and expose the problematic representation of women in Romantic poetry (both in the poems themselves and in the group of poets considered part of the canon). Jacqueline Labbe, discussing the relationship between landscape and gender in Romantic poetry, reminds us "that gender both makes, and is made, that the process is self-*a*ffecting and self-*e*ffecting. And thus, although it is and must be open to challenge, the power represented by the eye relies on the stature—and gender—of the 'I'" (186).

Romantic poetry lays the foundation for a poetics of landscape that de-scribes colonial power structures because, as Makdisi points out, Romantic poetry produced "a new *mode* of understanding and representing such sites of cultural otherness" that involved mapping that otherness onto poetic space (*Romantic Imperialism* 12). Makdisi explains that this "specifically romantic" understanding of otherness associates it with "sites" or "zones" within the poems that emblematize "'other worlds' being surrounded and cut off by the space-time of modernization" and the imperialism to which it gave rise (12). Using Wordsworth's spot of time (appearing in Book XII of *The Prelude*) as a "central concept," Makdisi locates illustrations of this romantic mode of otherness in places the poet maps as "self-enclosed and self-referential enclaves of the anti-modern, each defined by its own unique structures of feeling and its own distinct temporality" (12). A location of this Romantic mode of otherness—such as Byron's Orient or Wordsworth's Nature—"is conceived as a hitherto untransformed enclave that, when discovered and colonized by the outside world, is seen to experience a fall which erases, or, rather, rewrites it by weaving it tightly into the history of the outside world" (12). This rewriting in response to colonization marks a "process of transition [that] can be seen as a struggle between what appears as a totalitarian system and a range of sometimes localized (and sometimes not) sites and zones and cultures of resistance, *beginning* though not *ending* in the romantic period" (12). Makdisi's discussion of this "romantic understanding of otherness" invites a broader examination of ways in which Romantic poetry allegorically landscapes confrontations with empire. This confrontation, as Alison Hickey has illustrated, may be seen quite plainly in works such as Wordworth's *The Excursion*, which includes the "twofold image" of the "imperial" snow-white ram and his "shadowy counterpart" reflected in the crystal flood beneath him (9.439-51). Like the imperial ram, the characters of the novels examined in this study are placed within a landscape that reveals their ambivalent or conflicted relationships to their colonial heritage through identification with and against the other.

## Why novels?

As these novels illuminate the inner worlds of individual postcolonial subjects, they interrogate and revise global colonial histories by considering how placement within or outside the cultural space of imperial tradition has shaped postcolonial identity. The novel has become the preeminent form for presenting postcolonial narratives that examine this space because the novel, as Edward W. Said asserts, historically has been "the aesthetic object" central to imperial discourse (xii). He explains that because "stories are at the heart of what explorers and novelists say about strange regions of the world they also become the method colonized people use to assert their own identity and the existence of their own history" (xii). Since "imperialism and the novel fortified each other to such a degree that it is impossible . . . to read one without in some way dealing with the other," the novel is the primary form postcolonial authors use to retell historically misrepresented stories (Said 84).

The novels examined in this study weave intertexts with Romantic poetry to sharpen their retellings of colonial history and reexaminations of colonial legacy. One could, of course, perform a comparative reading of Romantic and contemporary poetries, but creating a comparative framework that reads the novel in light of Romantic poetry provides for an investigation not only of the role of Romantic poetics in postcolonial narratives' retelling of histories, but also of how genre complicates the intertexts. By appropriating and manipulating genres within their narratives, postcolonial novelists mimic the ways in which colonial educators and historians have appropriated various forms of literature, such as Romantic poetry, and incorporated them into a larger colonial rhetoric that abstracts and substantiates cultural domination. This reapplication (and in some cases reclaiming) of colonially appropriated texts contributes to the articulation of postcolonial rhetoric that works to interrogate the very workings of empire. As Bahri suggests, a postcolonial novel can speak "*other*wise" through the "complex operation of variant codes," such as genre, within language (148). In these texts, Evelyn O'Callaghan explains, "narrative moves fluidly between literary styles (prosaic, parodic, dramatic, lyric, satiric) and techniques (reported speech, dialogue, 'stream of consciousness,' monologue, fantasy, and so on) . . . There is a sense in which the writing refuses, to use Wilson Harris's term, 'consolidation' by any language, register, or formal device" (7). This ability of the postcolonial novel to avoid consolidation derives, in part, from being able to draw on a varied range of literary traditions, such as Romantic poetry; the fluidity that results from drawing from these disparate traditions testifies to the diverse cultural histories that contribute to postcolonial narratives while also inflecting them with critiques of both works they reference and beliefs or attitudes those works are seen to represent.

## The realm of change

In *Romantic Revisions* I present an alternative to traditional approaches of reading postcolonial novels, focusing specifically on the novels' Romantic intertexts in order to explore their nuanced historical, literary-historical, social, and political references. As Bill Ashcroft, Gareth Griffiths, and Helen Tiffin explain in *The Empire Writes Back*, the colonially derived canon is not "a body of texts *per se*, but rather a set of reading practices (the enactment of innumerable individual and community assumptions, for example about genre, about literature, and even about writing)" (186). Developing alternative ways of reading, therefore, can serve as another strategy for interrogating the canon and de-scribing empire. The de-scription process "is not simply a matter of replacing one set of texts with another," but also involves "the reconstruction of the so-called canonical texts through alternative reading practices" that revise larger assumptions "about genre, about literature, and even about writing" (Ashcroft, Griffiths, and Tiffin 186-87). In *Romantic Revisions* I take on this task and suggest that the world may be understood through what Octavio Paz calls "a growing heap of texts . . . each slightly different from the one that came before it: translations of translations of translations. Each text is unique, yet at the same time it is the translation of another text. No text can be completely original because language itself, in its very essence, is already a translation—first from the nonverbal world, and then, because each sign and each phrase is a translation of another sign, another phrase" (qtd. in Bassnett and Trivedi 2).

By reading the Romantic intertexts of twentieth-century novels of the Americas, I trace the genealogy of the poetics of landscape from former British colonies in the Americas to the British Empire. The connections reveal the ways in which the Americas continue to be shaped by the legacy of British colonialism and the importance of Romantic poetics in illuminating both the operations of empire and the modes of resistance that thwart it: "All writers must go from now to once upon a time; all must go from here to there; all must descend to where the stories are kept . . . And all must commit acts of larceny, or else of reclamation, depending on how you look at it" (Atwood, *Negotiating* 178). The goal of these writers, in Atwood's words, is to bring something useful "back to the land of the living"—"the realm of change" (178-79). These novels, in their reformulation of Romantic poetics, work to change our conceptions of the Americas through a new understanding of how the legacies of British colonialism influence our own social and political realities.

By analyzing the Romantic intertexts, I aim not only to highlight the fact that these novels invoke Romantic poetry at crucial moments, but also to explain why understanding this reframing of Romantic poetics is important for reading the novels' overall critiques of American manifestations of British imperialism. The nature of the critique, of course, varies with the particular narrative; while Fitzgerald uses Keats's "Eve of St. Agnes" in one of the most important scenes in the novel to demonstrate how US materialism has evolved from that of its imperial parent, Kincaid uses Wordsworth's poetry to describe how Romantic poetry itself was used to shape British subjects' worldviews. In addition to the nature of the critiques, the frequency with which the novels present Romantic intertexts also varies; Wordsworth's daffodils haunt the protagonist throughout Kincaid's *Lucy*, but the reframing of Keats's poem appears less frequently in *The Great Gatsby*. I am not asserting that these novels are rewritings of Romantic poems, or that Romantic poetics are the only ones operating in these texts. What I am claiming is that a diverse group of twentieth-century novelists from across the Americas uses Romantic intertexts to highlight and critique the relationship between British and American imperialism. Furthermore, I claim that these intertexts, read collectively, suggest that modern-day American authors reframe British Romantic poetry to illustrate new politics of location.

## Chapter summaries

In chapter 1, "Wordsworthian Intertexts in Kincaid's *Lucy*," I argue that Kincaid's *Lucy* radically renegotiates Wordsworth's identity-centered poetics to encompass a larger worldview, rewriting Wordsworth's voiceless Lucy of the "Lucy poems" to show how poetic genius grows out of—and in spite of—a colonial education. I examine how *Lucy*'s references to Wordsworth's lyric poem, "I wandered lonely as a Cloud" inscribe a "daffodil gap" (representing the difference between what is taught in colonial education and lived in colonial experience) that reflects adapted British colonial practices within US and Caribbean settings. In chapter 2, "Specters of US Empire in Atwood's Fiction," I analyze Atwood's short story, "Death by Landscape," which also rewrites Wordsworth's Lucy poems, to frame the importance of landscape for Atwood's *The Handmaid's Tale*. I suggest that in its contemporary evocation of America's Puritanical history, *The Handmaid's Tale* exposes US imperialist tendencies by using landscape as a figural medium that brings the specters of US imperialism into relief. In chapter 3, "McCarthy's *Blood Meridian*, Byron, and the US Frontier," I contrast the novel's gratuitous frontier violence and idealized depictions of the early eighteenth-century American frontier in Byron's poetry. The novel provides a critique of Byron's images of the American Arcadia in *Don Juan* and invokes images from his apocalyptic poem "Darkness" to gesture ironically toward a more realistic view of the consequences of Manifest Destiny as the US expanded its territory westward. In chapter 4, "Keatsian Echoes and US Materialism in *The Great Gatsby*," I argue that Fitzgerald's fiction, with its persistent focus on British fashion, depicts the bitter irony of the passage of the "style of man" from Britain to the US: Instead of bringing a new style in vogue, the people of the US, who so fiercely fought for their independence, merely adapted the British imperial model to fit their bigger waistlines. After tracing the novel's preoccupation with European styles and fashions, the chapter demonstrates that by invoking "The Eve of St. Agnes" in the novel's famous shirt scene, Fitzgerald critiques the US culture of consumption that both derives from and makes possible the US's superpower. In chapter 5, "The Coleridgean Poetics of *Palace of the Peacock*," I discuss how *Palace of the Peacock* reworks the rhetorical form of apostrophe to de-scribe the colonization of Guyana's landscapes. This chapter shows how Harris highlights problems of language and address associated with the colonialism by reimagining Coleridge's "Rime of the Ancient Mariner." By reading the rearticulations of Coleridge's "Rime" in *Palace*, this chapter examines not only Harris's application of Coleridge's synthetic mode of composition, but also his own radical reimagination of the possibilities for dialogue through poetics of landscape based on call and response.

To synthesize these chapters, a conclusion, "British Legacy in the Americas," follows them. The conclusion summarizes their claims and discusses how the readings collectively contribute to an understanding of the role Romantic poetics play in reframing American social and political landscapes. Then an epilogue, entitled "Angels in America Guard and Guide," closes the study. It examines the broader effect of these poetics that is seen in other media and in popular culture at large. In staging the influence of British Romantic poetry on the vision of American artists, the epilogue draws upon William Blake's visionary conception of "Universal Empire" and Tony Kushner's *Angels in America* to consider what these revisions tell us about the adaptation of Romantic figures for present-day America.

# Chapter One

## Wordsworthian Intertexts in Kincaid's *Lucy*

I have chosen to focus the first chapter of *Romantic Revisions* on Kincaid's *Lucy* because it illustrates the concept that is most crucial for contextualizing the four chapters that follow—that the relationship that postcolonial American writers and their subjects have with the English Romantic tradition varies according to their respective frames of reference. In *Lucy*, a young Caribbean woman who has recently moved to New York to become an au pair describes her coming of age. Living in the US helps bring Lucy to a state of self-awareness: as her worldview expands, she is better able to articulate where she is going and where she has been. By contrasting Lucy's US experiences with those of her host mother, Mariah, Kincaid suggests that the legacy of British colonialism is different for someone from a formerly British island in the Caribbean than it is for a person born and raised in the US. One of the ways in which these legacies differ involves language itself; we can imagine Lucy speaking an English that does not sound like the English spoken by Mariah. Although the spoken word is important in the novel's mapping of colonial legacies through language, it is the written one that ultimately reveals the disparities arising from politics of location.

Kincaid reinforces the importance of the written word for colonial experiences in one of Lucy's dreams, recounted near the beginning of the novel. In this dream, Lucy examines the label of one of her nightgowns that reads, "Made in Australia" (9). The dream is interrupted when the American-born maid wakes Lucy; however, Lucy tells us that "as I opened my eyes, the word 'Australia' stood between our faces, and I remembered then that Australia was settled as a prison for bad people, people so bad that they couldn't be put in a prison in their own country" (9). That the name of the former colony becomes literally spelled out between these two domestic workers reinforces the relationship between language and colonial legacies. It also leads the reader to question the histories of these women's ancestors—how they came to be involved in the settlement of the American colonies—and the difference of their worldviews. Kincaid suggests that their views are different, that they see the word Australia differently.

Words are important to Lucy in a way they are not to other characters in the novel. Because Lucy is an avid reader and aspiring writer, her engagement with literature—particularly the British canon—figures prominently in her growth process and reflects her changing worldview. Kincaid demonstrates the importance of English Romanticism to Lucy's imagination of herself in relation to place through her reactions to William Wordsworth's poetry. With repeated and explicit references to Wordsworth's work, Kincaid invites *Lucy*'s readers to consider the ways in which she appropriates Wordsworthian poetics as she relates the efforts of Lucy, her protagonist, to displace the same poetics with her "vow to erase from my mind, line by line, every word" of his poem (18). This poem, which Kincaid uses to highlight *Lucy*'s intertextual connection to Wordsworthian poetry, is his famous lyric about daffodils, "I wandered lonely as a Cloud." Several literary critics and scholars have used these allusions to daffodils as the point of departure for postcolonial interpretations of the text, convincingly arguing that Lucy's anxiety about Wordsworth's poem "creates opportunities for the de-scribing of empire, the continuing process of dismantling colonial regimes of power in language" (I. Smith 803). Moira Ferguson notes that "the fact that William Wordsworth wrote several 'Lucy' poems raises the question of Kincaid's possible ironies" ("*Lucy*" 241), Bénédicte Ledent writes that "'Lucy' is ironically also the title of one of Wordsworth's poems . . . suggesting that [Kincaid's] Lucy cannot really escape colonial tutelage and in some way also belongs to Wordsworth's world, whether she wants to or not" (60), and Christine Prentice suggests that Lucy's "very name evokes the persistence of this burden"—a colonially instituted conception of herself as "the interiorized, contemplative subject of the epitome of Romantic Englishness" (217).

Although critics and scholars have limited their discussion of *Lucy*'s Wordsworthian intersections almost exclusively to the daffodil poem, I argue that this allusion is not a localized literary effect; rather, it is that Wordworth's entire oeuvre has important interpretive significance for the novel as a whole. Not only does Kincaid name *Lucy*—this autobiographical bildungsroman—after the most mysterious and intriguing woman (absent) in Wordsworth's poetry, she further utilizes the narrative space Wordsworth creates for the "Lucy" character to deploy a complicated response to Wordsworth's poetry and the literary tradition it both represents and diverges from. *Lucy* pays homage to the potentialities for self-centered poetics that Wordsworth's work makes possible, but it also represents a radical departure of consciousness that depicts Lucy's expanding worldview, telling a story that rewrites the voiceless Lucy inscribed in Wordsworth's poems while giving voice to a poetic genius grown out of—and in spite of—a colonial education.

## Using Wordsworthian poetics

Kincaid has testified to the importance of the education that she herself received as a child in Antigua—which at that time was a British colony—for her development as a writer: "One of the things that inspired me to write was English poets, even though

I had never seen England," Kincaid explains. "I memorized Wordsworth when I was a child, Keats, all sorts of things. I got stuck with a lot of things, so I ended up using them" (qtd. in Bonetti 130). Kincaid contends that memorizing the works of Wordsworth and other British authors allowed her to learn "a lot of things about language" that she could "use against the people who educated [her] very well" (qtd. in Ferguson 175). Said explains the importance of this "use" of canonical texts by postcolonial writers and places the reappropriation it enables in historical context: "We now know that these non-European peoples [Caribbean or Indian natives] did not accept with indifference the authority projected over them, or the general silence on which their presence in variously attenuated forms is predicated. We must therefore read the great canonical texts, and perhaps also the entire archive of modern and pre-modern European and American culture, with an effort to draw out, extend, give emphasis and voice to what is silent or marginally present or ideologically represented . . . in such works" (66).

Focusing on Kincaid's adaptation of Wordsworthian poetry in *Lucy*, I consider what Kincaid has learned from Wordsworth linguistically and examine how and why she appropriates Wordsworthian poetics. That those who educated her forced her to memorize Wordsworth's poems complicates Kincaid's use of Wordsworth in *Lucy*: Kincaid, the author, appropriates Wordsworthian poetics in her own narration of *Lucy*, while Lucy, her protagonist, abstracts Wordsworth the poet by associating him with the forced recitation that is part of larger modes of colonial control. There is an autobiographical impetus for Kincaid's engagement with Wordsworth, poet of the "I"; Kincaid has indicated that her works—particularly her novels, *Annie John* and *Lucy*—are autobiographical (qtd. in Perry 494). But these works are not autobiographies in the traditional sense; they are also revisions. O'Callaghan states that "this autobiographical form allows a sort of re-vision, a radical re-shaping of a life, seen and recounted from the inside" (7). O'Callaghan's discussion of autobiographical "re-vision" describes the work of Kincaid and shows why we should not read Kincaid's works as strictly autobiographical. Kincaid tells Donna Perry that she writes fiction rather than autobiography because she likes to give the events of her life "more powerful meaning": "One of the things I found when I began to write," she says, "was that writing exactly what happened had a limited amount of power for me" (494). Jana Evans Braziel has categorized Kincaid's writing as "alterbiography," which "attempts to understand the genre of autobiography as gendered, sexuated, and above all, racialized" (*Caribbean Genesis* 8). Readers too often, however, have tended to elide the distinction between Lucy's response to Wordsworth and Kincaid's invocation of Wordsworthian poetics. Exploring the nuances of the different engagements with Wordsworth by Lucy, the character, and Kincaid, the author, more fully illuminates the extent to which Kincaid uses Wordsworthian poetics to subvert the colonial domination he is often seen to represent.

Noting that "I had never read a West Indian writer when I started to write," Kincaid asserts that if she were to identify where her writings come from, she would point to major British authors, including Wordsworth (qtd. in Ferguson 169).

Kincaid resists association with a distinct "Caribbean writing tradition," clarifying that she is "from the British Caribbean." She explains that, as a subject of the British Empire, she was taught under a colonial educational system that emphasized the English literary tradition. Although her own writing grows out of this English body of work, it undermines traditional English notions of authority while drawing attention to the traditions that have been eclipsed by her colonial education: "What tradition is that from? That is the English tradition. You know most people, especially people from my generation, had an education that was sort of an English public-school education. We got kind of the height of empire. They were trying to erase any knowledge of another history, another possibility. So we learned Shakespeare, the King James version, Wordsworth, and Keats. That's the tradition. I'm of the English-speaking-people tradition. British people, not English people" (qtd. in Ferguson 168). A close reading of *Lucy* reveals that Kincaid responds to the English tradition by using Wordsworthian poetics that both reflect upon the erasure of Carib and African histories by British colonists and depict the consequences of this erasure for herself and her development as a writer: "I started to write out of this need . . . to settle demons and settle scores and all sorts of things. So . . . driven to write. I'm not interested in things for their own sake. I'm only interested in explaining something for myself" (qtd. in Simmons 5).

Wordsworth's poetry provides Kincaid with a literary space within the British tradition from which she could challenge imperial authority while telling a story of her own. Wordsworth, the poet who placed the "I" at the center of epic poetry, represents the conscious exploration for and of the self that most interests Kincaid; consequently, the entire body of his work could be of use in her project. Known for works such as *The Prelude: Or, Growth of a Poet's Mind*, Wordsworth often is associated with the egotistical sublime, but inscribed within this seemingly unified subjectivity is a reliance on alterity that haunts the Wordsworthian "I" with the possibility of displacement or radical re-vision that is inherent in its original conception. Deborah Elise White discusses the productivity of the Wordsworthian "I" in terms of reflexive recognition of the imagination:

> When Wordsworth invokes its power in Book VI of *The Prelude*, he says to "his own soul": "I recognize thy glory." The structure of reflexive recognition is fundamental to this centralizing and individuating character. Imagination throws the "I" outward and draws it back as if engaged in an unending game of fort-da . . . By the positing and development of imagination through and as a reflexive structure . . . Romantic texts often offer a more, not less, sophisticated account of "ideology" and "illusion" than that offered by contemporary criticism. The very instance with which they confront the problem of the identity in the "I" that recognizes itself or the poem that is about poetry enables, far more than it obscures, an equally insistent confrontation with alterity. (1-3)

In *The Prelude*, we see this confrontation with alterity when Wordsworth evokes the distance between the selves of the "I" as a "wide . . . / vacancy" that registers the consciousness of "some other Being" within his own "self-presence": " A tranquilizing spirit presses now / On my corporeal frame, so wide appears / The vacancy between me and those days, / Which yet have such self-presence in my mind, / That, musing on them, often do I seem / Two consciousnesses, conscious of myself / And of some other Being" (2.27-33). Kincaid takes advantage of the "vacancy" Wordsworth derives within the poetical imagination to interpolate her protagonist Lucy, who at once represents both the subjective "I" and the "other Being," into Wordsworth's poetry.

Wordsworth's poems exhibit a fascination not only with probing the presence of that which is other within his own consciousness, but also with writing about those who previously had been ignored within poetical discourse or were thought to be inappropriate subjects of poetry. In the preface to *Lyrical Ballads* (1802), Wordsworth espouses a revolutionary break with traditional conceptions about poetry, theorizing that "incidents and situations from common life" presented in "language really used by men" should be the "principal object" of poetry (743). "Low and rustic life" serves as a primary focus for Wordsworth's "experiment" with poetic language in *Lyrical Ballads*, and in this sense Wordsworth can be said to have democratized poetry by including those who were typically outside of the poetic frame of reference (741-43). Laura Doyle, however, argues that "Wordsworth's sublime ego . . . gathers energy by humbly appropriating to itself . . . the voices of the 'folk' who work the soil . . . Wordsworth transforms folk manners and the objects 'to which they are attached' into the materials of racialized nationhood, but he does so in an imagery that naturalizes the process so successfully as to make it invisible . . . Clearly a nationalist nativisim is integral to Wordsworth's sublime poetic, which he eventually builds up into the image of the 'Poet of the Imagination' who is at once noble conqueror and humble shepherd" (31). In *Lucy*, Kincaid exploits this tension of democratization and appropriation that is at the heart of Wordsworth's "sublime ego" and projection of nationhood by giving voice to one of the best-known poetical subjects that Wordsworth's poems silenced.

To a greater degree than all of Wordsworth's other works, the Lucy poems provide a particularly inviting space for Kincaid to reconfigure the Wordsworthian "I" within a postcolonial context. Frances Ferguson labels the Lucy poems, "the lyrics that are probably his most famous," as invitingly "problematic" (173), explaining that "the chief difficulty in talking about these poems lies in our uncertainty about what the name 'Lucy' refers to. For the Lucy poems make quiet mockery of ideas of poetic representation which involve an imitation of reality; by continually denying Lucy any place in the present, Wordsworth seems to move toward a poetics in which representation involves a recognition of Lucy's absence rather than a representing in acknowledgment of her remembered presence" (174).

Before discussing this crucial "recognition of Lucy's absence" in the poems named for her, it is necessary to consider another problematic quality of the poems—the fact that Wordsworth did not group them together or even name them as such. The conventional designation of the Lucy poems derived from readers' preoccupation with their problematically absent subject. As Mark Jones notes, "the 'Lucy Poems' never existed as such in Wordworth's day, but were invented by Victorian critics and editors shortly after his death" (ix). Jones explains the critical consensus: "a true 'Lucy Poem' is an untitled lyrical ballad that either mentions Lucy or is always placed with another poem that does, that either explicitly mentions her death or is susceptible to such a reading, and that is spoken by Lucy's lover" (11). In this categorization, which relies heavily on the implied absence of Lucy, the Lucy poems consist of the five poems that begin "A slumber did my spirit seal," "She dwelt among th' untrodden ways," "Strange fits of passion I have known," "Three years she grew in sun and shower," and "I travell'd among unknown Men."

The designation of these lyrics as "Lucy poems" after Wordsworth's death is significant because this co-optation sets a precedent for readers' using the poet's language to give life to their own entirely distinct, but also inextricably related, literary beings—precisely what Kincaid accomplishes in her novel *Lucy*. As this artificially created group of poems has assumed an identity of its own in literary history, it has created a particular imaginative place in which critics and other writers can explore the presence or absence of Lucy, whoever or whatever she may be. Kincaid, for one, devises a character that occupies the same discursive space as the Lucy of Wordsworth's Lucy poems, but signifies alternative possibilities based on different cultural and historical realities. These alternatives to Wordsworth's poems continue the project of rewriting the poems that Wordsworth himself began with his multiple drafts.

The different drafts of the poems are important in investigating the issue of Lucy's absence because, as Frances Ferguson notes, "Lucy is given a voice only in the deleted final stanza of the 1799 manuscript version of 'Strange fits of passion' ('Her laughter light' which rings in the speaker's ears)" (175). In the published versions of the Lucy poems, the name Lucy appears only in the contexts involving: her death ("When Lucy ceas'd to be" ["She dwelt" 11] and "How soon my Lucy's race was run!" ["Three years" 38]); the spaces she used to inhabit before she died ("Lucy's cot" ["Strange fits" 15], "The bowers where Lucy played" ["I travell'd" 14], and "the last green field / Which Lucy's eyes surveyed" ["I travell'd" 15-16]); her instruction ("Such thoughts to Lucy I will give" ["Three years" 34]); and the possibility of her death ("If Lucy should be dead!" ["Strange fits" 28]). This list of references to Lucy emphasizes not only the previously mentioned absence of Lucy in the poems, but also Wordsworth's care to write Lucy out of the poems. In these poems, Wordsworth traces an apparition of Lucy that reflects upon the state of mind of the speaker rather than telling us about Lucy herself.

Geoffrey Hartman describes Lucy as an "intermediate modality of consciousness rather than an intermediate being," explaining that the "poet describes her as dying at a point at which she would have been humanized" (158). Lucy functions as a projection of consciousness not only of the speaker, Hartman asserts, but also of Wordsworth, who "when [he] depicts an object . . . is also depicting himself, or, rather, a truth about himself, a self-acquired revelation" (5). This assertion that Lucy can be read as Wordsworth "depicting himself, or, rather, a truth about himself, a self-acquired revelation" also applies to Kincaid, who has suggested as much in interviews about the autobiographical underpinnings of *Lucy*. Ross extends Hartman's reading by arguing that this assertion of self-identity relies heavily on re-inscribing traditionally gendered hegemonies and objectifying the female object: "The male's need for self-identity is repeatedly reenacted in [Wordsworth's] poems, and the female always serves that need as the object of his desire; ironically, though she is unattainable, she is always obtained . . . in that she is objectified—hence contained—by the contours of male desire." "By redetermining the place of women in his own history" Ross asserts, "Wordsworth has necessarily predetermined his own place in our history," making his work ripe for both feminist and postcolonial critiques ("Naturalizing Gender" 391). Applying this analytical framework to the Lucy poems, he claims that "Wordsworth uses Lucy to try to save himself from Nature's snatch-away game by claiming that absence intensifies desire, fosters memory, and promotes the resolution of the poetical mind to determine itself" (402).

Wordsworth's Lucy, who is absent and lacks linguistic, self-determining agency, presumably has been lost in this "snatch-away game." In *Lucy,* Kincaid resolves to engage in her own self-determining poetics not by re-inscribing the absence of Wordsworth's Lucy, but rather by reinserting Lucy into the game, which becomes a war of words. As Kincaid resurrects Lucy, however, she reforms the setting, and the terms of the game consequently change. Removed from the "heath, this calm and quiet scene" of Wordsworth's poem ("Three years" 40), Lucy resurfaces on an American shore. She is a British citizen, fresh off the boat, but—in an important rewriting of Wordsworth's Lucy—her place of origin is a Caribbean island, not the British mainland. Literary critics consistently read Lucy's place of origin as Antigua, since that is where Kincaid is from, even though it is not specified in the novel. J. Brooks Bouson, for example, suggests that although the novel tells us that Lucy comes from "a small unnamed island in the Caribbean," those "readers knowledgeable about Kincaid's life readily identify [the island] as Antigua" (70). Kincaid indicates that she intentionally does not identify the island Lucy comes from: "I didn't want to specify because I didn't want any preconceptions about the place" (qtd. in Perry 508). As the novel unfolds, the reader realizes that the geographical location—whatever Caribbean island it may be—complicates and revolutionizes the game itself, for what is at stake is much larger than authorial consciousness; the terms are put to the task of de-scribing an empire.

## Embodying a postcolonial spirit of place

Because of the Lucy poems' nationalist undertones, their involvement in de-scribing the British Empire can be seen as a kind of poetic justice. Although Wordsworth composed the Lucy poems in Germany during and after his visit to Goslar, the poems "are in purely an English mode" (Hartman 162). This mode takes on particular importance in the Lucy poems, in which Lucy represents "an embodiment of *English* spirit of place" (Hartman 213). Describing Wordsworth's evocation of England—in the words of his December 1798 letter to Coleridge—as an act of "self-defence," Frances Ferguson suggests that Wordsworth's "writing of the Lucy poems seems to have represented not merely a re-Anglicizing of the ballad form but also an attempt to figure forth a microcosmic English literary history in them" (179). She locates this history in the Lucy poems by tracing their "overt memorialization of Lucy" to "the terms of the poet's love for England": "Because he can only give his blazon of England by recalling aspects of the landscape in terms of Lucy, he implicitly includes it in his plaint" (185). This plaint also represents the inflection of nationalist sentiment upon the poet's "desire," most overt in the poem "I travell'd among unknown Men," which confines female productivity to a gendered English domestic space ("She I cherish'd turn'd her wheel / Beside an English fire" [11-12]) while opening the "Lands beyond the Sea" (2) to exploration and possible exploitation by the English explorer. Moira Ferguson has identified the interaction between *Lucy* and "I travell'd among unknown Men" as the "clinching one" in terms of Kincaid's Wordsworthian ironies. She points out that, in this poem, "a patriot narrates how he cherishes the image of Lucy in a cottage turning her wheel and contemplating green fields as she expires. The very idea of Kincaid's Lucy coming from a drought-ridden, arid Antigua and constructing a garment from cotton threads of empire while gazing on lush well-watered English pastures is ludicrous, a mockery of empire in general and Wordsworth specifically as a preeminent cultural icon" ("*Lucy*" 241). As Ferguson suggests, the absence of Lucy's body or voice in the poems heightens her associations with the English landscape, and one could argue that what Wordsworth mourns when he mourns his Lucy is in fact England itself. Thus, by invoking Wordsworth's Lucy, Kincaid can respond not only to Wordsworth's poems and their place in a larger literary tradition, but also to England and its physical and political landscape.

Kincaid critiques colonial landscapes—both British and American—through the eyes of Lucy, who is able to compare and contrast geopolitical landscapes as a result of her travels. As Gary Holcomb asserts, in *Lucy*, Kincaid "deploy[s] the tropes of travel as a means of deconstructing the imperialist ideology written into the very genre of travel literature":

> Lucy, exploring and negotiating the borders of transnational identity . . . is an *immigrant* who becomes a *traveler*, capsizing the hierarchies of subject agency. Recognizing that the subjectivity of travel writing operates at the center of colonial domination, Kincaid, with *Lucy*, assails the certitude written into who may write travel and who may not. Kincaid's seizure of the agency permitted the travel writer is a powerful assault on colonialism because it attacks the very mechanisms built into racist hierarchy: the master-slave construction, the received notions of dominance and submission, the inheritance of colonizer and colonized, the untested arrangement of the tourist and the native, the physical economy of the first-world consumer and the third-world producer. (297)

Although Holcomb does not consider Kincaid's overturning of travel-writing conventions in the context of Wordsworth's poetry, doing so helps explain why Wordsworth as a literary and historical figure and his poem "I wandered lonely as a Cloud" are so important to the novel. In contrast to the exclusively masculine mobility in Wordsworth's poems seen, for example, through the "travel[er] among unknown men" and the poet who "wander[s] lonely as a Cloud," Kincaid genders journey feminine by recounting the immigration of her female protagonist in *Lucy*'s first section, "Poor Visitor." Even after Lucy has spent some time in the US, she remains a visitor in the sense that she still calls her mother's house in the Caribbean "home," while seeking different places, both in terms of geography and sociopolitical space, with the impulse to be "going somewhere new again" (143). It is worthwhile to note that Lucy begins her narrative (and the novel itself) with the assertion that when she arrived in the US, "It was my first day" (3). When Lucy enters the US, she becomes a new woman. She is afforded a new range of opportunities, but—as an Afro-Caribbean immigrant—is also marked as different. In fact, the members of her blonde-haired, blue-eyed host family call her "the Visitor" because it seems as if she were "not a part of things," as if she "were just passing through" in a manner less fancy-free than that of the speaker of Wordsworth's lyric (13).

As the novel begins, Lucy, who as yet remains unnamed, gives the following description of her traveling fantasy: "all these places were lifeboats to my small drowning soul, for I would imagine myself entering and leaving them, and just that—entering and leaving over and over again—would see me through a bad feeling I did not have a name for" (3). These mobilities, both the imaginative license and her physical immigration to the United States, are crucial for Lucy's self-consciousness, for saving her "drowning soul." That she does not have a name for this "bad feeling" (in addition to the fact that she herself has not been named at this point in the novel) suggests that Lucy lacks both the linguistic productivity and the self-reflexivity to identify what it is that ominously looms over her consciousness. In this instance, Lucy mirrors Wordsworth's Lucy, who "is presented as prehuman and prelinguistic," dying "at the threshold of humanization" (Bewell 202; Hartman 160). Although Lucy, upon arriving in the US, envisions her future as "a large gray patch surrounded by black, blacker, blackest," by leaving the West Indies (as Kincaid herself once did), Lucy takes the first steps toward enlightening herself and mastering her self-expression (6, 65). When considering "what is needed in an environment to create an artist," Kincaid has said that "you certainly need a moment where you're silent and you listen. Which is not possible in Antigua. Everything is too intense. Everything crowds in. It's small. It's smaller than small, so it's larger than large" (qtd. in Garis 44).

Lucy's experience is similar to Kincaid's in that, by expanding her worldview, she frees herself from the overwhelming confinement of her homeland and initiates the self-exploration that will inform her future creative work. These opportunities arise for Lucy not because she comes to the US, the proverbial land of opportunity, but because after she leaves her home, placing distance between herself and her domineering mother, she is better able to name the "bad feeling" she has and trace it to its colonial roots. Lucy says that she imagined that "with my one swift act—

leaving home and coming to this new place—I could leave behind me, as if it were an old garment never to be worn again, my sad thoughts, my sad feelings, and my discontent with life in general" (6-7). Instead she finds herself discontented in this "new place," noting that "when I left my home I had wrapped around my shoulders the mantle of a servant" (95). Lucy's discussion of her unhappiness both at "home" and in the US draws attention to the ways in which colonial histories—and their on-going racial and gendered hierarchies—affect one's place in terms of geographical, social, and political contexts. Katherine Sugg associates Lucy's negotiation of place with that of postcolonial women writers more generally, "in the narrator's paradoxical refusal of the past—one that is embedded in a relentless, even obsessive invocation of it—*Lucy* offers an evocative model of gendered exile and narrative authority in contemporary postcolonial women's writing. This rewriting of female selfhood and the relation to 'home' circles around 'the past' via narratives that both embrace nostalgic affect and yet refuse the narrative trajectories that are part of our common romantic plots for women's relations to home, exile, community, and family" (157).

Underscoring the importance of place in the novel, Lucy sings "put yourself in my place, if only for a day; see if you can stand the awful emptiness inside" over and over to herself as a self-effacing mantra (8). Upon arriving in the US, Lucy's domestic place consists of the maid's room (though she "was not even the maid"), which she describes as being "enclose[ed] like a box—a box in which cargo traveling a long way should be shipped" (7). In addition to alluding to Lucy's ancestors' experiences on the slave ships traveling to the Caribbean and other slaves' experiences traveling to the US, this description more subtly harkens back to Wordsworth's Lucy, who remains unseen, enclosed underground in a coffin. The significant difference with Kincaid's Lucy is that although she is metaphorically buried alive, she can always leave her au pair position and seek those imagined "lifeboats" that will save her suffocating soul. Kincaid's Lucy, though discontented, is resourceful, intelligent, and fearless: "If I did not know everything yet, I would not be afraid to know *everything* as it came up. That life might be cold and hard would not surprise me" (153). Lucy's leaving home can be read as one "cold and hard" lesson in which she learns about her place. As Lucy sees more of the world, she comes to understand dominion, the source of the "bad feeling" for which she does not have a name. After overhearing the word "minions," she muses, "[it] would haunt someone like me; the place where I came from was a dominion of someplace else" (37). Lucy becomes "so taken with the word 'dominion'" that she begins to tell a story about "the place where [she] grew up," marking her entrance into the war of words (37-38).

Like her character Lucy, Kincaid began telling stories because of a "desire for a perfect place, a perfect situation" that Kincaid indicates came to her "from English Romantic poetry": "It described a perfection which one longed for," she explains, "and of course the perfection that one longed for was England. I longed for England myself. These things were a big influence, and it was important for me to get rid of them. Then I could actually look at the place I'm from." Kincaid says, "[although] I would not have ever, ever been able to say, 'You know, I really need to write this, I really need to get rid of these images' that's what I was doing" (qtd. in Bonetti 130-31). In *Lucy*, Kincaid depicts her longing for England, the motherland, through Lucy's love-hate relationship with her mother, whom she has to leave behind in order to assess her influence more clearly. In the words of Belinda Edmondson, *Lucy*'s "central thesis . . . becomes how Lucy can learn to integrate her love for her mother(land) when her selfhood is defined and maintained through an absolute opposition to what that mother(land) has intended for her to be" (159-60). Similarly, Laura Niesen de Abruna asserts that like Annie in *Annie John*, Lucy's "personal alienation [from her mother] is explored directly and then as a metaphor for the alienation of the daughter-island from the mother-country . . . The metaphorical exploration offers a criticism of the neo-colonial attitudes" in Lucy's life (15), and Prentice argues that "in rehearsing the problematic of the mother-daughter relation—in subjective terms a veritable life and death struggle for each—the (post-)colonial daughter's relation to her mother is shown to be situated in a mutually over-determining discursive relation between the colony and the imperial metropolis" (217). Insisting that her "past was her mother," Lucy at first thinks, "I had spent so much time saying I did not want to be like my mother that I missed the whole story: I was not like my mother—I was my mother" (90). Lucy soon realizes, however, that she is not "like [her] mother," who "should not have thrown away her intelligence [and] should not have paid such little attention to [Lucy's]" (123).

Finding her own voice, Lucy writes her mother a letter that reflects her feelings about empire more generally; it is "a cold letter" that "pointed out the ways she had betrayed herself," emphasizing that "she had betrayed [Lucy] also" (127). She closes her letter to her mother by insisting, "I would not come home now . . . I would not come ever" (128). Lucy explains: "I had come to feel that my mother's love for me was designed solely to make me into an echo of her; and I didn't know why, but I felt that I would rather be dead than become an echo of someone. That was not a figure of speech" (36). On an interpersonal level, Lucy consciously avoids being like her biological mother and Mariah, her surrogate mother, but in a broader sense she wants to avoid being subsumed within the imperial cultures of Great Britain or the United States. In attempt to defy the various types of dominion these cultures represent, Lucy turns toward language itself. Not only does she make her refusal to return home permanent by writing it down, she also uses her au pair position to teach Mariah's children her own lessons about place and language, about telling stories and subverting power, although "Mariah did not believe in this way of doing things" (45).

## Mapping the daffodil gap

Setting in motion a revolutionary reparation for the silencing of colonial subjects, Kincaid constructs an imaginary arena in which she can rewrite Lucy in a way that allows her to make use of modes of British domination that were transmitted through Romantic poetry. To create this opportunity, she summons Wordsworth's presence to her narrative with an obvious allusion to his lyric "I wandered lonely as a Cloud," which was originally published in *Poems, in Two Volumes* (1807):

> I wandered lonely as a Cloud
> That floats on high o'er Vales and Hills,
> When all at once I saw a crowd,
> A host of dancing Daffodils;
> Along the Lake, beneath the trees,
> Ten thousand dancing in the breeze.
>
> The waves beside them danced, but they
> Outdid the sparkling waves in glee:—
> A Poet could not but be gay,
> In such a laughing company:
> I gaz'd—and gaz'd—but little thought
> What wealth the shew to me had brought:
>
> For oft when on my couch I lie
> In vacant or in pensive mood,
> They flash upon that inward eye
> Which is the bliss of solitude,
> And then my heart with pleasure fills,
> And dances with the Daffodils.

When Mariah, who represents both the US and the privilege of its upper class, tells her that she "is made to feel alive" by seeing daffodils bend in the breeze (17), Lucy recalls reciting the poem in a performance at her school in the British Caribbean. While she explicitly refers to the poet, she never names Wordsworth specifically, but the nightmare she has that evening confirms that the poem indeed is "I wandered lonely as a Cloud":

> I remembered an old poem I had been made to memorize when I was ten years old and a pupil at Queen Victoria Girls' School. I had been made to memorize it, verse after verse, and then had recited the whole poem to an auditorium full of parents, teachers, and my fellow pupils. After I was done, everybody stood up and applauded with an enthusiasm that surprised me, and later they told me how nicely I had pronounced every word, how I had placed just the right amount of special emphasis in places where that was needed, and how proud the poet, now long dead, would have been to hear his words ringing out of my mouth. I was then at the height of my two-facedness: that is, outside I seemed one way, inside I was another; outside false, inside true. And so I made pleasant little noises that showed both modesty and appreciation, but inside I was making a vow to erase from my mind, line by line, every word of that poem. That night after I had recited the poem, I dreamt, continuously it seemed, that I was being chased down a narrow cobbled street by bunches and bunches of those same daffodils that I had vowed to forget, and when finally I fell down from exhaustion they all piled on top of me, until I was buried deep underneath them and was never seen again. I had forgotten all of this until Mariah mentioned daffodils, and now I told it to her with such an amount of anger I surprised both of us. (17-19)

In addition to establishing the Wordsworthian intertextual connection to "I wandered lonely as a Cloud" that many critics have discussed, this passage reveals Kincaid's project of rewriting Wordsworth's *Lucy*. When reciting Wordsworth's poem, Lucy, like the Lucy of the poems, does not have a voice of her own. The poet's—not her own—words ring out of her mouth. The "two-facedness"—evocative of Fanon's *Black Skin, White Masks*—reinforces this dispossession of her voice that she recognizes in the performance of her show, which echoes the "sh[o]w" the daffodils put on for Wordsworth in the original poem (18). The vow Lucy makes to "erase from [her] mind, line by line, every word of that poem" recalls Wordsworth's inscription of Lucy that writes her out of the poem. Further connecting Kincaid's Lucy with Wordsworth's Lucy is her nightmare of being buried alive beneath the daffodils and never being seen again, recalling the Lucy of Wordsworth's "She dwelt," who "liv'd unknown, and few could know / When [she] ceas'd to be" (9-10).

When Lucy tells Mariah her story "with such an amount of anger [she] surprised both of [them]," the passage breaks from the Wordsworthian inscription of Lucy. Lucy's surprise at her tirade parallels the surprise she experiences at the audience's enthusiastic response to her recitation, but it also marks a turning point in her narrative. When sharing her dream with Mariah, Lucy performatively erases the traditional absence of Wordsworth's Lucy and begins asserting her own growing selfhood by giving linguistic form to her consciousness. Ian Smith discusses this erasure in terms of "(mis)use" of the Wordsworthian poem: "The temporal chasm opened up by the daffodils fetishizes pre- and post-, before and therefore, [so that, to better] engage Wordsworth [one must] meet head-on the challenge of negotiating a place from which to deploy the creative, deliberate '(mis)use' of intertexts . . . in the discursive act of re-articulation and, sometimes, linguistic rebellion" (806). Smith reads Kincaid's use of Wordsworth's "I wandered lonely as a Cloud" as one such act of "linguistic rebellion" in which "the language of canonical texts, is adapted, taken over, re-contextualized, barbarized and reproduced to meet the current needs of a people shaped through a historical process of interculturation" (806). The evolution of the form of the language is very important to this process of recontextualization. It is no coincidence that, in Kincaid's novel, Lucy's expression of self-consciousness departs from Wordsworth's lyrical base and takes a narrative form. As Said argues in *Culture and Imperialism*, because "stories are at the heart of what explorers [and colonizers] have to say about strange regions of the world," narration "also become[s] the method colonized people use to assert their own identity and the existence of their own history" (xii). I argue that Kincaid's appropriation of Wordsworth's Lucy poems constitutes a similar act, even if that group of poems hasn't been associated with the colonial project to the degree that the daffodil poem has.

Dorothy Wordsworth's writings show that the language of colonization is related at least conceptually to Wordsworth's writing of "I wandered lonely as a Cloud." In one of her journal entries, dated 15 April 1802, she discusses the probable "subject of these Stanzas," the "single impression" that acted "upon [Wordsworth's] imaginative faculty" as he wrote the poem (see Alun R. Jones 171). In this excerpt from the entry, she recalls the following scene after seeing a huge expanse of daffodils in Gowbarrow Park: "When we were in the woods beyond Gowbarrow park we saw few daffodils close to the water side. We fancied that the lake had floated the seeds ashore and that the little colony had so sprung up . . . There was here and there a little knot and a few stragglers a few yards higher up but they were so few as to not disturb the simplicity and unity and life of the one busy highway" (qtd. in Alun R. Jones 171). The "simplicity and unity of life" of the "little colony" come across in the poem they inspire, which describes the "host" of "Ten thousand dancing in the breeze" (4, 6). While daffodils—because they are firmly rooted and are available as the result of travels—might be suggestive figures for colonies, that the daffodils provided such "laughing company" and provided undervalued "wealth" for the poet hints at the bitter ironies of reading the daffodils metaphorically as a colony (10, 11). Although Wordsworth probably did not intend "I wandered lonely as a Cloud" to espouse British colonization, it has become one of the staples in colonial education in part because terms of colonization (albeit unconsciously or associatively) figure in the poem.

The peripheral language of colonization notwithstanding, the poem's use in a colonial context can be explained by its genre. Ian Smith asserts that "Romantic poetry [with] its evocation of the beauty of nature is a perfect tool for empire" because "colonized people can be made to celebrate nature in a totally de-contextualized way, rapt in poetry's rhythmic cadences, treasuring its signs as free-floating signifiers" so that "they can be distracted from seeing the history of nature as conquered, appropriated and made the site of forced labor" (817). The daffodil has become one such signifier that mystifies English imperial presence and privileges English over native landscapes. This decontextualization of nature also applies to the Lucy poems, which supplant Lucy's absence with the poet's memory of her that both pervades and becomes embodied by the natural landscape, which serves as its own "signifier" of England. Tiffin contends that Romantic poetry "played an important part" in the "idealization of British and European flora" such as the daffodil and that "*The Royal Readers* and *The Irish Readers* were instrumental in this process": they were "being used in schools throughout the Empire from the late nineteenth century till well after independence . . . The *Readers* contained poetry about the English countryside and about flowers, and Wordsworth's poem 'I wandered lonely as a cloud' was an enduring favourite" ("Flowers" 60).

Because "I wandered lonely as a Cloud" has appeared prominently in the curricula of colonies in which daffodils do not naturally grow, the image of the daffodil itself has taken on an ironic significance within postcolonial discourse, representing the experiential disparity between the colonizer and the colonized: "The gap between the lived colonial or post-colonial experience and the imported/exported world of the Anglo-written . . . has often been referred to by Commonwealth post-colonial writers and critics as 'the daffodil gap'" (Ian Smith 806). As Betty Joseph explains, Kincaid uses temporal, not merely geographical, distance to mark the disparity signified by the daffodil gap: in Lucy's "nine-year lag in seeing a daffodil . . . Kincaid offers us a mode of reading that interrupts by way of a disruptive temporality the assumed power of a 'universal' concept" (75). Tiffin explains that this gap develops from acts of forced recitation that produce—like the Lucy poems themselves—a consequential erasure of the female subject: "In . . . Kincaid's *Lucy*, female school children recite English poetry to approving audiences, and . . . it is [this] recitation—the learning by heart of poetry and its reproduction before audiences—which is depicted as both a technology of interpellation and metonymic of the Anglo-colonialist erasure of the black Caribbean female body" ("Cold Hearts" 913). One of Lucy's dreams subconsciously enacts this type of erasure. In this dream, Lewis, Mariah's husband, chases a naked Lucy outside the house while Mariah eggs him on. While he never catches Lucy, she eventually falls into a hole, out of sight. The ending of this dream refigures the containment of Wordsworth's Lucy underground, but the dream itself focuses more on the erasure of the physical body, particularly the black female body, by foregrounding Lucy's naked body before she disappears.

In describing the mechanism of this bodily erasure, Tiffin points out that the text, a literal master narrative, has the capacity to enter and actually to control the productive capacity of the body:

> Texts, as a number of cultures recognize, actually enter the body, and imperial education systems of this century interpellated a colonialist subjectivity not just through syllabus content or the establishment of libraries within which passive colonials might absorb the lessons of the master, but through memorizing the English script, i.e. taking it into the body and re-producing before audiences of fellow colonials that which had been absorbed by heart/mind. Recitation is thus a ritual act of obedience, usually by a child performer, who in reciting an English litany speaks as if he/she were the imperial speaker/master rather than the subjectified colonial so often represented in those very passages. ("Cold Hearts" 913)

Tiffin's discussion about the interpellation of the colonial subjects by the English script has relevance for *Lucy* not only because of the recitation scene in which Lucy strongly feels the mark of the foreign text on her body ("outside false, inside true"), but also because Kincaid's overall project powerfully and subversively draws upon this strategy of bodily interpellation. At the center of this strategy is Kincaid's conception of a character—Lucy—who represents a purposeful aberration of and gives an entirely new life to Wordsworth's Lucy. In this new life, Lucy embodies a linguistic potential, which Kincaid emphasizes by entitling one of *Lucy*'s sections "The Tongue," representing the inevitable connection of the body with parole, the speech act. This bodily interpolation continues throughout the novel: Kincaid challenges Wordsworthian authority by interpolating Lucy—a literal foreign body—into the referential space of Wordsworth's poems. By reinvesting Lucy with a voice, Kincaid makes the absences present in this space productive; as Homi Bhabha writes, this interpolation works "to decentre ideology by making its absence speak . . . transform[ing] the repressions of the text, its 'articulate silences,' into a form of knowledge" ("Representation" 107).

## Recalling the after-image

One technique Kincaid uses to invoke this Wordsworthian referential space throughout the novel involves reappearances of the daffodil image in the text. As Hartman proposes, specific images such as the daffodil take on the important role of "*after-image*" in Wordsworth's poetical imagination: "An *after-image* of this kind [like the daffodils] plays an important role in many of Wordsworth's poems. It expresses the possibility of the renewal (or at least recurrence) of a certain experience by including that possibility in the very structure of experience. As a mental reflex, the after-image elongates the encounter, and an image *of* something, it may also suggest an indefinitely extended action. Not any action, of course: it is the image, itself repeated . . . The after-image echo may occur at a distance from the original experience, and still be part of it" (269). Wordsworth's "echo," the repetition of the original "after-image," not only visually "expresses the possibility of . . . renewal" that Wordsworth finds inherent in language itself, but also betrays that the "possibility" of displacement haunts Wordsworth in "the original experience." F. Ferguson describes Wordsworth's echo as "a structural incarnation of thoughts linking 'origin and tendency' inseparably" (166). Suggesting that "we can discern more about Wordsworth's sense of the problematics of echoing by expanding the notion beyond isolated poems and by seeing it as more formal than thematic," she argues that the Lucy poems themselves "participate in this mutually echoing process, heaping poem after poem on one mysterious object" (173).

Taking advantage of the potential temporal and spatial gaps that the echo introduces in Wordsworth's poems, Kincaid appropriates Wordsworth's use of the daffodil after-image to stage the imperial presence that the poems themselves represent within colonial education. The image of the daffodil has come to represent Wordworth's work and the greater English literary tradition in a postcolonial context because, as Bhabha has explained, "the major debate that has shaped our view of 'colonial literature' and identified the concepts by which we read it and write about it has been 'image analysis'" ("Representation" 99). In the passage in which Lucy remembers reciting the daffodil poem, Kincaid projects her own daffodil after-image that both critiques the daffodil in the context of Wordsworth's poems and highlights the significance of the echoes of her daffodil after-image that punctuate the rest of the novel.

By mapping Wordsworth's lyrics referentially onto the site of forced recitation, Kincaid invokes the echoes that Wordsworth inscribes in his poems while conveying that Lucy literally echoes his words when she reads his poem aloud. The idea of the echo haunts Lucy, who says, "I didn't know why, but I felt that I would rather be dead than become just an echo of someone. That was not just a figure of speech" (36). The novel extends the possibilities under which Lucy could "become just an echo of someone" beyond the obvious echoing of Wordsworth, whose "words ring[]" out of her mouth, and of the Lucy of his poems to a broader colonial scope (18). Lucy describes her fear, for example, that her "mother's love for [her] was designed solely to make [Lucy] an echo of her," a fear that applies not only to her domineering mother—who "would have been mystified as to how someone who came from inside her would want to be anyone different than her"—but also to England, the mother country (36). At a moment when Lucy "was about to break apart," Lucy recalls that "the only thing that would keep [her] alive" was her will not to be merely an echo of her mother (123).

*Lucy*'s daffodil after-image—Lucy's memory of the "old poem [she] had been made to memorize"—immediately follows Mariah's assertion that she "feel[s] so glad to be alive" when she sees daffodils "in bloom and all massed together" and "a breeze comes along and makes them do a curtsy to the lawn stretching out in front of them" (17). "So Mariah is made to feel alive by some flowers bending in the breeze," Lucy muses, "How does a person get to be that way?" (17). In response to Lucy's question "How does a person get to be that way?"—a question which itself echoes throughout the novel (e.g., 20, 26, 41)—Kincaid uses the daffodil after-image to launch a complicated response that illuminates the legacies of colonial domination. This response begins with Lucy recounting a dream she has the night after she recited the poem. In this dream, she "was chased down a narrow cobbled street by bunches and bunches of those same daffodils . . . until [she] was buried deep beneath them and never seen again" (18). This first echo of the daffodil highlights the contrast between Lucy, who betrays her anxiety about reciting the poem and the daffodils it references in her dream, and Mariah, who mimics Wordsworth's language when she talks about the daffodils and "feel[s] alive" when seeing them.

The disparity in the two women's responses to the daffodils draws attention to the differences in their postcolonial experiences. Mariah's affinity for the daffodils—in contrast to Lucy's negative associations with them—suggests that she has a worldview closer to Wordsworth than does Lucy. Given the daffodils' import within postcolonial studies, Mariah's and Lucy's vastly different reactions to them represent larger differences between British legacies in the US and the Caribbean. The US has modeled itself after its imperial parent, Kincaid suggests, with its tradition of manifest destiny and displays of global superpower. Through her depictions of Mariah and other representative US figures in the text, Kincaid traces this imperial genealogy and answers Lucy's question about how "a person get[s] to be that way" (17).

Mariah desperately wants Lucy to "see things the way she d[oes]," but Lucy does not share her history or frame of reference. Lucy is acutely aware of the attitude of US-American entitlement that Mariah (despite her philanthropic intentions) and her friends display unconsciously: "Like her, all of [them] were well off but they made no connection between their comforts and the decline of the world that lay before them. I could have told them a thing or two about it. I could have told them how nice it was to see them getting a small sip of their own bad medicine" (72). For all of her anger, Lucy develops a genuine affection for Mariah that makes her want to protect her from her own realities:

> it could be said that her kindness was the result of her comfortable circumstances, but many people in her position were not as kind and considerate as she was. And that was the reason that I couldn't bring myself to point out

> to her that if all the things she wanted to save in the world were saved, she might find herself in reduced circumstances; I couldn't bring myself to ask her to examine Lewis's [Mariah's husband's] daily conversations with his stockbroker, to see if they bore any relation to the things she saw passing away forever before her eyes. Ordinarily that was just the sort of thing I enjoyed doing, but I had grown to love Mariah so much. (72-73)

Lucy tries to explain the way she feels to Mariah, who attempts to understand where she is coming from, but others in her circle dismiss Lucy as an exotic novelty. Mariah's friend Dinah, for instance, says that Lucy is simply "from the islands": "the first thing she said to me when Mariah introduced us was 'So you are from the islands?' I don't know why, but the way she said it made a fury rise up in me. I was about to respond to her in this way 'Which islands exactly do you mean? The Hawaiian Islands? The islands that make up Indonesia, or what?' And I was going to say it in a voice that I hoped would make her feel like a piece of nothing, which was the way she had made me feel in the first place" (56). That Kincaid uses the phrase "the way she had made me feel in the first place" is important because it draws attention to the variety of places that this passage references. Physical location, of course, is important, as is place of origin, but social position, class status, and racial identification also determine one's place in society. With Lucy's asking how Mariah became the person she is, Kincaid leads the reader to consider not only Mariah's privileged position, but also Lucy's place relative to her. Thus, the reader gains insight into how Lucy, too, got to be the way she is.

Lucy's anger can be traced in part to racial inequalities that exist in the Caribbean, but are brought into focus after her immigration to the US. While taking a train trip with Mariah and the children, Lucy notes that the "other people sitting down to eat dinner all looked like Mariah's relatives; the people waiting on them all looked like mine" (32). Although Lucy notes that race largely determines who serves whom, she suggests that the issue is not simply black and white, qualifying her earlier comment with the "closer observation [that] they were not at all like my relatives; they only looked like them" (32). Lucy's Afro-Caribbean heritage sets her apart from African Americans, but because both groups are coded as "black," they are both subject to racial discrimination. The history of violence against black people in the US haunts Lucy as a present possibility. On the train, after musing about the racialized master-servant dynamic, she has trouble sleeping, imagining that "thousands of people on horseback were following me, chasing me, each of them carrying a cutlass to cut me up into small pieces" (32).

Despite her nightmare vision of the Klan, Lucy falls asleep eventually, but Mariah wakes her up early that morning because they "were passing through some of those freshly plowed fields she loved so much" (33). About this landscape Lucy only says, "thank God I didn't have to do that" (33). After this comment, Mariah postpones telling Lucy what she has been looking forward to telling her for a long time—that she has "Indian blood"—because she's afraid that Lucy will "take it the wrong way" (39-40). Lucy does recoil when she hears Mariah's proclamation, noting that "underneath everything I could swear she says it as if she were announcing her possession of a trophy. How do you get to be the sort of victor who can claim to be the vanquished also?" (40-41). Lucy expresses her surprise at Mariah's revelation: "To look at her, there was nothing remotely like an Indian about her. Why claim a thing like that?" Lucy explains that her grandmother is a Carib Indian, but that she does not "go around saying that [she has] some Indian blood in [her]" (40). In Lucy's eyes, Mariah's claim to a Native American heritage elides the colonial history that has created her privileged position.

Kincaid uses the daffodil after-image in one of Lucy's dreams to emphasize the ways in which colonial histories affect current race relations. In this dream, Lewis is chasing Lucy around the house, and the ground Lucy runs on "[is] yellow, as if it had been paved with cornmeal" (14). Moira Ferguson, who argues that "yellow is the jaundiced marker of white cultural identity," reads this yellow road as a reimagination of the yellow daffodils (*Jamaica Kincaid* 112). In addition to abstracting daffodils on the road, Kincaid figures Mariah and Lewis themselves as daffodils. Lucy describes them and their four children as "six yellow-haired heads of various sizes [that] were bunched as if they were a bouquet of flowers tied together by an unseen string," thereby associating Lewis and Mariah to the colonial legacy of the daffodil image (12). The dream of Lewis chasing Lucy prefigures both Mariah's attempts to trap Lucy within her au pair position when Lucy wants to leave and the "master business" Mariah enacts when trying to make Lucy feel like a slave-servant who is obligated to stay (143). This and other of Lucy's dreams illustrate that her immigration to the US and her employment as an au pair teach Lucy a great deal about the negotiations of place and power through race throughout history. Lucy learns "that the origin of [her] presence on the island—[her] ancestral history—was the result of a foul deed," and she notes the legacy of that deed in the "insist[ence]" that black immigrants, like Lucy, "be the servant[s]" and those who are privileged, like Mariah, "be the master" (135, 143).

As Tiffin notes, "[t]hroughout the novel Mariah and Lewis (the new American 'slave owners' of the Caribbean *au pair* Lucy) are associated with yellow, with daffodils, with Wordsworth's poem, and with an oppressive kind of disembodiment" ("Flowers" 64). This "oppressive kind of disembodiment" becomes even more visible when Mariah physically brings Lucy to daffodils, revisiting the site of her recitation of Wordsworth's lyric. Mariah "cover[s Lucy's] eyes with a handkerchief," leads her to "a spot in a clearing," "remove[s] the handkerchief," and tells her to "look at this" (28). What Lucy sees when she opens her eyes is a field of daffodils, which she has never actually seen before: "Along the paths and underneath the trees were many, many yellow flowers the size and shape of play teacups, or fairy skirts. They looked like something to eat and something to wear at the same time; they looked beautiful; they looked simple, as if made to erase a complicated and unnecessary idea. I did not know what these flowers were, and so it was a mystery to me why I wanted to kill them. I wished that I had an enormous scythe; I would just walk down the path, dragging it alongside me, and I would cut these flowers down at the place where they emerged from the ground" (29).

Reversing the earlier dream in which the daffodils trample Lucy, in this passage Lucy fantasizes about attacking the daffodils, which are reconstituted in the expository postcolonial context of Wordsworth's poem to "erase a complicated and unnecessary idea." As Ian Smith suggests, "the scene materializes Wordsworth's daffodils poem, its images and rhythms summoning once again the opening stanza with its revelatory moment for the poet" (813-14). By "cut[ting] these flowers down at the place where they emerged from the ground," Lucy can disarm the colonial orchestration of bodies that the daffodils figuratively represent. The daffodils' "beautiful" and "simple" veneer mirrors both the metaphorical mask Lucy wears when she recites Wordsworth's poem and Wordsworth's figuration of Lucy as a "violet by a mossy stone" or "like a rose in June" ("She dwelt" 5; "Strange fits" 6). These characterizations can be seen throughout Wordsworth's work; in fact, Judith Page claims that "in Wordsworth's poetry there is no female sublime, and hence no female identity apart from male perception" (25). Frances Ferguson gestures toward the implications of such gendered depictions, suggesting that "these flower similes and metaphors become impediments rather than aids to any imaginative visualization of a woman" (175). Kincaid overwrites the dainty characterization of the daffodils in this passage to mock this male perception, which is further undercut by Lucy's violent reaction to the image. In contrast to the violence Lucy feels toward the daffodils, however, the lyrical language with which Kincaid describes the beauty of the scene recalls Wordsworth's language in the poem. In a sense, Kincaid competes with Wordsworth's lyric beauty while at the same time undercutting its colonial legacy through Lucy's violent reaction to it.

While Lucy imagines doing violence to the daffodils, her inability to respond physically illustrates how the body becomes implicated by interpellation. When Lucy recalls her indecision about how to explain to Mariah the feeling she has about the daffodils—"that it wasn't exactly daffodils, but what they would do as well as anything else"—she reveals that her "heart and . . . thoughts were racing so that every time [she] tried to talk [she] stammered and by accident bit [her] own tongue" (29). As Wordsworth suggests in *The Prelude*, overwhelming emotion frustrates linguistic expression, amounting to writer's (or speaker's) block for the artist: when "A vital breeze" becomes "A tempest, a redundant energy / Vex[es] its own creation" (1.45-47). John Beer suggests that Wordsworth's drafts of *The Prelude* reveal the work as "a poem of process," noting that "the most striking feature of the first drafts is that they show him concerned with the side of his emotional memory that took him away from ordered and rational response, reminding him rather of dealings that had been touched by fear or the workings of extreme energy" (*Romanticism* 66). But while Wordsworth might have experienced a type of writer's block because of emotional memories, Kincaid suggests that Lucy's attempts at linguistic expression face much more formidable barriers, compounded by gender and years of colonial rule. Like Wordsworth's Lucy, Lucy's "form" is molded "silent" even in "the motions of the storm" ("Three Years" 22-24). Tiffin argues that the gender-inflected colonial silencing that Lucy experiences may be explained in terms of interpellation: "Through

Wordsworth's poem the politics of aesthetics has already been absorbed into Lucy's heart; she is dressed in it, but she has also eaten it, internalised it . . . Learning *by heart* the culture of others strangles self-expression—the absorption of their aesthetics, indeed their 'tongue,' cuts off one's own" ("Cold Hearts" 918).

## Framing her own worldview

Frustrated by her attempts at articulating her consciousness, Lucy decides to explore visual media through which she can wordlessly appropriate the power of the gaze, which, unmediated by language, would allow her to frame her world from her own perspective. One medium she uses for this end is the camera, which, as Moira Ferguson points out, "is empowering because it sets up distances and defines a distinct place and space for the gazer . . . with a camera memories can be rearranged, boundaries can be fudged . . . photos can tell a lie and cover things up. Perhaps more to the point, photos can even the score. With a camera, a barricade is always present" (*Jamaica Kincaid* 121). This "barricade" of the lens works to compensate for the barricade Lucy encounters in language, and she uses the camera to capture a glimpse of her worldview, "a picture that no one would ever take—a picture that would not end up in one of those books, but a significant picture all the same" (80). Lucy explains, "I was trying to imitate the mood of the photographs in the book Mariah had given me," adding, "though in that regard I failed completely, I was pleased with them all the same" (120).

As Lucy tries to imitate the "mood of the photographs in the book," Kincaid rewrites Wordsworth's "I wandered lonely as a Cloud," which he groups in a collection of poems called "Moods of My Own Mind." Even Lucy's photography can be seen as a functional metaphor for Kincaid's rewriting of Wordsworth in *Lucy*, which, although it does not reproduce Wordworth's poems, invokes them powerfully to create "a significant picture" of colonial influences on the growth of one young girl's mind. Mary Lou Emery has described this "significant picture" in terms of "counter-discursive revisions of *ekphrasis*" that "narrativize the links between representation and the social relations of colonialism and neo-colonialism" (262). "Turning to the narrative devices through which visuality is figured," postcolonial writers, like Kincaid, "are drawn especially to the classical rhetorical device of *ekphrasis*—defined as the verbal description of a work as visual art"—because of its association with "epic narratives of conquest and empire-building and with the construction of masculine identities." For this reason, Emery notes, "these writers return to a device that dialogically formalizes processes of identity formation in the context of colonialist expansion" (262). Kincaid's ekphrastic passages, I suggest, are not limited to her descriptions of Lucy's photographs, the pictures framed in Mariah's house, and the paintings in the museum, but include her invocations of the daffodil after-image, which denaturalize and demystify the image of the daffodil in Wordsworth's poem as well as the "scene" of the English landscape that his poetry projects ("Three Years" 40). Ironically, Kincaid's ekphrasis of Wordsworth's poetic images relies heavily on

Wordsworth's own poetics, which capture "the complexity of what happens when eye and object meet" (de Man 125). Kincaid uses Wordsworth's "delicate interplay between perception and imagination," seen, for example, in the "flash upon that inward eye" in "I wandered lonely as a Cloud," to examine how the images he projects affect Lucy's worldview (de Man 40, 125).

Behind the lens of the camera, Lucy loses some of the colonial inhibitions that make her self-conscious, enabling her to direct her gaze out at the world, rather than self-critically toward herself, and to frame her own images. That Lucy is directing her gaze out, like a reporter or critic, is evidenced by the fact that she has no pictures of herself (120). Projecting her sights outward, Lucy can appropriate the phallic gaze and become a voyeur in her own right, making a Sunday-afternoon routine to "go for a walk in the park and look around, then pick out the men [she] imagined [she] would like to sleep with" (88). Unlike Wordsworth's Lucy, who has "no force" and "neither hears nor sees," Kincaid's Lucy scopes the field and participates in economies of desire to realize her body's (re)productive power ("A Slumber" 5-6). She describes "how surprised [she] was to be thrilled" with sex, saying that she "had not known that such pleasure could exist and, what was more, be available to [her]" (113). After Lucy learns to (love to) live in her own skin, she can focus her attentions again on herself, this time consciously considering her "self" and what she wants it to be.

In the last section of the book, triumphantly entitled "Lucy," Lucy claims to be "making a new beginning again" (133). For the first time Lucy is named in the text, and the reader learns that she relishes being named after Milton's rebellious Lucifer, which (in terms of agency and poetical tradition) diametrically opposes her to Wordsworth's Lucy. Although Lucy's appearance has remained the same, she notes some inner changes: "[t]he things I could not see about myself . . . those things had changed, and I did not yet know them well. I understood that I was inventing myself, and that I was doing this more in the way of a painter than in the way of a scientist" (134). Although she does not "see" these changes, Lucy now envisions herself as an artist, who, like the poet in Wordsworth's *Prelude*, invents herself with "the earth . . . all before [her]," who has the freedom of mind to "look about" and, if she follows her own intuition, "cannot miss [her] way" (1.15-19). Like the boy in *The Prelude*, Lucy grows from a child to an artist-poet-(wo)man. She tells us, "One day I was a child and then I was not . . . I had begun to see the past like this: there is a line; you can draw yourself, or sometimes it gets drawn for you; either way, there it is, your past, a collection of people you used to be and things you used to do. Your past is the person you no longer are, the situations you are no longer in" (136-37). In recognizing her life as "two banks, one of which was [her] past . . . the other [her] future," Lucy exhibits the self-presence of the poet in *The Prelude*, who thinks of "the vacancy between [him] and those days" that appears "so wide" that he seems to be "two consciousnesses" (5-6; 2.28-32). Lucy decides that she is going to be the person "who draws herself," and, with this in mind, she "tr[ies] to explain to [her]self, by speaking to Mariah, how [she] got to feel the way [she] even now feel[s]" (137).

In another of Lucy's dreams, one that she has "over and over," Lucy dreams about an unidentified present, wrapped in her mother's madras headkerchiefs, which lies at the bottom of a deep, murky pool. Lucy is never able to "[get] to the bottom" of this mystery, but she knows that it is something that "would make [her] exceedingly happy" (87). This "present," I argue, puns on the "present" time, and the mystery of this present affords Lucy the ability to imagine it as she chooses. That the present is submerged and wrapped in matriarchal garment can be seen to frame it in terms of Wordsworth's Lucy, whose inscribed absence continues to haunt the present text.

Recalling the dream Lucy has of a present wrapped in her mother's headkerchiefs, Mariah gives Lucy a "present" that she found "while going through her old things" (87, 162). This present is a notebook, dyed bloodred—symbolizing the menarchal coming-of-age encapsulated in this female bildungsroman—that contains no writing, reminding Lucy that "[her] life stretched out ahead of [her] like a book of blank pages" (163). Yet in this notebook, after seeing her written name, Lucy can write "only this: 'I wish I could love someone so much that I could die from it'"—which is presumably the Romantic end of Lucy in Wordsworth's poems (164). Afterwards, she feels so ashamed that she weeps over the text, and her tears drown out the words.

Noting that Wordsworth's Lucy poems are in a "curiously mixed generic mode—part love poem, part epitaph," Frances Ferguson considers these "Lucy love-epitaphs [to be] a poetic history of the various stages in the poet's accession of knowledge" (176). She argues that the Lucy poems, "one quasi-continuous whole made up of five separate poems," figure "problems about poetic representation and naming" (184). According to Ferguson, the "progressive diminishment of Lucy's existence in these poems . . . suggests that they may serve as paradigmatic cases in coming to terms with Wordsworth's elusive notions of poetic language" (174). In *Lucy*'s final scene, Kincaid returns to this notion of the "elusive notions of poetic language" and provides the context to show why her own poetic enterprise is confounded by the historical legacies of both patriarchy and the colonial condition. At this moment, Lucy's antagonism with the shadow of Wordsworth's Lucy, who has been following her throughout the narrative, becomes literally spelled out. Although Kincaid's Lucy has learned to "draw herself" through pictures and words, the trace of Wordsworth's Lucy and the gendered containment she represents manifest themselves in her written expression. In the words of Gayarti Chakravorty Spivak (writing about Wordsworth), "there is . . . a trace of something else in seemingly self-contained origins" ("Sex and History" 325). As Tiffin and others have suggested, Lucy resists the bodily interpolation of this "final act of scriptorial obedience" by blurring the words with her tears ("Cold Hearts" 918), representing an "enactment of cultural revenge, of the dissolution of authorities, of others both family and foreign who overshadowed her life and her decisions" (M. Ferguson, *Jamaica Kincaid* 131). Moira Ferguson concludes that Lucy "reveal[s] the duplicity of the colonizing economy by mapping herself onto earlier texts" to create "a new postcolonial cartography" with which she "is ready to write" (131). Lucy explains, "It was my past, so to speak, my first real past—a past that was my own and over which I had the final word" (23).

In mapping the growth of the young writer's mind, Kincaid's *Lucy* mirrors Wordsworth's *Prelude* while narratively conceiving the modern Caribbean writer who leaves home to find herself and unpack her postcolonial baggage. Edmondson observes that "Tiffin's assessment that Lucy's body has 'erased a final act of scriptorial obedience' links this final writing act to Lucy's earlier imprisonment within the master narratives of colonialist discourse, represented first by her schoolgirl recitations of Wordsworth and later by 'new' Euro-American feminist theory introduced by her white, liberal employer to 'explain' Lucy as an entity" (83). She then asks, "If Lucy's *body* is the locus of black, Caribbean female resistance to colonialist/white feminist cooptation, then what does this mean for her *writing* as an oppositional strategy? Is writing for the Caribbean woman writer then always a form of 'scriptorial obedience,' a rewriting of already-written narratives—a *treason* to the body's reality? Is the ultimate authentic narrative for the Caribbean woman writer no narrative at all?" (83). Edmondson concludes that "for Kincaid, the narrative she writes must articulate a Caribbean female subjectivity that has no literary antecedents: hence, the body, as the carrier of female experience, is more authentic than the word" (83). I would argue, on the contrary, that *Lucy* engages these literary antecedents head-on and explores the contradictory ways that they both enable and frustrate the articulation of Caribbean female subjectivity. Furthermore, by using Wordsworth to, in her own words, "invent" herself and "ma[ke her] present different from [her] past," Kincaid extends Wordsworth's autobiographical project and shows how a reiteration of this project reads differently in her own gendered, postcolonial context (qtd. in Bonetti 130).

# Chapter Two

# Specters of US Empire in Atwood's Fiction

In her 2002 book on writing, *Negotiating with the Dead*, Atwood claims that "we are all living in the shadow cast by the Romantic movement, or in the fragments of that shadow" (xxvi). *Negotiating with the Dead* deals more extensively with the effect of the "Romantic cult of the writer as a great man" on post-Romantic writers than on Romantic poetry itself, but it points toward the importance of the Romantic "shadow" in Atwood's other works (51). A Romantic influence ominously marks Atwood's short story "Death by Landscape" and her novel *The Handmaid's Tale*, both of which use intertexts with British Romantic poetry to stage the disappearance of their female protagonists. Like Jamaica Kincaid's novel *Lucy*, "Death by Landscape" and *The Handmaid's Tale* are haunted by the absent Lucy of William Wordsworth's Lucy poems and equate this absence with erasure that occurs in a distinctly American—and decidedly imperial—context. Casting a shadow of her own on both the United States and the larger North American continent, Atwood invokes Romanticism in "Death by Landscape" and *The Handmaid's Tale* to depict empire's human costs, which come to light when her characters, Lucy and Offred, vanish in imperial landscapes. Linda Kauffman, writing about these human costs in the context of *The Handmaid's Tale*, notes that "the appropriation of the female body and voice is . . . closely allied with other political acts of appropriation and conquest" (226). Atwood's intertexts with Romanticism make the connection between "the appropriation of female body and voice" and larger-scale acts of imperial usurpation manifest.

## Lucy and others absent, but present in the landscape

Like Kincaid's novel *Lucy*, Atwood's short story, "Death by Landscape" engages the problematic absence of Lucy in Wordsworth's Lucy poems by telling the story of another Lucy character that evokes the fate of Wordsworth's Lucy, which I discuss in chapter 1. In "Death by Landscape," Lucy's story, told via her childhood friend Lois, culminates in a dire and ambiguous ending that recalls that of Wordsworth's Lucy: While at summer camp, Atwood's Lucy seemingly vanishes into the landscape. Despite the title, it is not clear that Lucy dies when she disappears because her body is never found. More important than the question of whether or not Lucy is actually dead, however, is Lois's insistence that Lucy is alive and inside her personal space: "Everyone has to be somewhere, and this is where Lucy is. She is in Lois's apartment, in the holes that open inward on the wall, not like windows, but like doors. She is here. She is entirely alive" (57). Where Lucy seems to be—or at least where Lois imagines her—is within the Canadian landscape paintings showcased in Lois's apartment. Although placing Lucy within the paintings' landscapes is, admittedly, fantastical, by creating such an association Atwood draws the reader's attention to landscape itself. Landscape, Atwood suggests, does not resemble scenes one might view through "windows," but "doors" through which one travels to gain more direct access to the scene itself. The story of Lucy's disappearance in "Death by Landscape," in fact, opens its own door into a North American landscape haunted by those displaced and exterminated during European settlement.

"Death by Landscape" begins by discussing Lois's recent move into a Toronto waterfront condominium. Living in the condominium is a huge relief to Lois, who is now a widow with grown children, because she does not have to worry about the natural world encroaching on her space, "about the lawn, or about ivy pushing its muscular little suckers into the brickwork, or the squirrels gnawing their way into the attic and eating the insulation off the wiring, or about strange noises" (49). Lois limits her contact with nature, but ironically, her most prized possessions are landscape paintings by famous Canadian artists. Although these paintings are worth a great deal of money, Lois values them not because they are investments, but because they mediate her engagement with a traumatic event from her childhood. When Lois was fourteen and at summer camp, she went on a canoe trip during which her best friend, Lucy, disappeared. Lucy's disappearance has become the defining moment of Lois's life: "She can hardly remember, now, having her two boys in the hospital, nursing them as babies; she can hardly remember getting married, or what Rob looked like. Even at the time she never felt she was paying full attention. She was tired a lot, as if she was living not one life but two: her own, and another, shadowy life that hovered around her and would not let itself be realized, the life of what would have happened if Lucy had not stepped sideways and disappeared from time" (57). Lois's paintings provide the canvas through which she can both contain and propagate the existence of this "shadowy life."

Lois's association of Lucy with the paintings' landscapes both invokes the sublimation of Lucy into nature in Wordsworth's poems and points to the ways in which such landscapes operate socially and politically in forming identities and negotiating power. Wordsworth's Lucy poems, as discussed in the last chapter, constitute the speaker's subjectivity through his reflections on Lucy's death and return to nature, with the "fond and wayward thoughts [that] slide / Into a Lover's head" upon his imagining Lucy dead: "No motion has she now, no force; / She neither hears nor sees, / Rolled round in the earth's diurnal course / With rocks and stones and trees" ("Strange Fits" 25-26; "A Slumber" 5-8). Altering the dynamic between the speaker of the Lucy Poems and the Lucy who "neither hears nor sees," Lois imagines an exchange, a type of scopic dialogue between Lucy and herself that is mediated by the paintings. She looks for Lucy inside a painting, but cannot see her, while Lucy is able to look out from the painting onto Lois, "involving [her] in its twists and turns of tree and branch and rock" (49, 57). The striking similarities of the natural figures that Wordsworth and Atwood associate with Lucy—"rocks and stones and trees" and "tree and branch and rock," respectively—become even more significant in light of the differences in how the two Lucys act, or interact, in their literary frames of reference; while Wordsworth's Lucy has "no motion" and "no force," Atwood's Lucy succeeds in drawing Lois into the painting. What Atwood draws attention to in "Death by Landscape" is not, however, the difference between her Lucy character and Wordsworth's, but rather the importance of landscape as imagined but naturalized space that mediates subjectivity.

Not unlike Lois's paintings, "Death by Landscape" functions as a canvas that frames landscape and draws attention to its associations with the Romantic tradition that Atwood negotiates in other pieces, most notably *The Handmaid's Tale*, in order to de-scribe empire. "Death by Landscape" asks the reader to acknowledge the importance of landscape, to consider, in Mitchell's words, "not just what landscape 'is' or 'means' but what it *does*, how it works as a cultural practice" (*Landscape* 1). The story provides glimpses of how landscape works culturally by directing the reader to examine its processes of subjectivization and marginalization, which place some subjects in relief while obscuring others, as well as its processes of objectification, which disenfranchise subjects by transforming them into naturalized objects. "Death by Landscape" suggests that in order to analyze this cultural work of landscape, one must always take into account not only who creates a landscape and what the landscape contains, but also what the landscape excludes, objectifies, subjectifies, or marginalizes.

"Death by Landscape" highlights these issues for the reader with its allusion to Wordsworth's Lucy poems, which create a landscape in which Lucy is notably absent. Marlon B. Ross asserts that Lucy's absence from Wordsworth's poems reflects the historical subordination of women, and that the poems further naturalize this power dynamic by subsuming the person Lucy within a natural space: "What we recognize when we uncover Wordsworth's relation to the female figures who inhabit his landscape is that the poet exploits the socio-historical experience of woman's subordinate position, transforming that culturally fabricated status (a socio-historical fact) into a natural and essential place (a transcendent idea)" ("Naturalizing Gender" 391). This "natural and essential place" reappears in "Death by Landscape," although it is slightly transformed to represent the different sociohistorical power dynamics at play in the creation of North American places (i.e., Canada and the US). When discussing the creation of North American places by European settlers, I consider place to be, in Gillian Rose's words, a geographical concept that takes into account "a specific set of interrelationships between environmental, economic, social, political, and cultural processes—what Lukermann has called a 'bounded element complex'"

(41). As Gilbert and Tompkins clarify, "colonial space was inscribed according to the imperatives of settlement, initially by European cartographers whose segmentation, classification, and hierarchisation of space transformed it into a *place* that could be known and inhabited" (145). In both the Lucy poems and "Death by Landscape," one can trace an identification of colonial space involving, on the one hand, the idealization of a marginalized other and, on the other, the naturalized erasure of that "other" subject by those framing the landscape. Because "Death by Landscape" explicitly frames landscape in terms of both aesthetic and cultural considerations, it serves as a productive text for examining Atwood's preoccupation with the relationship between landscape and power. In this story Atwood presents landscape's importance for identity by showing it as "a medium of exchange between the human and the natural, the self and the other" (Mitchell, *Landscape* 5). The paintings in "Death by Landscape" focus the story on the ways in which landscape functions in literary canvases, specifically drawing correspondences with Wordsworth's Lucy poems to examine the intersection of landscape, the self, and the other.

Mark Bruhn's "Margaret Atwood's Lucy Poem" provides a helpful starting point for examining the negotiation of identity in "Death by Landscape." Bruhn argues that Atwood invokes Wordsworth's "memorial poetics of the altered self" in her representations of subjectivity, but that she alters his poetics by differentiating the self from the other in a way that creates a new "postmodern art of otherness" (450-52). Noting that in both "Death by Landscape" and the Lucy poems the speaker or protagonist is an adult who laments the loss of a Lucy character that "seems simultaneously to be both herself and an earlier, youthful, and now defunct version of the speaker's or protagonist's self" (452), Bruhn suggests that Atwood "revises, by complicating and denaturalizing, the subjective meaning of Wordsworth's Lucy," thereby creating a "comparative representation of subjectivity" (453). He argues that Atwood complicates the "subjective meaning" of Wordsworth's Lucy by basing Lois's identification with Lucy on her otherness—that she wanted to be like Lucy because Lucy was "precisely . . . what she was not" (453)—and that Atwood denaturalizes Wordsworth's Lucy by "dissociat[ing] the living Lucy from Nature and expos[ing] the cultural constructions that undergird her value to Lois" (454).

Bruhn argues that Wordsworth's Lucy is merely an outdated version of the speaker himself: "In Wordsworth, Lucy's otherness is figured solely in her femininity, which is itself . . . hardly evoked. Indeed, this sole distinction from the presumably male speaker granted, Lucy is otherwise indistinguishable from what he himself was as a child" (453). Bruhn and Ross emphasize gender differently in their arguments about the poetics of otherness in Wordsworth's Lucy poems, but they are both helpful for considering what is at stake in the death of the feminized other and her association with the landscape, whether that other be a "defunct version of the speaker's or protagonist's self" or a female figure who represents "the socio-historical experience of a woman's subordinate position" (Bruhn 452; Ross, "Naturalizing Gender" 391). For both critics, Lucy's death becomes an occasion for speaker's authority, even if it involves mourning a younger, inferior version of himself.

To demonstrate how Atwood uses Wordsworth's Lucy for this comparative representation of subjectivity, Bruhn uses the language of the visual to highlight the distinctions between traditional landscape paintings and Lois's paintings. These distinctions, he suggests, describe the differences in Wordsworth's and Atwood's representations of subjectivity:

> Both writers intend to represent a multiple, processive, and otherwise textured subjectivity, to give what Wordsworth calls "a *picture* of the mind," Atwood "a *geography* of the mind." The fundamental difference in their apparently similar poetics, however, may be illustrated in the contrast Lois draws between "the old, tidy European" landscape paintings and the ones she's collected, where instead of "a gentle hill, a curving river, a cottage, a mountain in the background, a golden evening sky," one finds "a tangle, a receding maze . . . no backgrounds . . . no vistas; only a great deal of foreground that goes back and back, endlessly, involving you in its twists and turns." (117-18)
>
> For Atwood, Wordsworth's "picture of the mind" implies that it is too tidy, too carefully arranged; it is beautiful in its way, but false, or at least incomplete, for it fails to illustrate what even Wordsworth in his most searching poetic moments had to admit, the psychic truth that "you can become lost almost as soon as you step off the path and into the still largely uncharted, bewildering terrain of the self." (456)

In "Death by Landscape," Lucy provides a contrast by which Lois can more clearly grasp her own identity. Bruhn points out that Lucy is different from Lois and the other Canadian girls at the camp because she comes from the US, "where comic books come from, and the movies" (51). Unlike Lois, Lucy is rich and does not know how to live in the woods. Compounding Lucy's inexperience with the natural world is her lack of interest in (learning about) what she does not know: "There were things Lois knew that Lucy did not. Lucy scratched the tops off all her mosquito bites and had to be taken to the infirmary to be daubed with Ozonol. She took her T-shirt off while sailing, and . . . she burned spectacularly, bright red, with the X of her bathing-suit straps standing out in the alarming white; she let Lois peel the sheets of whispery-thin burned skin off her shoulders. When they sang 'Alouette' around the campfire, she did not know any of the French words. The difference was that Lucy did not care about the things she didn't know, whereas Lois did" (52). Lucy, bright red with an X on her back that shines an "alarming white," is clearly marked as different. The glaring white X also maps Lucy in the landscape, and the sunburn that brings this mark into relief is a sign of bodily harm that, along with her mosquito-bite scabs, symbolizes her ill-fated encounters with the natural world and foreshadows her eventual disappearance into it.

Although Bruhn is right to assert that Atwood's revision of the Lucy poems reflects a "comparative representation of subjectivity" that figures the other differently than Wordsworth does, his argument does not adequately account for the role of landscape in mediating this comparative subjectivity. Atwood's figuration of landscape in this story, in fact, provides the conditions for the comparative subjectivity to which Bruhn alludes. Negotiations of subjectivity are not limited to the most important interpersonal relationships in a person's life; they also involve the larger environment of which they are a part. As the narrator of *The Handmaid's Tale* reiterates in the novel, "Context is all" (144, 192). Analysis of Lois's memories of the events preceding Lucy's departure provides insight into the larger contexts of Lucy's disappearance, how these contexts constitute landscape, and why landscape is important for representations of subjectivity.

Lois first meets Lucy at Camp Manitou, a summer camp for girls, which, like others of its type, "favoured Indian names" (50). The name "Manitou" itself carries significance for the story. For many Native American tribes, the term "Manitou" represents "the manifestation of spiritual power, a manifestation that could occur in almost any form" applying both to figures of the landscape, such as "the sun, the moon, and . . . thunder" and to that which is "unknown" or other (Dowd 17-18; Salisbury 38-39). Neal Salisbury explains that conceptualizing that which is other in terms of Manitous allowed Native Americans (First Nations in Canada) "without experiencing a radical discontinuity in worldview," to "accommodate themselves to the more abrupt changes accompanying European colonization" (39). In "Death by Landscape," Atwood invokes the conception of Manitou as she landscapes the story to account for the Native American peoples whom European colonization has displaced and virtually erased from the North American landscape.

In addition to its "Indian" name, Camp Manitou adopts structures and activities that mimic First Nations' traditions, like its "totemic clan system," which classifies the campers by age groups according to species names: "Chickadees, Bluejays, Ravens, and Kingfishers" (51). Atwood here acknowledges that gender, even more determinately than age, orders these hierarchies: "In those days, thinks Lois, it was birds for girls, animals for boys—wolves and so forth—though some animals and birds were suitable and some were not: never vultures, for instance; never skunks, or rats" (51). The fact that no one was associated with undesirable animals—vultures, skunks, or rats—suggests that the species choice reflected upon the children they represented. Since wolves and such animals are higher on the food chain, so to speak, than birds, Atwood seems to imply that gender hierarchies—like racial stereotypes—become manifest even in grouping young children.

Before Lucy and Lois embark on the canoe trip during which Lucy disappears, Cappie, the camp leader who is also known as "Chief Cappeosota," gives them a "special send-off" (52). She paints "three streaks of red across each of her cheeks with a lipstick," ties "a twisted bandana around her head [with] a row of frazzle-ended feathers around it," and wraps herself "in a red and black Hudson's Bay blanket" (53). The counselors, "also in blankets but with only two streaks of red," participate, "beat[ing] on tom-toms made of round wooden cheeseboxes with leather stretched over the top and nailed in place" (53). After the initial fanfare, Cappie addresses the girls, her "braves," in a manner of speaking that "is her idea—all their ideas—of how Indians talk" (53). She decrees: "You go on big water . . . You go where no man has ever trod . . . You bring back much wampum . . . Do good in war, my braves, and capture many scalps" (53). Atwood notes that for the girls to embark on this expedition, they must be figured as "braves." She explains that "this is another of [Cappie's] pretenses: that [the girls on the canoe trip] are boys, and bloodthirsty. But such a game cannot be played by substituting the word *squaw*. It would not work at all" (53). Substituting "the word *squaw*" would not work partly because the role-playing implies the conquest of virgin land, which has traditionally been figured in terms of a female who is, in turn, deflowered by the male conqueror-explorer. This figuration reflects historical practice, as Rose has noted: "historically, in geographic discourse, landscapes are often seen in terms of the female body" (87).

Cappie's injunction to her "braves" presents many problems beyond gendered representation and her assumptions about "how Indians talk." Her commands are laced with the colonialist rhetoric of European explorers and the US's doctrine of Manifest Destiny. While the girls are posing as Indians, the tasks she sets out for them—plundering "wampum," doing "good in war," and capturing "many scalps"—hauntingly recall the colonizing behavior of these girls' male ancestors: the exploitation, displacement, and virtual eradication of Native American tribes from the North American continent. The impulse to explore, claim, and settle the land, as Anne McClintock asserts, finds justification in "the myth of the virgin land [which is] also the myth of the empty land, involving both a gender and a racial dispossession": "Since indigenous peoples are not supposed to be spatially there—for the lands are 'empty'—they are symbolically displaced onto what I call *anachronistic space* . . . According to this trope, colonized people—like women and the working class in the metropolis—do not inhabit history proper but exist in a permanently anterior time within the geographic space of the modern empire as anachronistic humans, atavistic, irrational, bereft of human agency—the living embodiment of the archaic 'primitive'" (30).

Because First Nations' citizens have been symbolically (if not literally) wiped off the map, they can be figured in ways that suggest that they do not deserve to be there—that they are, in McClintock's words, "atavistic, irrational, bereft of human agency." Although the camp directors and the girls view this ceremony as a "game" (53), the concept of the "send-off" has bitter connotations in the context of Native American displacements. Furthermore, the Indian personae assumed by Cappie and the counselors illustrate that they envision Native Americans as primitive and demonstrate how easily, in the absence of historical or accurate cultural representations within a given context, those in power can create and disseminate misbegotten stereotypes of colonized groups. Acknowledging the poorly represented particulars of the ceremony, Lois notes that "Cappie was never one to be much concerned with consistency, or with archeology" (53). Lois remembers this "special send-off" and weighs the scene in the context of what she has learned about Native peoples since that summer, when she was fourteen years old: "Looking back on this, Lois finds it disquieting. She knows too much about Indians. She knows, for instance, that they should not even be called Indians, and that they have enough worries without other people taking their names and dressing up as them. It has all been a form of stealing"

(53). As Lois reflects on this experience as an adult, she acknowledges that what the girls were doing somehow constituted an ethical trespass. While Lois equates what McClintock describes as "racial dispossession" with "stealing," the story leaves for the reader to consider the "stealing" that exceeds child's play—"other people taking their names and dressing up as them"—and involves greater crimes that Lois does not consider. As far as Indians are concerned, Lois thinks she already "knows too much."

When Lois was a child, though, she "care[d] about the things she didn't know," including Indians and things she associated with them. This lack of real information about Indians is something that Atwood has discussed in relation to her own childhood: "In school, under the inaccurate heading of Social Studies, we were learning the Kings of England and the Explorers . . . Of the things I later discovered I wanted to know we were told next to nothing. Among these were the disadvantages of being a colony, political or economic, and even greater disadvantages of being Indian" (*Second Words* 85). Atwood later explains, "the schools I went to were still bastions of the British Empire. In school we learned the Kings of England and how to draw the Union Jack and sing Rule Britannia, and poems with refrains like, 'Little Indian, Sioux or Cree, Don't you wish that you were me?'" (*Second Words* 376). Unlike Atwood, Lois was not then aware of the "stealing," but "she loved the campfire, the flickering of light on the ring of faces, the sound of the fake tom-toms, heavy and fast like a scared heartbeat" (53). As an adult, she insists that "it was not funny, it was not making fun. She wanted to be an Indian. She wanted to be adventurous and pure, and aboriginal" (53). In many respects Lois's childhood desire to be an Indian resembles her identification with her friend Lucy, whom, Bruhn argues, she wants to emulate because Lucy is "precisely . . . what she was not." "Lois is trying on a persona," Bruhn explains, "that attracts exactly to the extent that it is not her own" (454). Given this mindset, the persona of the Indian should, in theory, attract Lois even more.

In *Playing Indian*, Philip Deloria examines the preoccupation of Americans—colonists, US citizens, and Canadians—with posing as Indians. He traces the phenomenon in groups ranging from the colonists of the Boston Tea Party to "children of angst-ridden upper- and middle-class parents," like Lois and Lucy, who "wore feathers and slept in tipis and wigwams at camps with multisyllabic Indian names" (7). Although Deloria differentiates between groups such as the Woodcraft Indians and the Sons of Daniel Boone, who "learned Americanness . . . by recreating the lives of the pioneer scouts who had tamed the wild American frontier," he argues that "Indian-white relations and Indian play itself have modeled a characteristically American kind of domination in which the exercise of power was hidden, denied, qualified, or mourned" (95, 97, 187). Deloria notes that following World War II (the same time Lois and Lucy attended the camp), Americans "turned to Indians as markers of something undeniably real," claiming that "Indiannness offered a deep, authentic, aboriginal Americanness, [the ability] to connect with a real Self, both collective and individual" (183). This connection, Deloria explains, does not represent a form of hybridity, but merely a state of opposition: "Playing Indian offered Americans a national fantasy—identities built not around synthesis and transformation, but around unresolved dualities themselves. Temporary, costumed play refused to synthesize the contradictions between European and Indian. Rather, it held them in near-perfect suspension" (185). "Death by Landscape," by refusing to hold the dualities of white and Indian in suspension, collapses the identities of Lucy and the Indian she pretends to be into the figure of Lois's "other," who disappears into the landscape. Rather than privileging either Lucy or the Indian as Lois's "other" persona, "Death by Landscape" manipulates its own literary landscape in order to conflate the two personae and uses the intertexts with Wordsworth's Lucy poems to ground this persona in the landscape.

By mapping the figure of the Indian—the Native American—onto the "modern" American and displacing them both into the landscape, the story problematizes what it means to be American. Because Native Americans have largely been written out of the grand narrative of American history and no longer represent what is quintessentially "American," Lucy, the visible "modern" American must vanish in order to evoke the Native Americans' fate and what the displacement of Native Americans from the cultural landscape means for American identity more generally. The central role that landscape plays in this examination of Americanness points toward ways that colonial (and postcolonial) American identity has always been negotiated through the landscape—whether in terms of habitation, cultivation, urbanization, or domination—and toward ways in which Native Americans have been excluded, marginalized, or demonized in the colonial landscape. In a sense, the distinctly Canadian landscape that Atwood creates brings itself into focus by taking Lucy hostage and, in doing so, bears witness not only to US settlers' displacement and eradication of Native Americans, but also to the struggle for First Nations' citizens to be appropriately recognized within Canada's political landscape.

As Lucy, cloaked in her Indian persona, steps off the path in the story, Atwood transports her to McClintock's "anachronistic space," where Native Americans have been all along. Lucy's displacement from the foreground of the narrative represents Atwood's recreation of the North American cultural landscape that acknowledges and represents the literal and symbolic displacements of Native American peoples from the continent. The disappearance of Lucy, transformed into a "brave," stages the conflation of what McClintock calls "the myth of the virgin land" and "the myth of the empty land" within an imperial landscape. According to Eva Mackey, with this landscape Atwood depicts "a place in which the presence of Aboriginal people has been erased, making the paintings an assertion of a . . . *terra nullius*" (127). Although I agree with Mackey that Atwood frames her recreated landscape in the paintings to mark the erasure of native populations manifest in the narrative, I argue that Atwood brings this erasure into relief through the conflation of the Native American with Lucy, the antithetical modern American, in a way that points more directly to the injustice of settlers' displacement of American Indians. To stage the setting for the conflation of the two Americans, Lois's paintings, with their images of "an island of pink wave-smoothed stone . . . a lake with rough, bright, sparsely wooded cliffs . . . a vivid river shore with a tangle of bush and two beached canoes [and] yellow autumn woods with the ice-blue gleam of a pond," recreate the locale in which Lucy disappeared during the canoe trip. The paintings include neither Lucy nor any other human figure, but portray the presence of the other, both Lucy and the Indian, trapped within the anachronistic space: "Despite the fact that there are no people in them or even animals, it's as if there is something, or someone, looking back out" (49). By describing this sense that someone is "looking back out," Atwood creates a trace of the Native American within the landscape that instigates a dialogic visual exchange with the viewer of the painting. This exchange, facilitated by the painting framework which makes landscape the focus, allows subjectivities to be negotiated between the self—the viewer—and the other within the medium of the painting.

By framing the landscape within the paintings, Atwood not only creates a medium through which subjectivity may be negotiated via landscape, but also implicitly creates an audience, comprised of both Lois and the reader, that sees or reads about the paintings and thereby creates this dialogic condition. The reader's role in observing the paintings is, of course, mediated through the language of the story, but this mediation of landscape through literature is central to Atwood's project, for the recasting of colonial landscapes in fiction is a means by which Atwood herself exposes and undermines imperialist power. In her examinations of "the narrative devices through which visuality is figured," Atwood, like other postcolonial writers, utilizes "the classical rhetorical device of *ekphrasis*—defined as the verbal description of a work as visual art" as part of "a rhetorical strategy" for highlighting the human costs of empire (Emery 262-64). As Mary Lou Emery explains, "*Ekphrasis* has long been associated with epic narratives of conquest and empire-building and with the construction of masculine identities. Therefore, [postcolonial women] writers return to a device that dialogically formalizes processes of identity formation in the context of colonialist expansion" (262). According to Emery, ekphrasis "has to do with social power as acquired or denied through forms of possession in several ways: the consolidation and possession of naturalized, divinely sanctioned, national, and masculine identity; the dispossession of female identity; and, on a more exclusively formal level, the attempt by writing to possess the image by rendering it verbally" (264). Atwood's ekphrasis of the paintings draws out the presence of Lucy, who at once represents the girl within the story, the Indian, and, more generally, feminized landscape through her association with Wordsworth's Lucy poems. By describing Lucy's presence within the paintings, Atwood critiques the way American imperial rhetoric naturalizes the conquest of the "virgin" land through seemingly innocuous aesthetic objects while representing those who are written out of nation-building narratives.

To signal her opposition to colonially motivated ekphrasis, Atwood revises the language of Romantic landscape poems to rhetorically reconfigure the "prospect" within the story and to call into question the idea of the "prospect" itself. "As a literary trope," Labbe writes, the prospect view "is familiar to readers of eighteenth-century literature as the most common vantage-point from which one may compose or order the elements of the loco-descriptive poem" (ix). The suggestion of a "prospect view" in "Death by Landscape" resonates with Wordsworth's poems, many of which are loco-descriptive, a term Wordsworth himself uses in the Preface to *Poems* of 1815 to characterize his poems that are "descriptive . . . of the processes and appearances of external nature" (627). Atwood underscores her revision of the prospect with the names of key locations in the story of Lucy's disappearance: Camp Manitou is located on the edge of "Lake Prospect," and the site where Lucy was last seen is called "Lookout Point" (50, 54). Mitchell argues that viewing landscapes in this way represents a form of nostalgia for a time when the whole earth was available for "endless appropriation and conquest": "more people now probably have an appreciation of scenic beauty, precisely because they are so estranged from it. Landscape is now more precious than ever—an endangered species that has to be protected from and by civilization, kept safe in museums, parks, and shrinking 'wilderness areas.' Like imperialism itself, landscape is an object of nostalgia in a postcolonial and postmodern era, reflecting a time when metropolitan cultures could imagine their destiny in an unbounded 'prospect' of endless appropriation and conquest" (*Landscape* 20). Defying these expectations about the Romantic prospect, "Death by Landscape" illustrates that landscape is not merely a scene one views, but rather a way of looking that reveals how one imagines her own (and others') place within naturalized space (Rose 87). Atwood's "Lookout Point" is not the location for a scenic prospect, but the site of Lucy's disappearance; rather than allowing Lucy to see the bigger picture, she hides Lucy in the picture itself.

When considering the "Lookout Point" from which Lucy disappears, Lois remembers that "what you were supposed to see from [the lookout] was not clear," but that the counselor leading the canoe trip said it was "just a view" (55). The distinction between "see[ing]" and "just . . . view[ing]" is crucial for the de-scription of empire and is precisely what Atwood makes clear in "Death by Landscape" through Lois's engagement with the paintings. Lois's fascination goes beyond appreciating their aesthetic beauty—merely viewing them—and constitutes a more substantial way of seeing, an insight that allows for a reading of what is inscribed in, but not necessarily written on, the landscape. This distinction between just viewing and seeing relates to the difference between Lucy, who "did not care about things she did not know," and Lois, who did (52). Although Lois does have the insight to recognize the presence of those trapped within the paintings' anachronistic space, she is at the same time a collector who owns these paintings, and this ownership carries with it a (deceptively false) sense of control over what she sees inside them. Rather than positioning the pictures "in the old acceptable manner of sprinkling art around so that it does not get too intrusive," Lois has hung these pictures in her apartment with a gallery-like presentation: "blocks of pictures, above and beside one another" (49). This focused arrangement of the paintings represents Lois's attempt to localize the trauma associated with Lucy's disappearance and to contain it within the framed art. The attempts at controlling this trauma through art, however, have seemed to backfire for Lois; instead of providing her with a sense of ownership and containment of the trauma, they captivate her and fill her with a "wordless unease" (49).

Lois's anxiety about the paintings undoubtedly involves the trauma of losing her good friend Lucy, but it also represents a more generalized apprehension of the Canadian role in the dispossession of native lands. Although the story creates a distinct suspension between Lucy, the "American," and the Indian, Lois's relation to these two figures remains more ambiguous. The suspension between the dialectical figures of the Indian and the US citizen points toward other, more nuanced oppositions of Canadian identity in the context of Lois's paintings, which are importantly by Canadian painters and of Canadian landscapes. Lois's paintings are by members of the Canadian Group of Seven and Tom Thomson, who is associated with this group. Founded in 1920, the Group of Seven initiated the first major Canadian art movement with a concerted focus on the sublimity of Canadian landscapes (*Beyond Wilderness* 3). It is also worth noting the similarities between Lucy's fate and that of Thomson, who died before the Group of Seven was officially formed. Thomson disappeared during a canoe trip in 1917, and his body was found (unlike Lucy's) in Canoe Lake in Algonquin Park (*Beyond Wilderness* 279).

Lois's imagination of the other—both Lucy, the "modern" American, and the Native North American—within these Canadian paintings begs the question of where Canadians fit into this picture and gestures toward the problem of defining a specifically Canadian national identity that, although distinctive from First Nations and modern US-American identities, remains closely bound with both. I argue that the story plays with Canadian identification with the US through Lois's associations with Lucy. While Lois identifies Lucy as her childhood best friend, she draws more attention to their differences than their commonalties; for example, Lucy had more money, did not care about what she does not know, and so on, suggesting that Lois defines herself in opposition to Lucy. When Lucy disappears, Lois not only loses her friend, but also feels "tried and sentenced" and "singled out, condemned for something that was not her fault" (57). Although the condemnation of Lois follows Lucy's disappearance, Lois would not be singled out if she did not associate so closely with Lucy in the first place. Read in terms of national allegory, Lois's feeling could on another level represent a more general Canadian response to their own mistreatment of First Nations in addition to guilt by association for the larger-scale US displacement and dispossession of Native Americans.

Atwood frames the landscape in the paintings in such a way that directs both Lois and the reader to avoid what Ronald Hatch calls "pioneer" vision: "some grand narrative or 'vision' that will allow [a person] to stand back and comprehend [her] relation to the land" abstractly and without considering her relation to the actual people, objects, and ecological features that constitute it (185). Labbe describes the "viewpoint" associated with this vision in terms of the climb to the lookout point and what it means for social landscapes: "This élite viewpoint leads to a valorization of the generalized landscape one sees when one climbs—socially and literally—high enough to oversee. What had been postulated as an aesthetic category, a metaphor of vision that indicated one's place on the educated eminence, becomes a social advantage: the viewer exchanges his interest in the artistically generalized landscape for a self-interested refusal to notice any *single* object, domain, or activity in the political or worldly landscape" (xi). By conveying a landscape in the paintings that contains "no backgrounds . . . no vistas[,] only a great deal of foreground that goes back and back, endlessly, involving you in its twists and turns," Atwood discourages one from "stand[ing] back" and taking a prospect view (57). Instead, she designs "a tangle, a receding maze, in which you can become lost as soon as you step off the path" and into the story's landscape (57). By drawing the reader in this way, Atwood insures that the historical and cultural realities of Native Americans are not abstracted or glossed over. These historical and cultural realities, which Atwood stages with Lucy's disappearance, involve bodily harm, dispossession, and disappearance.

It might seem to be poetic justice that Lucy, the US-American who "did not care about the things she didn't know," suffers the fate of Wordsworth's Lucy and vanishes into unknowable, anachronistic space. Lois, however, must bear the burden of seeing, but not viewing, what is there. She is so traumatized by her experience and her guilt—both of being the last to see Lucy and of stealing from the Indians—that she loathes proximity to the natural world. To assuage her anxiety, she moves to the condominium, where "the only plant life is in pots in the solarium" (49). Deloria suggests that anxiety like Lois's represents a larger national sense of guilt and unease. He explains that "while Indian people have lived out a collection of historical nightmares in the material world, they have also haunted a long night of American dreams" (191). It certainly has been a long night for Lois, for whom it "is increasingly an effort" to stir from the space of her apartment (57). Although Lois's paintings, like Wordsworth's Lucy poems, represent displacements of terrifying landscapes, they also embody the danger possible in such a place. Thus, while Lois's paintings ostensibly frame and harness the shadowy Lucy figure, they foster Lois's fear of the natural world and have come to serve as a type of prison for Lois instead.

The landscape Atwood creates in "Death by Landscape" de-scribes empire by inscribing the haunting presence of those forcibly removed from, and therefore absent in, the American landscape. Diana Brydon notes that in addition to critiquing Britain, the US, and other imperialist powers, Atwood is careful to also recognize "Canadians' complicity in colonization, in the genocide and marginalization of the country's indigenous inhabitants as well as in their own domination by foreign economic and cultural interests" (52). Atwood herself points out that "we sometimes forget, in our obsession with colonialism and imperialism, that Canada itself has been guilty of these stances towards others, both inside the country and outside it" (*Second Words* 282). As Atwood recasts American landscape in the story's paintings, she revises the imagined space in which Americans negotiate their identities to include the specters of Native American bodies. For Atwood, what is at stake in re-envisioning the American landscape is not merely accounting for the erasures of Native Americans, but more broadly exposing how, throughout American history, those in power have relied upon subordinating raced and gendered bodies within the body politic. Like "Death by Landscape," *The Handmaid's Tale* critiques the naturalization of the containment, control, conquest, and dispossession of bodies for political purposes through a reimagination of American landscape. Upon a much broader canvas, *The Handmaid's Tale* paints a futuristic dystopia that draws from American history to illustrate how the rhetoric of the "natural" underpins the disenfranchisement of women while examining ways that this disenfranchisement is both perpetuated and obscured.

## *The Handmaid's Tale,* seeing the "facts of this world" and bearing witness

While illustrating the importance of landscape for negotiating identity, "Death by Landscape" demonstrates that landscapes are created, that they can be manipulated for political purposes, and that they have implications for the body politic. "Politics," Atwood says, "is everything that involves who gets to do what to whom. That's politics . . . Politics really has to do with how people order their societies, to whom power is ascribed, who is considered to have power" (*Conversations* 149). Noting that "a lot of power is ascription," Atwood emphasizes the fact that writing is bound up with authority and that writing is, therefore, a primary means of negotiating political power (*Conversations* 149). Many of Atwood's works, like "Death by Landscape," engage the relationship between landscape and politics through what Catharine Stimpson terms "a languagescape" that symbolizes, portrays, and undoes imperial landscapes' ascription of power (764). Atwood's languagescape destabilizes the cultural underpinnings of empire because it deconstructs its landscape, which, as Mitchell explains, is "the 'sacred silent language' of Western imperialism, the medium on which it 'emancipates,' 'naturalizes,' and 'unifies' the world for its own purposes" (*Landscape* 13). Works from various genres—including short stories, novels, essays, and poetry—participate in Atwood's languagescape. For example, many of her poems decode the "sacred silent language" of imperial landscapes through their examination of ways in which these landscapes naturalize unequal social conditions to justify and maintain political power. "Social and political forms," Atwood explains, "get translated into poetry" (*Conversations* 118). Atwood's poems translate the aesthetic characteristics of landscapes to reveal their social and political implications. As Hatch observes, "instead of merely representing [landscape], Atwood uses the landscape to write about representation in general" (180).

Atwood's 1966 collection *The Circle Game* includes several poems that use landscape to write about political representation. In "An Attempted Solution for Chess Problems," for example, "The white king moves / by memories and procedures / and corners . . . forcing her universe to his / geographies: the choice imposes / vestiges of black and white / ruled squares on the green landscape" (30-38). Like "An Attempted Solution for Chess Problems," many Atwood poems explore the implications of patriarchal imperial landscapes for women. Poems such as "The Circle Game" focus specifically on how, when men and women negotiate power, the female body is cast within the terms of landscape, "names (to hold / these places / in their proper places)": "now you trace me / like a country's boundary / . . . and I am fixed, stuck / down on the outspread map / of this room, of your mind's continent . . . // transfixed / by your eyes' / cold blue thumbtacks" (iv.29-31, iv.32-45). The poems "Torture" and "A Woman's Issue" in Atwood's 1981 collection *True Stories* map women's bodies as "enemy territory" subject to violence, violation, and silencing for the consolidation of "uneasy power" broadcast in "a flayed body untangled / string by string and hung / to the wall, an agonized banner / displayed for the same reason / flags are" ("A Woman's Issue" 30-37; "Torture" 33-36). Atwood's poetry, like her fiction, often draws attention to the exploitation, violence, and inequalities that are naturalized in imperial landscapes. As she declares in "Notes Towards a Poem that Can Never Be Written," also in *True Stories*, when one sees "facts of this world" clearly, "Witness is what you must bear" (v.1; v.16). One work in which Atwood bears witness is her novel *The Handmaid's Tale*. As Said asserts, the novel is the preeminent form for bearing witness to imperial histories because it historically has been central to imperial discourse. Given the links between the novel and imperialism, the novel serves as the primary form postcolonial authors use to retell historically misrepresented stories.

Among Atwood's works that map out her political languagescape, *The Handmaid's Tale* addresses most explicitly and stages the political work of de-scribing empire by bearing witness to the "facts of this world." Unlike "Death by Landscape," which does not explore what Lucy is thinking and feeling, *The Handmaid's Tale* illustrates how landscape operates within imperial contexts to naturalize the subjugation of bodies and their placement within abject social spaces by exploring how the political landscape affects one woman's consciousness. The Handmaid telling the tale explains that her body is actually marked to contain her physically and mentally in her designated place: "I cannot avoid seeing, now, the small tattoo on my ankle. Four digits and an eye, a passport in reverse. It's supposed to guarantee that I will never be able to fade, finally, into another landscape. I am too important, too scarce, for that. I am a national resource" (65). As this quote suggests, *The Handmaid's Tale* emphasizes much more distinctly than the short story the importance of markings—both symbols and the written word—for constructing (or deconstructing) an imperial landscape. Through the pronouncements of the totalitarian, theocratic empire it describes, *The Handmaid's Tale* articulates the rhetoric that underlies Gilead, and, in so doing, draws attention to the ways that its landscape is constituted by language. By showing that language underwrites imperial landscape, *The Handmaid's Tale* suggests that language also can undo it. Indeed, the narration of the Handmaid's tale itself does the political work of de-scribing the empire about which it has spoken.

In *Landscape and Power*, Mitchell argues that an "account of landscape . . . has to trace the process by which landscape effaces its own readability and naturalizes itself and must understand that process in relation to what might be called 'the natural histories' of its own beholders" (2). With *The Handmaid's Tale*, Atwood offers an account of landscape that exposes this process in a palimpsest of historical narratives about the fictional Republic of Gilead, which has overthrown the US government and instituted a theocracy. Although other Atwood works use landscape as a figural medium of critique, what differentiates *The Handmaid's Tale* from her other works is the novel's specific focus on discourse (Hogsette 263). The novel is a retrospective narrative composite recorded by a woman who served as a Handmaid in Gilead, followed by a section called "Historical Notes," given by a professor approximately 200 years after she recorded her tale. The "Historical Notes" comment on "a certain reflective quality about the [Handmaid's] narrative" and characterize her tale as having "a whiff of emotion recollected, if not in tranquillity, at least *post facto*" (303). The reference to Wordsworth's Preface to *Lyrical Ballads* represents much more than the dismissal of the Handmaid's narrative as "naïve and nostalgic drivel," which critics such as David Hogsette have suggested (272). In fact, the claim that the Handmaid's tale does not, like Wordsworth's conception of poetry, take "its origin from emotion recollected in tranquility" is important for understanding the significance of the tale itself because it points toward the difficulty of bearing witness to life under the Gileadean regime.

Wordsworth describes poetic composition as a process by which one contemplates an emotion in a state of "tranquillity" until it takes on an existence of its own in the mind. Reminding the audience throughout her narrative that "Context is all," the Handmaid demonstrates that her confined position within Gilead not only obscures her understanding of her context within the regime, but also prevents her from achieving a transcendent experience once she is outside of it (144, 192). She even lacks the perspective to precisely recall the chain of events and her original emotions that accompanied them. As she tells her story, she admits that she is "not sure how it happened; not exactly" (263). The Handmaid attempts to return to her life under Gilead by using the present tense in the narrative, which was recorded after she escaped, but her disjointed recollection of the events and emotions betrays the absence of a unified vision and carries the desperate narrative impulse of survivor testimony. Unable to recollect her life in Gilead in a poetic mode, all the Handmaid can hope for is a reconstruction that provides glimpses of the state-sanctioned terror and its effect on the people to whom it was subjected (134, 140, 263). While *The Handmaid's Tale* is layered in its narrative about the Gileadean empire in terms of different historical moments, the novel is set in the future (Atwood set *The Handmaid's Tale* in the near future of the time of its writing, the early 1980s. Although this "near future" now has passed, it is still important to consider the novel as "speculative" fiction). In "An Interview with Margaret Atwood on Her Novel *The Handmaid's Tale*," which appears in the 1998 Anchor edition of the novel, Atwood classifies it not as a work of science fiction, but as "speculative fiction" that extrapolates an imagined future of an "imperial power" based on historical referents such as the Puritans in early America, the Germans in World War II, and the KGB in the former Soviet Union (317, 320). The future orientation of the novel works well for staging how the writing of histories affects readings of empire. Because Atwood's Gileadean regime represents a conglomeration of various imperial powers rather than one identifiable regime, the reader comes to the novel with fewer historical preconceptions. Thus, Atwood puts the reader in a position of knowing similar to that of the Handmaid, who tells the tale and draws attention to the importance of the narratives for deciphering what actually happened.

Being "in the dark" is the best metaphor to describe the Handmaid's state of knowing. Atwood divides the Handmaid's narrative into fifteen chapters, eight of which are entitled "Night." Atwood has discussed the importance of this framework: "*The Handmaid's Tale* is organized partly by the repeated 'Night' sections. There are periods of action, punctuated by periods of reflection" (*Conversations* 203). In the "periods of reflection," the "Night" chapters, the Handmaid is left to reflect upon her situation without knowing what is going on around her. Although she has some private meetings with her Commander, he does not offer detailed information about how the regime operates. The darkness metaphor appears again in the "Historical Notes," in which Professor Pieixoto concludes: "As all historians know, the past is a great darkness, and filled with echoes. Voices may reach us from it; but what they say to us is imbued with the obscurity of the matrix out of which they come; and, try as we may, we cannot always decipher them precisely in the clearer light of our own day" (311). The irony of his comments is that his talk has failed to illuminate the Handmaid's narrative not because of "the obscurity of the matrix," but because he is ideologically too close to Gilead's commanders to read the Handmaid's narrative objectively, though he purports to do just that. Instead of reading her tale, the Professor merely contextualizes it in terms of the darkness from which it arises. By illuminating the darkness, *The Handmaid's Tale* serves as a warning not only about manifestations of imperial power, but also about the histories that frame them. In "A Note to the Reader" that follows the novel, Atwood stresses that "History proves that what we have been in the past we could be again" (316). *The Handmaid's Tale* fictionalizes the return of imperial histories while depicting what is at stake in reexamining them.

Although constant surveillance and restricted freedoms limit the view of the Handmaid who tells the tale of the empire, her accounts are detailed and vivid enough to convey that the Gileadean empire exercised control over and disenfranchised its female subjects by controlling, containing, and violating their bodies. Piecing together parts of her narrative, the reader learns that after the fall of the US government, her money was taken from her, she (like all working women) was fired from her job, and she was separated from her husband and daughter. Chosen because of her "reproductive fitness" to be a Handmaid, she was forced into a reeducation center, where she was taught to be silent, to wait, and to maximize her chances for conception (306). She was told that her primary duty as a Handmaid was to be a walking womb and that she was responsible for conceiving, carrying, and giving birth to the Commanders' babies; if she failed to produce children, she would be shipped to the colonies, where she might be forced to shovel radioactive waste (248). Because she, like all of the Handmaids, was supposed to devote all of her energy to the reproductive function of her body, she was forbidden to read or write. This context is important for understanding that the Handmaid's very act of narrating her experiences itself constitutes resistance to the empire. The danger of her recordings was so real, in fact, the narrator remains unnamed in the narrative—she refers to herself only as "Offred" (Of-Fred), which is her patronymic from serving as Fred's Handmaid; as Bouson explains, "her name . . . also suggests the words 'afraid,' 'offered,' and 'off-read' (misread)" (137-38). Instead of focusing on the Handmaid's experience within the regime or the political implications of her narrative, Professor Pieixoto, who has transcribed, coedited, and published the Handmaid's tale roughly 200 years after it was recorded on audio tapes, is more concerned with its "Problems of Authentication" (300). Atwood presents Pieixoto's discussion of the tale in the "Historical Notes" that follow the Handmaid's narrative in the novel.

Professor Pieixoto's talk comes from the proceedings of the "Twelfth Symposium on Gileadean Studies," an academic conference held in the year 2195 (299). As Arnold Davidson has suggested, "In a very real sense, the future presaged by *The Handmaid's Tale* is already our history, just as the meeting of the Gileadean Symposium of 2195 could readily be incorporated into a contemporary literature or history convention" (116). The Professor's talk reveals that his preoccupation with uncovering factual information that will identify the Handmaid's Commander (and thus "authenticate" her narrative) blinds him from engaging with the account of the Gileadean empire present in the Handmaid's narrative. As Roberta Rubenstein has noted, "From the more 'objective' perspective of scholarly research, Professor Pieixoto . . . focuses less on the details of Offred's life than on the *men* who shaped it" (20). Rubenstein's critique points toward the Professor's patriarchal prerogative, which surfaces at other moments throughout his talk and underlies his own judgment of the Handmaid's narrative.

Rather than looking to the Handmaid's narrative for a critique of the Gileadean regime, the professor dismisses such attempts as "the occasion for a good deal of hypocritical self-congratulation" (302). He validates only those information sources that the regime generated or sanctioned, and instead of reading the Handmaid's recording as an alternative account to this imperially generated history, Pieixoto treats her tale as an exhibit or artifact that must be categorized and validated within the regime's history, not a work to be seriously considered as having an "authentic" history all its own. The Handmaid's account, he suggests, would be much more valuable if it included information from the Commanders about Gilead: "She could have told us much about the workings of the Gileadean empire, had she had the instincts of a reporter or a spy. What we would not give, now, for even twenty pages or so of printout from Waterford's [the man thought to be the Commander's] computer!" (310). By insisting on identifying the Commander in order to "authenticate" the Handmaid's narrative and by valuing his perspective over hers, the professor makes the mistake of confusing authority with authenticity and upholds the power dynamic that silenced the Handmaid in Gilead.

Atwood has said that at the center of *The Handmaid's Tale* is a "study of power, and how it operates and how it deforms or shapes the people who are living within [a] regime" like Gilead (qtd. in Rothstein C11). The narrator's tale illustrates how such a regime "deforms or shapes" the people within it by describing the view of the narrator, who sees herself as "a distorted shadow, a parody of something" (9). The professor's talk traces unwittingly this deformation to its source, revealing how Gilead's power operates through a rhetoric that naturalizes its control and containment of bodies. As Hilde Staels argues, the professor's "ironic repetition of Gileadean discourse" highlights the body-oriented rhetoric that "underlies the design" of the Gileadean empire (456). The Professor begins his talk with a bawdy joke that involves "enjoy[ing]" both the Arctic Char served at dinner the night before and the Arctic Chair(woman) who introduces him (300). This joke is indicative of a larger rhetorical pattern: the importance of the reinscription of Gilead's discourse for reading the novel becomes evident in his colleague's titling of Offred's narrative "The Handmaid's Tale," which, as the professor explains, puns on the "vulgar signification of the word *tail* . . . being . . . the bone, as it were, of contention, in that phase of the Gileadean society" (301). As Kauffman has pointed out, the conflation of "genre (tale) and gender (tail)" serves to further undermine the authority of the narrative (224). The sexist jests referencing the female body continue in the talk when the Professor dubs the "Underground Femaleroad" the "Underground Frailroad" (301).

Pieixoto's address, with its puns about women as sexual objects and its demeaning of women's bodies, reflects the rhetoric that the Gileadean Commanders used to underwrite their reduction of women to reproductive parts. Both Pieixoto and the Commanders identify Offred merely as a resource; Pieixoto uses her to further his academic career and the Commanders claim that she is a "national resource" for reproductive purposes (65). Lucy Freibert observes that Atwood's alignment of Pieixoto with the horrors of the Gileadean regime represents "an ironic indictment of a society that treats a woman's body as a pawn and her life as an academic question" (280). Because nothing before or within the tale indicates that "the narrative is unfolding within [the] different and larger context" of the Professor's lecture, the "Historical Notes," as Dominick Grace argues, "force a purely retrospective re-evaluation of the text" that brings rhetoric about the female body into focus (158). Although Grace finds "no analogue" for the "Historical Notes" at "the beginning of the text," one such analogue might be found in Atwood's dedications (158).

Atwood dedicates *The Handmaid's Tale* to one of her ancestors, Mary Webster, who survived an attempted witch hanging in Massachusetts and to Perry Miller, a professor under whom she studied while a graduate student at Harvard. Both of the novel's dedicatees have significance for reading Offred's narrative because they draw attention to the American society that was the historical predecessor of Gilead. Perry Miller's study of early America serves as an uncanny foil to Professor Pieixoto's estimation of Gilead in the "Historical Notes." Pieixoto analyzes Gileadean society roughly 200 years after Gilead's inception, and Miller discusses the American society that prefigured Gilead 200 years earlier. Considering Miller's work alongside Professor Pieixoto's creates a historical framework for the Handmaid's tale by highlighting a negotiation of power through language that persists across time. This negotiation takes place, as Offred's narrative reveals, in terms of a landscaping of bodies.

Miller's work contextualizes the importance of landscape in US literary history and helps illuminate how Offred's narrative constitutes an intervention in this history by de-scribing the imperial language that naturalized control over women's bodies.

Emphasizing the importance of the historical framework of the novel, Atwood tells the reader in her "Note" after the text that the "thing to remember is that there is nothing new about the society depicted in *The Handmaid's Tale* except the time and place" (316). Although Gilead—the place of this empire—is "new," Atwood insists that Gilead evolves from within the framework of US history: "I tried all kinds of possibilities," Atwood explains, "I set it in the States because I couldn't fly it in Canada" (*Conversations* 223). Atwood derives Gilead's totalitarian society from America's Puritan roots, explaining in an interview that concludes the novel: "The society in *The Handmaid's Tale* is a throwback to the early Puritans whom I studied extensively at Harvard under Perry Miller, to whom the book is dedicated. The early Puritans came to America not for religious freedom, as we were taught in grade school, but to set up a society that would be a theocracy (like Iran) ruled by religious leaders, and monolithic, that is, a society that would not tolerate dissent within itself. They were being persecuted in England for being Puritans, but then they went to the United States and promptly began persecuting anyone who wasn't a Puritan. My book reflects the form and style of early Puritan society and addresses the dynamics that bring about such a situation" (318).

Challenging the romanticized idealization of the US as a nation founded for religious and other freedoms, Atwood demystifies early US-American society, which, while being part of the British Empire, relied on domination all its own to create a "monolithic . . . society that would not tolerate dissent within itself." Atwood asserts that these historical identifications run deep and that "dynamics that [could] bring about" an imperial society like Gilead underlie the current US cultural landscape (318). Bloom echoes this sentiment in the introduction to his edited collection of essays on *The Handmaid's Tale*: "Atwood makes [an important] point when she warns us about the history of American Puritanism, which is long and dangerous. Its tendencies are always with us, and speculative fictions from Hawthorne to Atwood legitimately play upon its darkest aspects" (2). When asked how the creation of her imagined republic of Gilead would be possible, Atwood replies that if one were to try to "take over the United States," he would most likely succeed by saying, "I have the word from God and this is the way we should run things." She notes that "there are a number of movements in the States saying just that, and getting lots of dollars and influence," maintaining that the country's transformation into a theocratic regime is an actual—and underacknowledged—possibility (318).

Atwood's dedication of *The Handmaid's Tale* to Miller suggests that the novel contributes to and even intervenes in the field of US studies which he helped found by conducting a study of power on and through a distinctly US landscape. Atwood describes *The Handmaid's Tale* as a "throwback" to Miller, and she draws upon Miller's scholarship on early US-American society to form a backdrop for her own illumination of the imperialism that has haunted the United States from its inception.

One can read *The Handmaid's Tale* as haunted by the ghosts of US imperialisms past by considering ways in which the novel restages horrors of American slavery. Kauffman argues that "the closest corollary to the Gileadean system is slavery in the American South, when black women were similarly prized as breeders" (234). One distinction Atwood makes between slave women and the narrator, however, is that Offred chose from her few heinous options to be a Handmaid, while slaves had no such choice (94). There are strong parallels, though, between slave narratives and Offred's narrative. As Magali Cornier Michael points out, "much like American slave narratives, her story not only points to the oppressive structures that victimize her but also allows her to move beyond the role of victim, creating herself as an individual with whom the reader can sympathize and identify" (136).

Miller's critical works, such as *Errand into the Wilderness* and *Nature's Nation*, posit a rhetorical connection between landscape and US society that Atwood adapts in the context of her own languagescape in *The Handmaid's Tale*. In an essay from *Nature's Nation* entitled "Shaping the American Character," Miller discusses the conscious effort of nineteenth-century US writers "to prove that we too were a nation in some deeper sense than mere willfulness" by projecting "the embodiment of America as rooted in the soil" (10). He explains that although "Indians" have had the longest-standing relationship with the land, US writers such as James Fenimore Cooper established a literary tradition that produced "our legends, our misty past, our epic figures, our symbolic heroes," which arose, as through Manifest Destiny, from the natural environment (5, 10): "We may have come to the land by an act of will," Miller observes, "but despite ourselves, we have become parts of the landscape" (11). While he concedes that early US writers such as Cooper might have had "noble" intentions, he intimates that "to our ears something rings terribly false in their hymns to the natural nation" (11).

In *The Handmaid's Tale*, Atwood evokes the falsity of the "natural nation" through a parody that depicts such extreme degradation of the natural environment of what was US that the landscape— not to mention the majority of its citizens—is barren and infertile. To emphasize the disastrous effects of Americans "becom[ing] part of the landscape," Offred describes the interaction of man and the natural environment in terms of infectious pollution: "The air got too full, once, of chemicals, rays, radiation, the water swarmed with toxic molecules . . . meanwhile they creep into your body . . . your very flesh may be polluted, dirty as an oily beach, sure death to shore birds and unborn babies" (112).

Despite—or perhaps because of—the destruction of the natural environment, Gilead adapts the rhetoric of the natural to authenticate its reign. The narrator's Commander actually identifies nature as a justification for the regime, telling her that the operations of the regime constitute "Nature's plan" and that "All we've done is to return things to Nature's norm" (237, 220). As Verena Bühler Roth states, "In *The Handmaid's Tale* the idealization of the natural is practised in a world in which actual natural spaces have been destroyed or are absent" (154). She explains that "the ideology of the natural is a kind of substitute for this absence, and it is primarily used to define gender roles" (154). The Commanders in Gilead use this "ideology of the natural" to legitimize their commandments, which institutionalize the practice by which women function as womb machines. Atwood wryly observes in the interview following the novel that Gilead "is a society in which you have a sort of 'farming' of women" (319). This pseudo-agricultural "farming" mentality serves as the basis for the Handmaids' training and indoctrination; the future Handmaids are told: "Not all of you will make it through. Some of you will fall on dry ground or thorns. Some of you are shallow-rooted . . . Think of yourselves as seeds" (18).

Atwood has expressed the fear that readers of *The Handmaid's Tale* would consider the novel as representing "feminist propaganda of the most outrageous kind, which was not really what I intended"; rather than specifically focusing on the plight of women, she asserts that "I was more interested in totalitarian systems" (*Conversations* 215). By highlighting the use of naturalizing rhetoric to underwrite the totalitarian state in Gilead, Atwood not only landscapes the Gilead of her novel, but also critiques and denaturalizes the mythology of the United States as "nature's nation." As Atwood traces Gilead's naturalizing rhetoric to the early American nationalist narratives, she evokes that which has been obscured in the rhetoric of the "natural nation": the exploitation of the natural environment and native peoples of North America, as well as the usurpation of the rhetoric of the natural for patriarchal domination, both of which have been effaced in the US's national mythology.

Within the context of Gilead's politically motivated naturalizing rhetoric, nature itself takes on an unexpected subversive quality and serves as an inspiration for resistance to the regime. The narrator muses about the subversiveness of nature when examining the Commander's wife's garden, the only natural (although domesticated) space in the novel: "There is something subversive about this garden of Serena's, a sense of buried things bursting upwards, wordlessly, into the light, as if to point, to say: Whatever is silenced will clamor to be heard, though silently" (153). These flowers symbolize and prefigure Offred's own acts of resistance, including what appears to be her escape from Gilead at the end of her narrative: "I step up, into the darkness within; or else the light" (295). Refusing to be silenced by Gilead, the Handmaid tells a tale that simultaneously reconstructs Gilead's landscape and allows her to constitute her own subjectivity. This poetic mode aligns her with the great tradition of other American writers, such as Walt Whitman and Henry David Thoreau, whose works draw upon British Romantic poets' negotiations of the self through landscape to create a distinctly US Romantic tradition. While at Harvard, Atwood took an "American Romantics" class with Miller, whose work on the American Romantics informs *The Handmaid's Tale* as much as his study of Puritan society does (see Atwood, "Writing *Susana*").

Miller writes about the US-American Romantics in *Nature's Nation*, where he traces their understanding of "The Poet" to Wordsworth (177). While noting the initial US "hostility" to Wordsworth, Miller argues that Thoreau and his contemporaries were influenced by the Preface to *Lyrical Ballads*, which Miller describes as proposing "a new kind of utterance—he was talking about poetry but his prescriptions would apply as well to prose—in which the writer should strive by might and main to look steadily at the subject" (176). This poetics of landscape, Miller explains, would not take the form of "a photographic reproduction of the scene," but would with "passion come into literature . . . as emotion recollected in tranquility" (180). Miller identifies Thoreau's *Walden* as "one of the supreme achievements of the Romantic Movement—or to speak accurately, of Romantic Naturalism" (181). Incorporating its own Wordsworthian connection with direct reference to "emotion recollected [but not in] tranquillity," *The Handmaid's Tale* utilizes a Romantic poetics of landscape that follows in *Walden*'s tradition to describe a distinctly US-American landscape (303). Instead of using "Romantic Naturalism" like *Walden* does to depict a utopian idyll, however, *The Handmaid's Tale* adapts Romantic conceptions of landscape and the imagination to stage a dystopic nightmare. Thus central to Atwood's depiction of the dystopia in Gilead is her ability to portray the Handmaid's perspective and convey her state of mind. As part of Gilead's imperial design, restrictions on women's freedom to read and write, as well as other basic human rights, reduce opportunities for resistance and alienate and demoralize its subjects. Atwood's challenge in depicting how a regime like Gilead warps people within it involves capturing the perspective of someone like the narrator, who is denied a voice, while exposing the imperial rhetoric that naturalizes her silencing. Composing the Handmaid's narrative in a Romantic mode that uses descriptions of her surroundings as stimuli for self-reflection allows Atwood to meet this challenge. By framing Offred's narrative in a way that shows how what around her affects her imagination of herself, Atwood reveals the psychological effects of the means by which Gilead's Commanders exerted control over their republic.

During his address to the Symposium, Pieixoto describes the Handmaid's tale in terms of Romantic poetics when he equates the Handmaid's "account" with the definition of poetry Wordsworth espouses in the Preface to *Lyrical Ballads*, which characterizes poetry as arising from "emotion recollected in tranquillity" (302). Atwood, however, alters Wordsworth's language when Pieixoto applies it to Offred's account, changing the phrase to "a whiff of emotion recollected, if not in tranquillity, at least *post facto*" (303). Because the Professor serves as a model of how not to read the Handmaid's tale, Atwood invites the reader to consider the very serious issues that underlie his sarcastic and dismissive remark. Invoking Wordsworth in the novel allows Atwood to draw attention not only to her adaptations of his poetics of landscape, but also to a closer examination of how Gileadean society affects the Handmaid's self-conception. Wordsworth, the poet who charted the growth of the poet's mind in *The Prelude*, represents the negotiation of the self through that which is external. By including Wordsworth in a discussion of the Handmaid's tale, Atwood creates a context through which she can map the "prospect" of Offred's mind in relation to Wordsworth's state of "tranquillity." In *The Rhetoric of Romanticism*, Paul de Man explains that in Wordsworth's poetry tranquillity represents a type of vision that allows for the reading of landscapes: "Tranquillity is in *this* place on *this* earth, and it exists for the poet who can hear its voice, not because he is endowed with supernatural wisdom, or because he can dwell beyond the boundaries of space or of life, but because he possesses the kind of double vision that allows him to see landscapes as objects, as well as entrance gates to a world lying beyond visible nature. 'Tranquillity,' it seems, is the right balance between literal and symbolic vision, a balance reflected in a harmonious proportion between mimetic and symbolic language in the diction of the poem" (132).

By drawing attention to the fact that the Handmaid's recollections were "not [made] in tranquillity," Atwood emphasizes that tranquility was not possible in her "place" because Gilead prevents the "balance between literal and symbolic vision" that de Man finds in Wordsworth's poetry. Instead of allowing Offred to "see landscapes as objects, as well as entrance gates to a world lying beyond visible nature," Gilead restricts Offred's "literal" vision by casting her as an object within its imperial, "symbolic" landscape. The irony of the Professor's comparison of the Handmaid's state of "tranquillity" with that of Wordsworth is that instead of having "double vision," she is not allowed to see clearly at all: "Given our wings, our blinkers, it's hard to look up, hard to get the full view, of the sky, of anything . . . But we can do it a little at a time, a quick move of the head, up and down . . . We have learned to see the world in gasps" (30). Because Offred only "see[s] the world in gasps" and is spatially constricted, she lacks the capacity to see the big picture of the Gileadean regime and her place in it. "What I need," she says, "is perspective": "Perspective is necessary. Otherwise there are only two dimensions. Otherwise you live with your face squashed against a wall, everything a huge foreground, of details, close-ups, hairs, the weave of the bedsheet, the molecules of the face . . . Otherwise you live in the moment. Which is not where I want to be" (143). The narrator describes her objectification within Gilead as being part of a landscape that she has no control framing. Ironically, Gilead's strategy for maintaining Offred as a reproductive resource involves enclosing her within an insular landscape that is very womb-like in its own right, containing Offred's body, wrapping her in darkness, and making her dependent on those in power for information about her own situation and what is happening more generally within and outside of Gilead's borders.

Offred's lack of perspective resembles the paintings in "Death by Landscape," which had "no backgrounds . . . no vistas, only a great deal of foreground that goes back and back, endlessly, involving you in its twists and turns" (57). Atwood explains: "You're dealing with a character [in *The Handmaid's Tale*] whose ability to move in the society was limited. By the nature of her situation, she was very circumscribed. She couldn't communicate well with people. It was too dangerous. She was boxed in. How do you tell a narrative from the point of view of that person? The more limited and boxed in you are, the more important details become . . . Details, episodes separate themselves from the flow of time in which they are embedded—a flow which tends to be monotonous—and become significant, luminous" (*Conversations* 216). The similarity of the confinement of Offred's landscape with the mode of containment in the short story associates her situation with that of Lucy, with the important qualification that unlike the other Lucys, she possesses a voice and a physical presence. Within the confines of Gilead, however, this presence seems more like a curse than a blessing. The narrator says "in the moment . . . is not where I want to be," yet she returns there in her recollections, composing them in the present tense.

In the narrator's attempt to reconstitute her subjectivity after her escape from the Gileadean regime, she recollects the "moment[s]" that changed her life so drastically. She repeatedly emphasizes that her narrative is a "reconstruction," explaining, "All I can really hope for is a reconstruction" (134, 140, 263). Because she saw the world in "gasps," it is no wonder that her narrative is episodic and fragmented. As Martine Watson Brownley explains of *Bodily Harm*'s Rennie, Offred's "narrative fragmentation . . . suggests her inability to synthesize and understand her experiences" (77). Unlike Gilead, whose "genius," according to Professor Pieixoto, "was synthesis," the Handmaid is left with a scattering of memories that she tries to bring together to recollect herself through language (307). Marta Dvorak asserts that in depicting Offred's association of narrative fragments, "Atwood shows . . . the world through what Coleridge termed the secondary Imagination, involving a structuring process, and elaboration, that 'dissolves, diffuses, dissipates, in order to re-create'" (145). This Coleridgean association further contextualizes Offred's account within Romantic poetics.

Having used "litanies . . . to compose [herself]" and illicit Scrabble games with the Commander as tools for exercising the language skills Gilead denied her, Offred highlights the importance of language for putting the pieces back together (110, 139): "I compose myself. My self is a thing I must now compose, as one composes a speech. What I must present is a made thing, not something born" (66). Offred describes her self-composition as a mode of survival, suggesting that "it's the body's way of seeing to it that I remain alive, continue to repeat its bedrock prayer: *I am, I am*. I am, still" (281). In addition to demonstrating Offred's defiant refusal to be erased within the imperial landscape, this repetition of "I am" represents another instance in the novel in which Atwood engages Romanticism in order to describe the effects of Gilead's totalitarian regime on its subjects. Offred's echoing of "*I am*" recalls Samuel Taylor Coleridge's discussion of "I AM" in the *Biographia Literaria*, where Coleridge himself repeats the phrase "I AM" in his description of Imagination, "the living power and prime agent of all human perception," which he envisions as "a repetition . . . of the eternal act of creation in the infinite I AM" (*Major Works* 313). Given that Coleridge's theorization of the Imagination contributes to his broader speculation about the role of the subject in organizing the world, his formulation of "I AM" represents the transcendental activity of the mind that unifies and consolidates in order to bring a world view into being; the activity that Coleridge describes as "I AM" can, in fact, be seen as the basis for the recollections in "tranquillity" that Wordsworth describes in the Preface to *Lyrical Ballads*.

Atwood's invocation of Coleridge's "I AM," like her reference to Wordsworth's Preface, summons Romantic ideas about the power of the subject to create a representation of his world that projects self-consciousness in order to illustrate that Gilead's subjects lack this power, and, as a result, by necessity have a very different sense of self-consciousness. Instead of representing the transcendence of recognizing, in Coleridge's words, "that the self-consciousness may be the modification of a higher form of being . . . which must lie beyond the possibility of our knowledge," Offred's assertion, "I am" represents survival on a basic, bodily level (*Major Works* 300). For Offred, "I am" is a self-constituting mantra that is "the body's way of seeing to it that I remain alive" (281). In light of Offred's preoccupation with survival, the Professor's suggestion that her tale represents "emotion recollected, if not in tranquillity, at least *post facto*" takes on new meaning. Offred's struggle to stay alive prevents her from achieving the distance from her existence in Gilead that would provide her with "tranquillity," and her focus on keeping her body living eerily coincides with the regime's reduction of her to her physical parts. Because of Offred's psychological confinement within her physical body, her transcendent moment never comes. Thus, evidenced by the present tense of her narrative, there is no post facto in Offred's tale, no time in which she can distance herself from the horrors of Gilead, and no space where she is free of bodily danger. But, despite the lack of transcendent perspective, Atwood undermines the Professor's dismissal of the Handmaid's tale and invites the reader to consider the accomplishment of its very existence. Although there is no post facto in the tale itself, there is one for the Gileadean regime.

Like the protagonists of other Atwood novels, Offred is haunted by the very real possibility of bodily harm, which she endures by abstracting her mind from her body. She intimates: "I can't think of myself, my body, sometimes, without seeing the skeleton" (112). Because Gilead reduces the narrator to the sum of her reproductive parts, she develops a sensation "of absence, of existing apart from the body" (160). Within the Gileadean regime, as Professor Pieixoto notes, women like the Handmaid signified only reproductive capability. After being objectified in this way, Offred explains: "I avoid looking down at my body, not so much because it's shameful or immodest [as in Gileadean doctrine] but because I don't want to see it. I don't want to look at something that determines me so completely" (63). Although the Handmaid denies the scopic, her narrative returns again and again to images of her own body and those of other women in order to try to contextualize the transformation surrounding women's bodies under the Gileadean regime and to understand the implications that being part of this larger imperial landscape has for the person she has become. She evokes the image of her friend, Moira, whose feet "looked like lungs" because they had been shredded by "steel cables, frayed at the ends" for attempting to escape the reeducation center. "It was the feet they'd do, for a first offense," Offred says, "After that the hands. They didn't care what they did to your feet or your hands, even if it was permanent . . . For [their] purposes your feet and your hands are not essential" (91). In another instance, the narrator observes that she and her fellow Handmaids are "containers," since "only the insides of our bodies are important"; we are "two-legged wombs, that's all: sacred vessels, ambulatory chalices" (96, 136). Offred recognizes that the Gileadean commanders have inscribed her and other women's bodies as objects within an imperial landscape in order not only to produce children, but also to disenfranchise women within the body politic. She remembers that before the regime she "lived in the blank white spaces at the edges of print," which "gave [her] more freedom" (57). Now, her body itself has been inscribed; on her ankle, the "tattoo, a cattle brand [that] means ownership" marks her to prevent her from "fad[ing], finally, into another landscape" and the freedom it represents (254, 65). Although the Handmaid, who formerly "lived in the . . . spaces at the edges of print," was not actually part of the "master" narrative before the rise of the Gileadean empire, after the regime comes to power she loses the right to write and becomes merely a page upon which the Commander's words may be written in "a Braille he can read" (254).

Atwood provides an indication of the futility of women's attempts to make their own marks on Gilead's landscape through an ongoing focus on the graffiti Offred finds in the room she occupies in the Commander's house, where the former Handmaid, who hung herself, once lived. Atwood figures this room, with its ironic resonances with Virginia Woolf's *A Room of One's Own*, as a contested space that Offred first rejects—"not *my* room, I refuse to say *my*"—and then claims: "My room, then. There has to be some space, finally, that I claim as mine, even in this time" (8, 50). To make the room feel more familiar and herself feel more a conqueror than an occupied territory, she consciously and meticulously explores the room (51). In the cupboard "where the darkest shadow fell," she makes an amazing discovery:

> there it was, in tiny writing, quite fresh it seemed, scratched with a pin or maybe just a fingernail, in the corner where the darkest shadow fell: *Nolite te bastardes carborundorum.*
>
> I didn't know what it meant, or even what language it was in. I thought it might be Latin, but I didn't know any Latin. Still, it was a message, and it was in writing, forbidden by that very fact, and it hadn't yet been discovered. Except by me, for whom it was intended. It was intended for whoever came next. It pleases me to ponder this message.
>
> It pleases me to think I am communing with her, this unknown woman . . . It pleases me to know that her taboo message made it through, to at least one other person, washed itself up on the wall of my cupboard, was opened and read by me. Sometimes I repeat the words to myself. They give me a small joy. (52)

In addition to providing Offred with a sense of solidarity, her discovery gives her hope that there are opportunities for resistance within this space where she has been cast as an object; that she, too, can make her own mark; and that if she sends a message, it will eventually reach her intended audience.

Until Offred asks the Commander to translate the words she discovered in the cupboard, she repeats them to herself as a self-sustaining mantra and even invokes them in her prayer to God (92). Resurrecting these scrawled words from "the darkest shadow," Offred makes them visible by writing them on a piece of paper—a crime in Gilead—and gives them to the most powerful figure to whom she has access, the Commander. Instead of marking a defiant triumph of resistance to the regime, Offred's inscription makes a mockery of her and her attempt to understand what it means. The Commander laughs at the words, calls them a "joke," and shows her where he as a schoolboy wrote those same lines in a textbook (186). On the pages where these lines are written, Offred also notes a defaced picture of Venus de Milo and a painting called *The Sabine Women* adjacent to the word "cunt" (186-87). These pages contextualize the Commander's original statement within an aestheticized composition of dismembered, violated, and degraded female bodies that reference violence against women from the time of the Greek and Roman empires to the present day. By situating these images of defiled women in a textbook, Atwood emphasizes the fact that young boys come to learn this attitude toward women from "older boys" and, perhaps, the educational system itself (187). Wherever the impulse to derogate women originates, evidence of it in the textbook helps explain why Offred's echo of the statement is a "joke" and why her words carry no force. Offred, realizing that the previous Handmaid learned the pseudo-Latin phrase, which means "Don't let the bastards grind you down," from this very textbook, "can see why she wrote [it]" (187).

After learning the origination of her predecessor's cupboard scrawl, Offred understands that the other Handmaid hung herself because she wanted to disengage from the body—which associates her with this field of desecrated women—and to "fade, finally, into another landscape" (187, 65). In describing the ways in which Offred views her own body, Atwood shows that the Gileadean empire's reduction of women to their reproductive parts warps the minds of these women so that they imagine themselves as others see them: objects within the Gileadean landscape. In a nightmarish adaptation of Wordsworth's vision from *The Prelude* in which "bodily eyes / Were utterly forgotten, and what I saw / Appeared like something in myself, a dream, / A prospect in the mind," Offred begins imagining her "flesh arrang[ing] itself differently" (2.73, 350-53). She sees herself as "a cloud, congealed around a central object, the shape of a pear, which is hard and more real than I am and glows red within its translucent wrapping" (73-74). The "central object" of this vision, which quite literally "appear[s] like something in [her]self," is an imaginary womb, representing her resignation to her reproductive destiny as her only "prospect" in Gilead.

In the course of Atwood's examination of how Gilead "deforms or shapes the people who are living within" it, she suggests that the state's political propaganda relies on an infectious rhetoric that interpolates its subjects and disciplines them into bodily subordination. Atwood draws attention to the fact that Gilead's Commanders created a landscape in which bodies serve as markers; there are no street signs in Gilead because women are not allowed to read (26, 18). Like empire itself, Gilead "knows no bounds" (23). In the reeducation center, Offred is instructed that "Gilead is within," and as she internalizes this concept, she imagines herself as an invaded territory within the larger imperial landscape: "I sink down into my body as into a swamp, fenland, where only I know the footing. Treacherous ground, my own territory. I become the earth I set my ear against, for rumors of the future . . . I have failed once again to fulfill the expectations of others, which have become my own" (23, 73). Danielle Schaub writes, "Atwood adopts, with subversive effect, the pattern of geographical discourse that Gillian Rose underlines. . . . While Rose notes that 'landscapes are often seen in terms of the female body' (87), Atwood's protagonist claims landscape and fuses with it to deconstruct male inscriptions of the female body" (91). Although Schaub is referring specifically to *Surfacing*, her analysis applies to *The Handmaid's Tale* as well. Offred continues to insist that she has sovereignty over her own body, that her body is "[her] own territory," but she reveals that "the expectations of others . . . have become [her] own," suggesting that the rhetoric that likens her to virgin territory has taken some effect and that her body itself has become a "treacherous" and contested space. Indicating her doubts about her ability to win the battle over her body, the narrator imagines that the "treacherous ground" within this landscape provides no exits; she imagines her skin to be "like a map, a diagram of futility, crisscrossed with tiny roads that lead to nowhere" (143).

The Gileadean Commanders' inscription of their subjects into a dystopic imagined space reinforces the subjects' sense of physical danger and regulates the body politic through threats of bodily harm. The narrator insists that although the landscape might appear "picturesque" from a distance, the threat of retaliation keeps it organized that way. "We must look good from a distance: picturesque, like Dutch milkmaids on a wallpaper frieze," she says, "Soothing to the eye, the eyes, the Eyes [Gilead's surveillance officers], for that's who this show is for" (212). Throughout the novel Atwood repeats the image of the hook to symbolize both the regime and its interpolative rhetoric with a physical mark on the landscape. Atwood uses the reappearing hooks as a leitmotif that conjures up the image of the bodies of dissidents who hang from the Wall. Offred remembers that when she and another Handmaid would pass the Wall, they would "stop, together as if on signal, and stand and look at the bodies" hanging from the hooks, which "have been set into the brickwork of the Wall, for this purpose" (32). Describing the hooks as "appliances for the armless," Atwood figuratively associates the hooks with the bodies that hang on them, "[o]r steel question marks, upside-down and sideways" (32). Placing hooks in Offred's cupboard and in the closet, Atwood tempts her Handmaid with a possible escape (52, 195). Imagining the bodies on the Wall, however, Offred banishes the thought: "I don't want to be a dancer, my feet in the air . . . I don't want to be a doll hung up on the Wall . . . I want to keep on living, in any form" (286).

Atwood allows the narrator to keep living through her narrative, which outlasts the Gileadean regime. Although the Handmaid is able to both survive the regime and preclude her erasure in its imperial landscape, the "Historical Notes" reveal how easy it is for one to lose sight of "the facts of the world" to which she bears witness. Professor Pieixoto concludes his talk by asking, "Are there any questions?" (311). The hook-shaped question mark that punctuates the novel serves as a hieroglyph that evokes the specters of violated bodies and warns of the possibility of Gilead's return.

# Chapter Three

## McCarthy's *Blood Meridian*, Byron, and the US Frontier

While *The Handmaid's Tale* imagines a possible imperial dystopia in the US, *Blood Meridian* returns to the 1800s to depict the conflicts that expanded US territory across the North American continent. Both novels invoke Romantic poetry to characterize US empire, but *Blood Meridian* more specifically portrays how the US developed its imperial power—by appropriating land, by charging discourse with racial distinctions, and by perpetuating myths about the US frontier. *Blood Meridian* opens with a brief glimpse of the main character, known only as "the kid," during his Tennessee childhood. By the end of the first page the kid is fourteen years old, running away from home and heading out West, but we learn in the meantime that the kid, who "can neither read nor write and [has] already a taste for mindless violence," does not follow in the footsteps of his father, a former schoolmaster who "quotes from poets whose names are now lost" (3). Although we do not see the father once the kid runs away, echoes of poets that we might associate with the father curiously resurface and complicate our reading of the novel. Immediately after contrasting the father and son, in fact, the narrator appropriates Wordsworth in concluding: "All history present in that visage, the child the father of the man" (3).

Several scholars have commented on this Wordsworthian intertext with lines from the poem "My heart leaps up when I behold." Adam Parkes, for example, argues that:

> In running away from home, the kid literalizes what is implied in McCarthy's use of Wordsworth's famous line, "The Child is father of the Man." In McCarthy's hands, this phrase suggests a self divorced from the Romantic notion of an organic, developing consciousness. The child is father of McCarthy's man not because he will become a man but because he plays the role of his own father, as if to suggest that such terms as *child* and *man* do no more than designate the roles that are available to the same character; either role, in other words, could be said to father the other. In this sense, the kid's biological father becomes irrelevant. Wordsworth, who redeployed

> this line from "My Heart Leaps Up" as the epigraph to "Ode: Intimations of Immortality from Recollections of Early Childhood," posited a fundamental relation between selfhood and memory, but from the outset McCarthy's narrator denies this version of the self's relation to time. (104)

Yoogin Kim, on the other hand, suggests that "McCarthy fixes the boy's identity to man's communal history . . . In a strange adaptation of the original Wordsworthian verse, McCarthy implies that all of history has produced the kid, whose existence extends, and even engenders anew the history of man" (173). The allusion to Wordsworth's verse so soon after the association of the father with unnamed poets seems to suggest that the poets' words have significance for the novel, even if the poets themselves remain unacknowledged. Poetry is important to the narration of *Blood Meridian* because it informs how we conceive of our history, how we read the novel, and how we see ourselves. At the very beginning of the novel, the narrator tells the reader to "see the child" (3). The Wordsworthian intertext that follows suggests that in order to fully conceive of the history present in his visage—the image of the US he represents—one must acknowledge the novel's engagement with Romantic poetry.

As Rick Wallach points out, the line "the child the father of the man" in *Blood Meridian* is not the only Wordsworthian intertext in McCarthy's oeuvre. In reference to *Cities of the Plain*, Wallach observes that "considering the elegiac tone of the epilogue, it is perhaps not surmising too much that we might perhaps trace much of the symbolic content of the stranger's dream to Wordsworth's 'Essay on Epitaphs.' All of this is especially poignant when we recall that McCarthy closed his first novel, *The Orchard Keeper*, with a very close paraphrase of Wordsworth's 'A Slumber did my Spirit Seal'" (60). Clearly McCarthy's larger body of work demonstrates an engagement with the Romantics' poems. *Blood Meridian*, I argue, does so to demythologize the US West.

Set in the mid-nineteenth-century Southwestern borderlands, *Blood Meridian* revises the history of the western US as it follows the kid and tracks the haphazard violence of the filibusters and scalphunters he joins during his journey out West. Like many who have discussed *Blood Meridian*'s critique of the frontier, Vereen Bell notes that when reading the novel, "we have the queasy feeling that we are being told, for the first time, the raw, unromantic truth about both sides in the war for the Southwest territories" (124). This unromantic portrayal exceeds the history of the territorial battles (which, as the novel shows, involves many more than two parties). In addition to representing the sheer brutality of the violence between cowboys and Indians, the novel's unromantic picture of American history involves demythologizing the conception of the US itself. This historical revision is "unromantic" in the sense that the novel pointedly diverges from the romance plots that characterized many early frontier narratives; Robert Jarrett, in fact, claims that "while the novel revises McCarthy's earlier fiction, the account of the kid's childhood in the opening pages also rewrites the American romance" (64). But this revision is "unromantic" also in the sense that it challenges the romantic idealization of the US seen in British Romantic poetry.

## Byron's influence on the US

George Gordon, Lord Byron, provides a distinctive vision of "America" that seems to be of particular importance to McCarthy's work. The collective depiction of the US in *Childe Harold's Pilgrimage*, "Ode on Venice," "Ode to Napoleon," *Don Juan*, and *The Age of Bronze*—none of which are expressly about the United States—demonstrates that "America" is nevertheless an important topos in Byron's writing. Byron's poetry returns again and again to America as if its very representation imparts a regenerative energy and licenses an empowering freedom. His "Ode on Venice," for example, which laments that "The name of Commonwealth is past and gone / O'er the three fractions of the groaning globe; / Venice is crush'd, and Holland deigns to own / A scepter, and endures the purple robe" (125-28), ends with a triumphant transmigration to America:

> Still one great clime, in full and free defiance,
> Yet rears her crest, unconquer'd and sublime,
> Above the far Atlantic!—She has taught
> Her Esau-bretheren that the haughty flag,
> The floating fence of Albion's feebler crag,
> May strike to those whose red right hands have bought
> Rights cheaply earn'd with blood. Still, still, for ever
> Better, though each man's life-blood were a river,
> That it should flow, and overflow, than creep
> Through thousand lazy channels in our veins,
> Damm'd like the dull canal with locks and chains,
> And moving, as a sick man in his sleep,
> Three paces, and then faltering:—better be
> Where the extinguish'd Spartans still are free,
> In their proud charnel of Thermopylae,
> Than stagnate in our marsh,—or o'er the deep
> Fly, and one current to the ocean add,
> One spirit to the souls our fathers had,
> One freeman more, America, to thee! (142-60)

In the poem's celebration of American freedom, Byron acknowledges the bloodshed of the American Revolution, but he deems the sacrifice worth the price, for it creates a society resembling that of idealized ancient Greek societies (it is worth noting here that the "red right hands" refer to those of the American colonists—not to those of the Native Americans—and that the phrase "red right hand" also represents an allusion to Horace's "Ode to Augustus Caesar"). With figures such as George Washington, "the tyrant-tamer," and Benjamin Franklin, Byron's poetry depicts the US's founding fathers as "prophets of young Freedom" (*The Age of Bronze* 382, 388). The characterizations of famous US-Americans such as Washington and Daniel Boone in Byron's work, as I discuss later, contribute to a composite picture of America as a nation that has freed itself from the chains of (British) empire, leaving its people, a "sylvan tribe of children," at liberty to explore the "unconquer'd and sublime" virgin landscape of the American Arcadia (*Don Juan* 8.65, 2; "Ode on Venice" 143).

Byron's depictions of the US contributed to a collective image of the new US identities because his poetry was so widely read around the world. Byron became immensely popular in Europe after the publication of the first two cantos of *Childe Harold's Pilgrimage*; he noted that he awoke one morning to find himself famous (Clubbe, *Byron* 33). His popularity spread rapidly beyond the continent and to the US with the increased publication of his works. The July 1814 issue of *Port Folio*, a Philadelphia magazine, observed that "the most fashionable writer now in England—and the fashion there is always sure to be the fashion here—is Lord Byron" (Clubbe, *Byron* 144). Even after Byron's popularity waned in England owing to his brazen affairs and scandals, he continued to be widely popular in the United States in the early-to-mid-nineteenth century. In the storefronts of US galleries, portraits of Byron were as common as those of Washington (Clubbe, *Byron* 143).

Byron was not only an icon in the US, but also in the Canadian territories. In fact, "Canada's first international literary celebrity," a "full-blooded Ojibwa Indian named George Copway (also known as Kah-ge-ga-gah-bowh, or 'Standing Firm')," includes an epigraph from Byron's poem "To the Countess of Blessington" in his 1851 conversion narrative entitled *Recollection of a Forest Life* (Hutchings 217, 231). The epigraph prefaces his chapter on hunting, evidencing Byron's influence in the ways that people from across the Americas imagined their own relationship to the land: "My life is not dated by years / —There are moments which act as a plough; / And there is not a furrow appears, / But is deep in my soul as my brow.—*Byron*" (*Recollections* 16). Like the "plough" in the poem, Byron made a mark that deeply affected how Americans saw themselves in relation to the world around them. Kevin Hutchings notes that although "these lines might seem a rather strange choice" as an epigraph to "a chapter that piously renounces the hunt and its associated rituals," they inscribe a sense of loss in which "Byron's use of the plough metaphor . . . takes on literal significance" (233).

Although Byron never visited the US or Canada, he had a great fondness for the American people. He remarked that he would prefer "a nod from an American [to] a snuff-box from an emperor" (Clubbe, *Natural Man* 5). Byron was delighted to hear of his popularity in the US and said that "the first tidings that have ever sounded like *Fame* to [his] ears" were those that proclaimed that he was "redde on the banks of the Ohio," which made him feel weirdly "*posthumous*" (Clubbe, *Natural Man* 1): "Whenever an American requests to see me—(which is *not* infrequently)," Byron writes, "I comply—1*stly*. because I respect a people who acquired their freedom by firmness without excess—and 2*ndly* because these trans-atlantic visits 'few and far between' make me feel as if talking with Posterity from the other side of the Styx" (Clubbe, *Natural Man* 1). In both of these quotations, Byron's relation of himself to America evokes a specter of death, which he does not associate with America (as does *Blood Meridian*), but instead uses to contrast the Old World with the New. Byron explained to US painter William Edward West that "Americans were worth studying as a people . . . because, devoted to their republic and living under democratic institutions, they represented the wave of the future" (Clubbe, *Natural Man*

6). For Byron, America represented an English-speaking society that provided an alternative to Great Britain and embodied the future of civilization while serving as "a Model of force and freedom & moderation." At the same time, the American people, whom he deemed far less refined than the British, exhibited an unsettling degree of "coarseness and rudeness" (Clubbe *Natural Man* 5). Byron reconciles these potentially contradictory images of the American—the valiant, forward-thinking republican and the gritty pioneer—in his poetry through the characterization of Daniel Boone, who comes to represent for the rest of the world the prototypical American frontiersman.

When news of Byron's death in Greece reached the US on 24 June 1824, people described a sense of overwhelming loss; it was almost as if the country had lost one of its founding fathers. In the months following the news, US publications dedicated more coverage to Byron than to any other European—even Lafayette, who was visiting the US at the time. In January 1825, the renowned *North American Review* printed a 47-page obituary that paid homage to Byron's life and works, in which Alexander Everett wrote: "The death of Lord Byron . . . has produced a deep and general feeling of regret throughout the country. The loss of a truly great poet is in fact an event that affects immediately, in their occupations and their pleasures, a much larger number of persons than that of a distinguished statesman or of a military conqueror" (qtd. in Robinson 52, 50). And US-Americans and Canadians continued to revere Byron years after his death. On a tour of the US during the 1830s, Frederick Marryat noted that "nine drawing rooms out of ten [had] a copy of Byron lying on the table" and that even in "the log cabins of Sault Ste Marie [Canada], the deepest backwoods of America, [he] came upon 'complete editions of Lord Byron's works'" (Clubbe, *Byron* 179). During this era, Byron was a much-loved literary figure. Harriet Beecher Stowe acknowledged in *Uncle Tom's Cabin* (1852) the impact that Byron's poetry had on her life and her work, proclaiming that he was "the single greatest literary and imaginative influence" on her writing (qtd. in Clubbe, *Byron* 178).

## *Don Juan*, Daniel Boone, and the US frontier

Cormac McCarthy, known for his reluctance to discuss his own works, has made no such sweeping claim about the degree to which Byron has influenced him. He has provided little insight into the works that influenced his writing of *Blood Meridian* other than saying that the "ugly fact is books are made out of books" (Woodward 29). Critics, however, have highlighted the Byronic undertones of McCarthy's work. Charles Bailey was the first scholar to associate McCarthy with Byron: "Certainly critics have remarked the echoes of Homer, Shakespeare, Melville, and Faulkner in the novels of McCarthy, but none, insofar as I know, cites Byron. *Cities of the Plain*, however, makes the connection unavoidable and, considering its position as the last of the Border Trilogy, also inevitable" (293). Bailey argues that the trilogy (the three Western novels written after *Blood Meridian*: *All the Pretty Horses*, *The Crossing*, and *Cities of the Plain*) follows a progression of heroic portrayals—the courtly hero, the tragic hero, and the antihero—seen in Byron's poems *Lara*, *Childe Harold's Pilgrimage*, and *Don Juan*. "In sequence," Bailey explains, "*Cities of the Plain* presents the anti-hero, introduced by Byron and developed in the American novel" (296).

Although Bailey's categorization of the progression of Byronic heroes in McCarthy's novels works well, I argue that McCarthy's engagement with Byron, and more specifically with *Don Juan*, begins in *Blood Meridian* years before he wrote the Border Trilogy. If, as Bailey suggests, John Grady Cole and Billy Parham of *Cities of the Plain* are associated with *Don Juan* because they broadly correspond to Byron's conception of the antihero (characterized by Don Juan), *Blood Meridian* presents a much more complex engagement with *Don Juan*, responding to the poem's overall lack of a hero in the context of the explicit depiction of America seen in Canto 8 of Byron's mock epic. When Bailey draws connections between *Don Juan* and *Cities of the Plain*, he qualifies this association by noting the characteristic Americanness of *Cities of the Plain*: "I do not mean to imply that the Border Trilogy, *Cities of the Plain* included, is simplistically a Byronic dirge for the passing of the hero. For one thing, *Cities of the Plain* is distinctly an American novel, not Byron's High Romanticism. It belongs to that literary genre called the Western, after all" (299). While Bailey assumes that the Americanness of *Cities of the Plain* works to disengage it from comparisons of Byron, I assert that the preoccupation with Americanness is what most interestingly ties *Don Juan* to *Blood Meridian*, and that *Blood Meridian* responds to and critiques the figuration of America within *Don Juan*, the rest of Byron's poetry, and the generic Western by using Byron's own mode of romantic irony.

Nick Monk, among other scholars, has criticized reading *Blood Meridian* as a Romantic text, claiming that "to argue, therefore, that what occurs in McCarthy's novels is an unadulterated Romantic dialectic would be to fail to recognize the ironic presentation of Romanticism/romanticism—a movement/genre that McCarthy's fiction represents as merely a blind offshoot of modernity, a futile cul-de-sac at the dead end of which lurks a crisis" (97). I suggest that the novel's presentation of romantic irony is much more complicated—and important—than Monk acknowledges. In my view, romantic irony in *Blood Meridian* is engaged in order to critique romanticized, sentimental representations of America and suggests that what results from the failure to account for the influence of romantic idealizations of America is indeed a crisis—a crisis of identity, a crisis of history, and, above all, a crisis of self-deception.

Before analyzing how *Blood Meridian* engages with Byron's poetry to form a critique of idealized representations of America, it makes sense to contextualize *Blood Meridian* with regard to romantic irony. Anne Mellor explains that romantic irony "grows out of philosophical skepticism and the social turbulence of the French Revolution and the American War of Independence; it posits a universe founded on chaos and incomprehensibility rather than a divinely ordained teleology" (vii). I argue that reading *Blood Meridian* through Byron's poetry demonstrates how the novel unmasks romanticized views of America. The "romanticized" images I am discussing here follow Schlegel's definition of the romantic as "that . . . which presents a sentimental theme in fantastic form" (Mellor 19). In that sense, "Romantic" images (those found in Romantic literature) might not be "romantic," and those images that are strictly "romantic" are not "romantic-ironic." Romantic-ironic images, instead of relying on fantastic, sentimentalized abstractions, work to undo romantic images, to "deconstruct mystifications of the self and the world" (Mellor 5). Although Byron's poetry is generally characterized as romantic-ironic, it contains elements of both romantic irony and romanticism. *Blood Meridian* invokes romantic irony both thematically and structurally to show that within the ever-expanding American frontier, the social turbulence and violent contest seen in the American Revolution has become even more wildly chaotic. The chaos of Western existence comes across not only in the plot of the novel, which haphazardly follows the drifting of the kid between groups of filibusters and scalp hunters with random scenes at various Southwestern locales, but also in the novel's structure, which is composed of a series of vignettes that are placed sequentially but only loosely tied together through narrative—much like Byron's *Don Juan*. As Mellor asserts, Byron's work serves as the locus classicus of English Romantic irony, with *Don Juan* its "greatest exemplar" (5, 31). The striking correspondences between *Don Juan* and *Blood Meridian* highlight the novel's engagement with romantic irony. Both works, for example, follow a young, relatively naïve protagonist's travels and crises, but there is no sense in either work that any higher purpose orders the progression of the text, or that the aimless direction of the mock heroic protagonist will ultimately be revealed as some sort of quest.

The lack of textual telos in *Don Juan* and *Blood Meridian* aligns both works with romantic irony and contributes to their larger critiques of Enlightenment discourse. Mellor points out that romantic irony in works such as *Don Juan* emerges "from [a] background of political revolution and post-Enlightenment distrust of the capacity of human reason to ascertain the laws of nature, or, indeed, any absolute truths concerning the ways of the world" (4). *Blood Meridian*, like *Don Juan*, demonstrates an engagement with Enlightenment discourse that specifically undermines the rationalization of imperial authority. This engagement becomes crucial to *Blood Meridian*'s critique of America, in fact, because it illustrates how Enlightenment discourse came to inform rhetorics of Manifest Destiny and the design of US empire. *Blood Meridian* signals its opposition to Enlightenment-based imperial thinking through the character of the judge, the novel's most frightening, cruel character and the kid's main antagonist. A giant, hairless man, the judge appears to be larger than life, and, in terms of his knowledge, he is. His expertise spans a wide range of fields, including law, history, biology, and chemistry, and he can speak an incredible number of languages. As Jarrett observes, "the judge's name suggests his interpretive function within the narrative: in the Southwestern border zone, devoid of law, the judge personifies the law of the narrative's events. His is the voice who supplies an apologetics and rational ideology for the gang's violence, murders, and massacres" (78). According to Jarrett, the judge not only represents the ethos of Manifest Destiny, he also acts as the novel's rational egoist: "The judge acts and speaks not merely as a diabolical agency . . . but as a nineteenth-century version of

Blake's Urizen, a representation of the unrestricted will to power of the transcendental Reason" (79). "His speech," Jarrett asserts, "clarifies his position as representative of the marriage of power and reason in the modernity of the West" (79).

In addition to contextualizing the scalp hunters' killings within the rationality of the US West, the judge also comes to embody the figure of the author who literally writes its historical record. Many readers have characterized the judge as an author of Manifest Destiny. Masters, for example, has argued that "the judge's impermeable, amoral logos . . . demarcates the judge's westward expansion as a *textual* enterprise" (25). Similarly, Fielder has observed that the judge serves as the novel's "embodiment and agent of the scriptural process" (32). He explains that "According to the judge, the 'truth' of a book is determined *not* by the degree to which it conforms to the external world it purports to represent, but rather by the extent to which it is able to *impose its own scriptural order on that external world.* Much like the rhetoric of Manifest Destiny, then, the judge's rhetorical gesture simply asserts the inexorable teleology and absolute authority of its own textual system" (40).

The judge's textual system is revealed in his notebook, complete with both his written accounts and his illustrations of ancient artifacts (which he destroys after sketching), flora and fauna, and portraits of actual contemporaries, the purpose of which, he says, is "to expunge them from the memory of man" (140). Through this simultaneous process of writing and expunging, the judge configures "the landscape of the Frontier . . . as a void waiting to be filled, as a tablet awaiting inscription, and as a world of broken language requiring order. In the judge, we see the violence of authorship, for the act of inscription implies a simultaneous erasure of an existent text" (Masters 26). The judge's authorship evidences a textual violence as it imprints his larger philosophy about the rational basis of man's existence upon US history: "The universe is no narrow thing and the order within it is not constrained by any latitude in its conception to repeat what exists in one part in any other part," the judge proclaims, explaining that "war is at last the forcing unity of existence. War is God" (245, 249). Thus the judge rationalizes the scalp hunters' slaughter of Native Americans and Mexicans within a higher order of Manifest Destiny. As Jarrett observes, the judge represents "a will, implicit in the Western mind and the historical impetus behind the American Western expansion, to wield an absolute power," to attempt to dominate both nature and men (80).

With its depiction of the judge's writing and expunging of the historical record (and the Manifest Destiny it represents), the novel itself participates in a process of construction and deconstruction that it enacts through narrative. In her discussion of romantic irony, Mellor explains that a sense of "never-ending becoming" constitutes an "aesthetic mode that sustains this ontological reality" of "the universe as chaos" (4-5). "The resultant mode that alone can properly be called romantic irony," she claims, "must therefore be a form or structure that simultaneously creates and de-creates itself" (5). *Blood Meridian* acknowledges this process of creation and de-creation when the novel makes clear that the tale is ending only to be told again. The act of simultaneous narrative construction and deconstruction comes across most powerfully in the conclusion, which shows that the story itself, manifested in the character of the judge, continues in a dance that will never end:

> Towering over them all is the judge and he is naked dancing, his small feet lively and quick and now in doubletime and bowing to the ladies, huge and pale and hairless, like an enormous infant. He never sleeps, he says. He says he'll never die. He bows to the fiddlers and sashays backwards and throws back his head and laughs deep in his throat and he is a great favorite, the judge. He wafts his hat and the lunar dome of his skull passes palely under the lamps and he swings about and takes possession of one of the fiddles and he pirouettes and makes a pass, two passes, dancing and fiddling at once. His feet are light and nimble. He never sleeps. He says that he will never die. He dances in light and in shadow and he is a great favorite. He never sleeps, the judge. He is dancing, dancing. He says that he will never die. (335)

An "enormous infant," like the newly formed, continuously expanding US, the judge says that he will never die, and the novel provides no indication that his dance will ever stop or that he will ever die. Instead, it ends with the judge "towering over them all," including the kid, whom the narrative has been tracking from the beginning. *Blood Meridian* leaves the reader with the sense that no matter whose story is told, what the judge says will eclipse the individual tale. As his dance begins again and takes center stage at the end of the novel, we get the sense that the killing will start again, too. The trace of his skull is illuminated, thinly veiling the future he embodies.

Byron's *Don Juan* also undoes the possibility of ending because it figures its "poetic language as *action*, as *process*" through its narrator's insistence that the poem itself is an ongoing "linguistic performance," much like the judge's speech (Mellor 72). Mellor concludes: "That is why the poem is never concluded, indeed hardly begun [as] the narrator insists at stanza fifty-four of the twelfth canto" (72). Crucial to the presentation of the poem as a performance is the distinction between Don Juan—the naïve, romantic character who participates in the action of the plot—and the ironic, experienced voice of the poem's narrator. Through the dual representations of the narrator and Don Juan, "Byron found a vehicle for his divided, romantic-ironic consciousness. In this poem, Byron carefully balances a romantic enthusiasm against a skeptical conviction of human finitude" (Mellor 42). In addition to the opposition between the narrator and Don Juan's character, the poem also alternates between epic and satiric impulses. *Don Juan*'s opening lines point toward its purposeful blurring of generic conventions: "I want a hero: an uncommon want, / When every year and month sends forth a new one, / Till, after cloying the gazettes with cant, / The age discovers he is not the true one" (1.1-1.4). In these opening lines, the narrator of *Don Juan* introduces the play between epic and satiric undertones that contributes to the comic rendering of Juan's tale.

While the narrator oscillates between satiric and epic modes, he at times regresses into romantic sentimentality. Tilottama Rajan has argued that "the point about Byron is that he too cannot be satisfied with irony, and approaches Juan through the eyes of a narrator whose occasional lapses into sentimentality keep unsettling the poem's commitment to realism" (265). She goes on to explain that "this paradox should give us pause as we contemplate the apparently anti-Romantic direction of Byron's career, from *Childe Harold's Pilgrimage*, which renounces the sentimental illusions of quest-romance and realizes the nothingness of human endeavors before the power of the ocean, to *Don Juan*, which tries to subsume the nihilism of *Childe Harold* by replacing Romantic irony with pragmatic irony" (265-66). *Blood Meridian*'s engagement with Byron hinges on the tension in his poetry between ironic critique and sentimentality. Building upon this tension, *Blood Meridian* provides a critique of the sentimental portrayal of America that is seen in *Don Juan* and other of Byron's poems by depicting a nihilist American tale entirely devoid of romance. Reading the phrase "his blood / Is all meridian," which appears in "To the Po," perhaps Byron's most sentimental poem, comparatively against *Blood Meridian* emphasizes this contrast between his poems' romanticized visions and the unromanticized images of the novel. "To the Po," an 1819 poem in which Byron reflects on his love for the married Countess Teresa Guiccioli, identifies the Po as a river that physically separates the lovers, but it notes that the river is the least of the obstacles that thwart their being together:

> Both tread thy bank, both wander thy shore,
> I near thy source, and She by the blue deep.
> But that which keepeth us apart, is not
> Distance, nor depth of wave, nor space of earth,
> But the distractions of a various lot,
> Ah! various as the climates of our birth!
> A Stranger loves a lady of the land,
> Born far beyond the Mountains, but his blood
> Is all meridian, as if never fanned
> By the bleak wind that chills the Polar flood.
> My heart is all meridian, were it not
> I had not suffered now, nor should I be—
> Despite of tortures ne'er to be forgot—
> The Slave again, Oh Love! at least of thee!
> 'Tis vain to struggle, I have struggled long
> To love again no more as once I loved.
> Oh! Time! why leave this earliest Passion strong?
> To tear a heart which pants to be unmoved? (35-52)

Byron describes "his blood" as "all meridian" to represent his affinity with southern climates and locales, which serves to bring him closer to Teresa, who is Italian. Byron's "blood" and "heart" gravitate toward her because he is a "Slave again" to "Love."

In contrast to the passionate romance of "To the Po," *Blood Meridian*'s title points toward the excessive violence portrayed in the novel and the blood-red color of the sky that reflects that violence. Jarrett notes that "the *blood meridian* of the title is used as an extremity, peak, or climax; the period covered by the events of the novel is chosen as the historical position when the bloodshed of the West is at its peak" (68). All the characters of the novel "have 'hearts of clay,'" as Jarrett observes (68), opposing them to the sentimental Byron, whose heart "pants to be unmoved." As Woodward notes, as a "man's novelist whose apocalyptic vision rarely focuses on women, McCarthy doesn't write about sex, love or domestic issues" (29). Although they differ in their respective foci on death and love, both *Blood Meridian* and "To the Po" represent the defiance of borders in pursuit of conquest, whether of the countess's affection or Manifest Destiny. Emphasizing the importance of border conflicts not only to *Blood Meridian,* but also to McCarthy's entire body of work, Jarrett discusses how the focus on borders shifts geographically in *Blood Meridian*: "The geographical movement of McCarthy's fiction to the Southwest in *Blood Meridian* redefines the definition of 'border' in his earlier fiction from a hill-valley of North-South border to one tilted along a Northeasterly to Southwesterly plane. By tracing the violent lives of the kid, the judge, and their various historical and fictional cohorts in the Glanton gang of scalp hunters, *Blood Meridian* intensifies McCarthy's early interest in the violence which accompanies the clash of cultures along geographical and cultural borders" (66).

The use of the term "blood meridian" in "To the Po" and *Blood Meridian* not only exemplifies the novel's refusal to validate romance or sentimentality, but also highlights the role that border crossings—both geographical and cultural—play in the violence that the novel's title represents. Reading *Blood Meridian* alongside "To the Po" complicates the consideration of border crossings by illustrating the arbitrary nature of borders themselves; the most striking example of this is the fact that the speaker's "blood / Is all meridian" even though it comes from a place in which it was "fanned / By the bleak wind that chills the Polar flood." Although borders do exist (represented in "To the Po" in the figure of the "Mountains" that separate the speaker's and his beloved's places of origin), they seem only to intensify, not thwart, desire, making those with "Passion strong"—both the poem's speaker and the novel's filibusters—"Slave" to the act of conquest itself.

Byron, who at the time he wrote "To the Po" was considering relocating to the Americas (Clubbe, *Natural Man* 3), was very interested in the exploration of the lands of the American frontier and enchanted by the opportunities of the fledgling American nation to expand its territory and influence across the continent. As John Clubbe explains, "in contrast to constricted, populated England, America seemed immeasurable, its features unknown or hardly known. The idea of the place, the enormous potential of seemingly infinite expanses, exhilarated Byron . . . the American West [was an] epic in itself" (*Byron* 144). Byron owned several books about the American frontier, but he particularly relished the journals of Lewis and Clark's expedition across the North American continent. After reading their account of the American West, Byron exclaimed that he "never envied any men more than Lewis and Clark" (Clubbe, *Byron* 144). Byron's preoccupation with the American frontier becomes manifest in *Don Juan* when he "unexpectedly introduces a sequence of stanzas describing the Arcadian existence of Daniel Boone, 'back-woodsman of Kentucky'" in the eighth canto (Clubbe, *Natural Man* iii).

In the eighth canto of *Don Juan*, Byron focuses specifically on the casualties of war he depicts with Don Juan fighting alongside the Russians against the Turks. But when Juan accompanies the Russian troops into Ismail, the narrator curiously breaks from the action, turning for the next eight stanzas to America and Daniel Boone. The narrator uses this sentimental digression on the American Arcadia not only, as he says, for a bit of "variety," but also to provide a foil for the upcoming battle in Ismail and the "great joys" of civilization to which it bears witness—"War, Pestilence, and the despot's desolation" (8.68; 537-40). As Clubbe explains, "Byron meant the Boone stanzas to jar when we come upon them in the midst of the realistic war cantos. He wished us to envisage an alternate existence to wars endemic to urbane (and European) civilization. The peaceful life Boone leads in Arcadia puts to shame Souvarow's conquests" (*Natural Man* 23). Laurence Goldstein supports this reading, suggesting that the turn from Boone to the Ismail is representative of a "movement of mind [that] can be found everywhere in Byron's verse," which in this case examines "this fallen world in which power usurps the place of continuity" (213). In contrast to the bloody confrontation seen with the Russian troops, the narrator associates those living in American Arcadia with Nature, far removed from the turbulence and madness of "cities caged" (8.62, 495). Daniel Boone, "the child / Of Nature," and his "sylvan tribe of children" live an idyllic existence that is tainted by neither "sword nor sorrow" (8.63-65, 503-16). Because they live a "Simple" life in isolation apart from civilization, they remain uncorrupted ("their thoughts had never been prey / Of care or gain"), and they live in peaceful harmony in the "back-woods" of the American frontier (8.61-66, 484-524). Clubbe argues that in these stanzas on Daniel Boone, Byron suggests that "Arcadia *is* necessary . . . because civilization will always remain with us. Man has a perennial need to create ideals to compensate for the failings of society, chief among which is the lust for power that war embodies. The important thing to realize is that however tempting we may find having power over others, it constricts our existence" (*Natural Man* 23).

With these images, *Don Juan* came to characterize both Daniel Boone and the American frontier for a worldwide audience. "The seven stanzas that Lord Byron devoted to Boone in the eighth canto of *Don Juan*," Clubbe asserts, "made him a world-wide celebrity, and he gradually became the one overshadowing figure of the frontier" (*Natural Man* ii). Byron's stanzas, according to Boone biographer John Faragher, serve as his "most famous" characterization "as 'natural man.'" Although "Americans could have read these lines in late 1822," Faragher explains, "they were reprinted scores of times throughout the century," which solidified Byron's portrait of Boone within the national imagination (328). Boone biographer Robert Morgan stresses that "the impact of Boone's story and legend on . . . Byron, and other writers of the Romantic era is only the beginning of the story of the Boone legend and biography," suggesting that the portraits that followed were heavily influenced by the Romantic model. "When viewed in the larger context of the colonial age," Morgan writes, "the Boone legend is in many ways typical of the way stories and figures of quest and conquest were romanticized, as Europeans conquered lands and peoples" (xv). Byron participates in this rewriting of history, glorifying Boone "the frontiersman as a spirit who kept in front of the civilization he himself brought into being" (Goldstein 212). In fact, in the 1822 edition, Byron promoted Boone, who was actually a colonel, to the rank of general, an error that was addressed in the US reprints (Lofaro 180). "For Byron," Michael Lofaro, another Boone biographer, explains, "Boone was an ideal example of Rousseau's natural man whose life in the wilderness gave him spiritual purity, serenity, freedom, simplicity, and good health" (180-81). With Byron's portrait, Boone became a symbol of these qualities for the American people as well.

## *Blood Meridian*'s anti-Arcadia

While the images of the US frontier produced by *Don Juan* and other works of British Romantic poetry painted a pretty picture of the realities of Western life, *Blood Meridian* casts a dark shadow of its own over these rosy, romanticized representations of frontier existence. The novel shows that although the frontier is indeed separate from the hubbub of US cities, it does involve contact with civilization, namely, the civilizations of native people who are totally alien to the settler. Responding to the Enlightenment conceptions of primitivism inscribed in *Don Juan*, McCarthy uses the unnamed figure of "the kid" to provide a jarring contrast to the "sylvan tribe of children" who, though simple, were not "savage," and had rifles that "were not yet used for trifles." When the kid first leaves home, John Cant explains, McCarthy offers us "a brief portrait of a youth who sets off into the world, and into the mythic west, in something approaching a 'state of nàture'" (162). What we get, however, is a journey full of violence and destruction. The kid and the gangs he joins, both Captain White's filibusters and Glanton's scalp hunters, are characterized by "mindless violence" (3). The kid is deemed eligible for the filibusters, in fact, because he viciously attacks a barman who refuses him a drink, cramming "the jagged remnant [of a bottle] into his eye as he went down" (25). Putting aside for a moment the gratuitous violence that marks even the nonbattle scenes in *Blood Meridian*, the glimpses we see of battle show just how unrealistic the depiction of the American frontier in *Don Juan* is. The contrast between Byron's portrayal and the actual realities of frontier life reinforces the irony of using it as a contrast for the representations of war between the Russians and the Turks in the eighth canto, an irony which the novel highlights by countering the Arcadian primitivism seen in *Don Juan* with an extreme savage primitivism.

The following passage conveys just one example of the overwhelming horror of the violence central to *Blood Meridian*'s anti-Arcadia:

> Now driving in a wild frieze of headlong horses with eyes walled and teeth cropped and naked riders with clusters of arrows clenched in their jaws and their shields winking in the dust. . . . until they had circled the company and cut their ranks in two and then rising up again like funhouse figures, some with nightmare faces painted on their breasts, riding down the unhorsed Saxons and spearing and clubbing them and leaping from their mounts with

> knives and running about on the ground with a peculiar bandylegged trot like creatures driven to alien forms of locomotion and stripping the clothes from the dead and seizing them up by the hair and passing their blades about the skulls of the living and the dead alike and snatching aloft the bloody wigs and hacking and chopping at the naked bodies, ripping off limbs, heads, gutting the strange white torsos and holding up great handfuls of viscera, genitals, some of the savages so slathered up with gore they might have rolled in it like dogs and some who fell upon the dying and sodomized them with loud cries to their fellows. (53-54)

The images of the Comanche attack in this passage are so frightening that the narrator describes them in terms of a sick fantasy, with "funhouse figures" moving about in "alien forms of locomotion." Instead of reinforcing *Don Juan*'s pastoral association of the frontier life with "Nature," *Blood Meridian* denaturalizes the existence of America's "sylvan tribe of children," who—instead of getting along harmoniously with natives and other frontier dwellers—are subject to, and themselves perpetrate, unnatural crimes against humanity. The perversion of the image of the American Arcadia in this passage is punctuated with the sodomy of the "unhorsed Saxons," which presents a counterpoint to the rape of the North American continent by European settlers. The American filibusters in this passage are linked to a tradition of European conquest by being described as "Saxons," connecting them to a savage, war-riddled history and emphasizing the continuation of that history, which originated in the European continent, by those of Saxon descent as its own type of Manifest Destiny in the New World.

Byron's figure of Daniel Boone, the "child / Of Nature," appears otherworldly when considered in relation to *Blood Meridian* and the kid, who clearly does not belong to the "sylvan band of children" depicted in *Don Juan*. Not only does *Blood Meridian* present a world from which heroes are absent, it also describes the frontier as an almost antipastoral landscape. The representation of this landscape contradicts *Don Juan*'s depictions of the American frontier and Boone himself, who has come to be "the apotheosis of the pastoral hero" (Salomon 66). Henry Nash Smith has described the transformation of the American frontier into the "poetic idea" of the American pastoral in his 1950 *Virgin Land: The American West as Symbol and Myth* (123). McCarthy points toward the groundlessness of this American pastoral dream of westward expansion at the beginning of *Blood Meridian*, during which the kid embarks on a pilgrimage markedly different from that of Childe Harold and travels west from his backwoods home, leaving the "flat and pastoral landscape" behind (4).

Landscape becomes important, as Sarah Phillips Casteel suggests, for "New World cultural production" because of "the Americas' composite character and their reluctant anxiety of origins" (9). As Casteel explains, "postcolonial writing of the Americas has continued to rely heavily on landscape to generate a distinctively American poetics. One strain of such landscape imagery takes the form of critical pastoralism, which, like settler colonial pastoralism, capitalizes on pastoral's capacity for emplacement" (12). By depicting the expansion of the newly formed US through the critical pastoral mode, McCarthy contributes to a "distinctively American poetics" of landscape that returns to Romantic conventions, if only to overturn them. Returning to the depictions of American Arcadia that Byron and his contemporaries helped perpetuate is necessary for postcolonial forms of the critical pastoral because of its relationship to emplacement that Casteel describes above. Byron's depictions of the American frontier in *Don Juan*, for example, inscribed the descendants of European settlers, exemplified by Daniel Boone, as the rightful occupants of the American territories. Daniel Boone, the "child / of Nature," is "not all alone" because "all around him grew / A sylvan tribe of children" who follow in his footsteps. Notably absent from Byron's landscape are American Indian tribes or Mexicans; he has cleared the scene for the US frontiersmen; "Serene, not sullen, were the solitudes / Of this unsighing people of the woods" (8.67, 535-36). In addition to countering the romanticized vision of the US frontiersman inscribed by Byron's cantos, *Blood Meridian* also describes the romanticized landscape. McCarthy highlights the importance of landscape to the novel, Cant explains, by making the "harsh landscape . . . a 'character in itself' whose propensity to 'imprint its own qualities on human characters' implies a move away from an anthropocentric cultural standpoint, the grievous consequences . . . being greatly increased by the West's largeness of scale" (158). Barcley Owens notes that in the novel, "even the landscape lacks any romance. Unlike the Border Trilogy, *Blood Meridian* is without pathos, pastoralism, or nostalgia" (7).

The most poignant example of the novel's resistance to the mythos of the pastoral American West, however, comes not from the landscape itself, but from what is literally written on the judge's gun: "Then about the meridian of that day we come upon the judge on his rock there in that wilderness by his single self . . . He had with him that selfsame rifle you see with him now, all mounted in german silver and the name that he'd give it set with silver wire under the checkpiece in latin: *Et In Arcadia Ego*. A reference to the lethal in it. Common enough for a man to name his gun. I've heard Sweetlips and Hark From The Tombs and every sort of lady's name. His is the first and only ever I seen with an inscription from the classics" (125). Whereas Byron invokes classical representations of a pastoral Arcadia in his idyllic description of the American West, McCarthy subverts this classical portrayal—on a rifle no less—to give a sense of the horrible reality of the violence of the frontier. *Blood Meridian* brings to light this history of conquest through the symbol of the judge's rifle in "the meridian of [the] day" and underscores the importance of this representation through the title of the book. The novel signals the subversion of myths of the American pastoral through association of the inscription with two of Nicolas Poussin's seventeenth-century pastoral paintings in which the phrase "Et in Arcadia Ego" (Even in Arcadia am I [Death]) appears ironically on a tomb (it is worth noting that Tom Stoppard's 1993 play *Arcadia*—which focuses on contemporary historians who look to unravel mysteries of Byron's life—is named after the inscription from Poussin's paintings that also appears on the judge's gun). "In the American Arcadia," Harold Bloom observes in the introduction to *Blood Meridian*, "death is also always there, incarnated in the Judge's weapon, which never misses" (x).

McCarthy unmasks the mythos of an American Arcadia in *Blood Meridian* by writing his own account of the West using people, places, and conflicts from historical records, which John Sepich details in *Notes on* Blood Meridian (1993). Byron's projection of the image of Arcadia upon America in *Don Juan* does not revolve as much on portraying the historical reality of the West as it does on serving a need to "compensate for the failings of society": "Arcadia *is* necessary, Byron seems to say, because civilization's vices will always remain with us. Man has a perennial need to create ideals to compensate for the failings of society, chief among which is the lust for power that war embodies" (Clubbe, *Natural Man* 23). David James and Philip Tew consider Arcadia to represent transformative possibility, suggesting that "Arcadia may be best regarded as a realm of action, of certain intersections full of innate contradictions, which it attempts to . . . mediate by . . . both foregrounding archetypal patterns of behavior . . . and by identifying an overriding trajectory of nature as fecund, generative, and transformative" (13-14). Although the conception of a pastoral American ideal might have given hope to Byron and his contemporaries, it also falsely shaped an image of America that obscured or disregarded the brutal realities of conquest central to the Western experience, contributing to a romantic American mythos that has remained prevalent hundreds of years after Byron's death. Richard Slotkin testifies to the prominence of this mythos in *Gunfighter Nation: The Myth of the Frontier in Twentieth Century America*: "The Myth of the Frontier is our oldest and most characteristic myth, expressed in a body of literature, folklore, ritual, historiography, and polemics produced over a period of three centuries" (10). Byron's poetry was among the first of these works to inform the development of the frontier myth.

*Blood Meridian* complicates this mythos by responding to works—like *Don Juan*—which helped create or perpetuate a false idealization of the American frontier. The novel's engagement with Byron's poetry, however, extends beyond merely refuting its romanticization of America and in fact draws upon the imagery and sense of desperation of what is perhaps Byron's most foreboding poem, "Darkness," to provide a sense of the darker side of the American Arcadia. *Blood Meridian* thus not only refutes the idealization of America seen in Byron's poetry to provide a sense of what the American frontier was not, but it also invokes Byron's poetry to depict a better picture of what the frontier was.

## "Darkness" and McCarthy's apocalyptic vision

Although the most striking correspondence between *Blood Meridian* and Byron's 1816 lyric poem "Darkness" involves the poem's ending, the novel invites its comparison to "Darkness" with its epigraph from Jacob Boehme: "It is not to be thought that the life of darkness is sunk in misery and lost as if in sorrowing. There is no sorrowing. For sorrow is a thing that is swallowed up in death, and death and dying are the very life of the darkness" (1). *Blood Meridian* can be read as a representation of "the very life of darkness" that characterized the American frontier, and Byron's poem "Darkness" provides insight into what that life was like. "Darkness" represents an apocalyptic vision of the earth that results after "the bright sun was extinguish'd, and the stars / Did wander darkling in the eternal space, / Rayless, and pathless, and the icy earth / Swung blind and blackening in the moonless air" (2-5). Without the light of day, the men in Byron's poem "forgot their passions in the dread / Of this their desolation" and "the brows of men by the despairing light / Wore an unearthly aspect, as by fits/ The flashes fell upon them" (7-8; 22-24). War, "which for a moment was no more, / Did glut himself again;—a meal was bought / With blood, and each sate sullenly apart / Gorging himself in gloom: no love was left; / All the earth was one thought—and that was death" (38-42).

*Blood Meridian* reproduces the poem's sense of desolation, loneliness, and alienating violence while reframing a fixation on death that comes across as the defining characteristic of the American frontier. Critics have often described *Blood Meridian* as its own apocalyptic vision: Bloom calls *Blood Meridian* "the authentic American apocalyptic novel" (v); Woodward notes McCarthy's "apocalyptic vision" (29); and Bell suggests that the novel provides a representation "of looking off into the heart of an imminent darkness [into] a small apocalypse, a primitive ceremony in which life and death have been forced to become one" (134). As Bell's allusion to Conrad suggests, *Blood Meridian*'s apocalyptic vision forms a critique of American imperialism and Manifest Destiny, which is represented by the judge, whose ongoing dance represents a paradoxical living death.

Within a US frame of reference, the opening line of Byron's "Darkness"—"I had a dream, which was not at all a dream"—has poignant significance for the realization of the "American dream" through westward expansion. Byron's "Darkness," as R. J. Dingly notes, "is defined largely by its absences" (22). Dingly explains that "the poem's very title indeed, Darkness, indicated the only quality positively present in Byron's moribund world, and its sound aligns it closely with the negative terminations in the body of the poem. Darkness, after all, can only be defined by an absent quality—it is no more than lightlessness" (22). Another of the poem's absences is the absence of dreamlike qualities from the poem. In March of 1815, a few months before Byron started writing the poem, he wrote these lines that anticipate the poem's turn away from the realm of dreams: "Then the moral coldness of the soul like death itself comes down; It cannot feel for others' woes, it dare not dream its own" (Fleming 269). *Blood Meridian* stages the moral depravity of the nightmare that is not a dream in the quality of its narration, which is at the same time jarringly detailed and historically accurate while also being nightmarish and fantastical. However, unlike in "Darkness," in *Blood Meridian* the negation of the dream is linked inextricably to the American setting, gesturing broadly to the emptiness of the "American dream." The frontier mythology "has created a symbolic vocabulary that has been employed to express and interpret the American Dream, to articulate, examine, and criticize American values" (Mogen, Busby, and Bryant 4). McCarthy applies this vocabulary to the novel to describe the impossibility of American dreams being realized on the frontier. Neil Campbell argues that "*Blood Meridian* [takes these] myths to their natural conclusion, 'to the west . . . toward the evening lands and the distant pandemonium of the sun'" (185). McCarthy sees that the pursuit of the 'American dream' in the West contains within itself the horrific inevitability of its own failure. Just as life is eternally reaching upwards but constantly shadowed by death, and just as the stars, however bright, are condemned to dust and nothingness, so too is man 'to bloom and to flower and die . . . His meridian is at once his darkening and the evening of his day'" (225).

As Campbell points out, images that invoke darkness ("the evening lands" and "his darkening and the evening of his day") predominate in the language with which McCarthy casts the frontier West as a "fatal environment." The harsh physical conditions and barren landscape contribute to the death that characterizes frontier existence, but, as the novel illustrates, the work of Manifest Destiny is largely responsible for this bloodshed. Steven Shaviro relates what he terms a "ritual" of Manifest Destiny to the emptiness of the American Dream: "*Blood Meridian* performs the violent, sacrificial, self-consuming ritual upon which our civilization is founded. Or better, it traumatically re-enacts this ritual . . . More blood is always needed to seal and renew the pact. The American dream of manifest destiny must be repeated over and over again, ravaging the indifferent landscape" (157). By depicting the reliance of Manifest Destiny on a continual cycle of bloodshed, *Blood Meridian* echoes the portrayal of war in "Darkness," who, personified, "glut[s] himself . . . / With blood . . . / Gorging himself in gloom" (39-41).

In terms of *Blood Meridian*'s anti-imperialist critique, the disillusionment of the dream corresponds to the fatality associated with Manifest Destiny, which, instead of bringing light to those across the continent, cast a dark shadow over their civilizations and eventually eclipsed them. In addition, as Toni Morrison has discussed in *Playing in the Dark: Whiteness and the Literary Imagination*, the literary association of blackness with death and social destruction has loaded the term "darkness" with a racialized, pejorative, and even apocalyptic significance that can be traced throughout US literature. *Blood Meridian* draws upon the literary racialization of darkness as it restages elements of Byron's poem "Darkness" to critique the ways in which the American dream has been dependent upon conquest and subordination of nonwhite peoples.

To account for the racialized significance of darkness in a US context, the novel adapts one of the final scenes from the poem and casts it in black and white. The novel does not limit its discussion of race in black and white terms, of course. *Blood Meridian* portrays the true diversity of the West, which, as Limerick notes, "with its diversity of Indian tribes, Hispanics, Euro-Americans of every variety, and blacks [is] a crucial case study in American race relations" (28). But the novel's restaging of "Darkness" deals starkly in racialized black and white. In the passage from the poem, everyone has starved to death but the last two men on earth, who are bitter enemies, and they gather around a fire. It is at this moment that they behold their true hideousness—and the mark of death:

> The crowd was famish'd by degrees; but two
> Of an enormous city did survive,
> And they were enemies; they met beside
> The dying embers of an altar-place
> Where had been heap'd a mass of holy things
> For an unholy usage; they raked up,
> And shivering scraped with their cold skeleton hands
> The feeble ashes, and their feeble breath
> Blew for a little life, and made a flame
> Which was a mockery; then they lifted up
> Their eyes as it grew lighter, and beheld
> Each other's aspects—saw, and shriek'd, and died—
> Even of their mutual hideousness they died,
> Unknowing who he was upon whose brow
> Famine had written Friend (55-69)

In contrast to Byron's generalization of the two enemies (he says that they are from the same city, nothing more), the narrator of *Blood Meridian* racializes the two enemies who, later in the novel, will gather around the same fated fire:

> In this company there rode two men named Jackson, one black, one white, both forenamed John. Bad blood lay between them and as they rode up under the barren mountains the white man would fall back alongside the other and take his shadow for the shade that was in it and whisper to him. The black would check or start his horse to shake him off. As if the white man were in violation of his person, had stumbled onto some ritual dormant in his dark blood or his dark soul whereby the shape he stood the sun from on that rocky ground bore something of the man himself and in so doing lay imperiled. The white man laughed and crooned things to him that sounded like words of love. All watched to see how this would go with them but none would caution either back from his course. (81)

Even in this instance in which the narrator describes the animosity between the black and white John Jacksons, one can read correspondences with Byron's "Darkness." The shadow here carries more significance than merely "shade," and the shapes cast by the sun on the ground seem to represent more than the outline of a man's frame. In this passage the racialization of darkness is clearly delineated, with the narrator associating "dark blood" and a "dark soul" with black Jackson.

Before black Jackson and white Jackson have their violent encounter around the fire, one of the men in the company offers a "wager as to which Jackson would kill which," placing his odds on "the blackie" (86, 87). A few days later, he gets the opportunity to reap his wager. "The sun to the west lay in a holocaust" on the night of the fated encounter, while "[a]ll the sky seemed troubled and night came quickly over the evening land and small gray birds flew crying softly after the fled sun" (105). On this night, in an invocation of Byron's poem, the narrator notes that all passed "into the problematical destruction of darkness" (105). The gang had two fires that night, one around which the Delaware Indians and the newcomers gathered, and around the other sat white Jackson, who shooed black Jackson away as he approached. In contrast to the fire scene of "Darkness," the men who face off in *Blood Meridian* each know who the other is. The specter of death that haunts both of them does not result from famine, as in Byron's poem, but is due to their participation in the scalp hunters' campaign, which contributes to the same overall project as that of Captain White's filibusters, who profess to be "instruments of liberation in a dark and troubled land," but in reality only ensure their own destruction (34). In the confrontation around the fire, black Jackson beheads white Jackson in one fell swoop, after which "[t]wo thick ropes of dark blood and two slender rose like snakes from the stump of [white Jackson's] neck and arched hissing into the fire" (107). The pair of twinned ropes of blood eerily enacts the ways in which the fates of black and white Jackson are intertwined.

As the judge tells black Jackson after his tarot card reading: "in your fortune lie our fortunes all" (93). Black Jackson picked the card of "El Tonto," the fool, from the tarot card dealer. Although the fool is associated with new beginnings and possibility, he is also expected to do something foolish. One might think that black Jackson's involvement with the scalp hunters is foolish both because it puts him in great danger (he is among the first of the group to die), and also because it contributes to an Anglo-Saxon domination of the continent and validates the rhetoric of Manifest Destiny. Jarrett explains how racism underlies the philosophical foundations of Manifest Destiny: "The rhetoric of Manifest Destiny justified territorial acquisition by combining racism with an appropriated version of the Puritan notion of predestination. The ideology of Manifest Destiny held that one race, the Anglo-Saxon, combined with the political form of republican government, comprised an elect nation that held the true title to the American landscape; justification for the individual and the communal enterprise of expansion and settlement lay in the subjugation of nature, both within man and without" (69). Although black Jackson wins the battle with white Jackson, he surely will not win the war, which, in the end, all of the scalp hunters will lose. That, according to the narrator, is ultimately "[h]ow these things end. In confusion and curses and blood" (40).

Black Jackson, however, is the subject of particular confusion. After the fight with white Jackson, he draws uninvited scrutiny from approaching Mexican troops. The judge gives a longwinded speech about race to a Mexican sergeant (whose men Glanton notably calls "halfassedlookin niggers" [84]), who has a problem with black Jackson's "dark vexed face" and refuses to shake his hand (84): "He [the judge] sketched for the sergeant a problematic career of the man before them . . . He adduced for their consideration references to the children of Ham, the lost tribes of Israelites, certain passages from the Greek poets, anthropological speculations as to the propagation of the races in their dispersion and isolation through the agency of the geological cataclysm and an assessment of racial traits with respect to climatic and geographical influences. The sergeant listened to this and more with great attention and when the judge was done he stepped forward and held out his hand" (84-85). Despite the gesture of goodwill, Jackson refuses to shake the sergeant's hand and asks the judge instead about what he told the sergeant. The judge replies that "[i]t is not necessary . . . that the principals here be in possession of the facts concerning their case, for their acts will ultimately accommodate history with or without their understanding . . . Words are things. The words he is in possession of he cannot be deprived of. Their authority transcends his ignorance of their meaning" (85). This discussion on the authority of words that carry no meaning ironically points toward the problematic discourse involving race, and, more broadly, its association to conquest. *Blood Meridian* gestures toward the import of words to territorial battles beyond the lives of the scalphunters it follows. As Mark Eaton argues, "the violence in *Blood Meridian* . . . is presented simply as one of the hard facts of frontier life . . . which needs to be viewed not in the old myth and symbol vein of American studies, but rather in the new paradigm of political domination and power" (157). *Blood Meridian* does not simply recast the myths that have come to characterize the frontier and—more generally—America, but instead deconstructs their larger mythos by examining their representations in terms of irony rather than symbolism. Unmasking the romanticized vision of the frontier as an American Arcadia and revealing the darkness at the heart of Manifest Destiny, the novel depicts the violence of the American West that has historically underlined and "still inform[s] our political rhetoric of pioneering progress, world mission, and eternal strife with the forces of darkness and barbarism" (Slotkin, *Fatal Environment* 12).

Several scholars and critics have read *Blood Meridian* as a commentary on more recent acts of US imperialism. Owens, for example, finds resonances with the Vietnam War, asserting that as "one of the most violent novels in contemporary American literature, *Blood Meridian* parallels its times. The mirror of art that McCarthy holds up to the nineteenth century reflects the ugliness of our own times as well" (20). Whether McCarthy specifically critiques recent US imperialism or not, his ironic portrayal of the "optical democracy" of the US-American frontier suggests that these claims for territory and power are in vain: "here was nothing more luminous than another and nothing more enshadowed and in the optical democracy of such landscapes all preference is made whimsical and a man and a rock become endowed with unguessed kinships" (247). In the brief epilogue to the novel, McCarthy presents a man making holes on the plain, presumably for a fence to enclose newly acquired territory. He describes the track of holes as seeming "*less the pursuit of some continuance than the verification of a principle, a validation of sequence and causality as if each round and perfect hole owed its existence to the one before it*" (337). The erecting of fences represents one man's attempt to create borders, but as *Blood Meridian* suggests, the fence he raises will not stand, and the fire in his hole will not last. The dance itself, however, will go on. And although Childe Harold's pilgrimage constitutes a very different journey than the kid's meandering, Byron's poem and McCarthy's novel leave the reader with sentiments more similar than one might imagine: "There is the moral of all human tales; / 'Tis but the same rehearsal of the past, / First Freedom and then Glory—when that fails, / Wealth, vice, corruption,—barbarism at last" (*Childe Harold* 4.964-67).

# Chapter Four

## Keatsian Echoes and US Materialism in *The Great Gatsby*

In *Blood Meridian* McCarthy focuses on the violence associated with expanding the US westward, making the human and cultural costs brutally apparent. F. Scott Fitzgerald likewise considers the costs of US empire, but he is concerned primarily with socioeconomic and political commentary. Instead of revisiting the 1800s, Fitzgerald writes on the age he made famous, the Jazz Age, a time when the US was emerging as the world's superpower. In his retrospective essay, "Echoes of the Jazz Age" (1931), he examines this shift in power and discusses the symbol he uses in his fiction to critique the shift's effects. Fitzgerald begins "Echoes of the Jazz Age" by "look[ing] back with nostalgia" on the era he named, chronicled in his fiction, and personified in his very public private life. He quickly shifts, however, toward a more ironic critical examination of why this period represents a turning point in US history, claiming that it marks the passage of "the style of man" to America:

> It was an age of miracles, it was an age of art, it was an age of excess, and it was an age of satire. A Stuffed Shirt, squirming blackmail in a lifelike way, sat upon the throne of the United States; a stylish young man hurried over to represent us to the throne of England. A world of girls yearned for the young Englishman; the old American groaned in his sleep as he waited to be poisoned by his wife, upon the advice of the female Rasputin who then made the ultimate decision in our national affairs. But such matters apart, we had things our way at last. With Americans ordering suits by the gross in London, the Bond Street tailors perforce agreed to moderate their cut to the American long-waisted figure and loose-fitting taste, something subtle passed to America, the style of man. During the Renaissance, Francis the First looked to Florence to trim his leg. Seventeenth-century England aped the court of France, and fifty years ago the German Guards officer bought his civilian clothes in London. Gentlemen's clothes—symbol of "the power that man must hold that passes from race to race."
>
> We were the most powerful nation. Who could tell us any longer what was fashionable and what was fun? (15)

Fitzgerald suggests that because gentlemen's clothes historically symbolize "the power that man must hold that passes from race to race," the US's acquisition of "the style of man," while seemingly "subtle" and superficial, signifies a much more meaningful transfer of global power from Great Britain to the US. Belonging to "the most powerful nation," Americans now had the prerogative to decide "what was fashionable and what was fun," but nonetheless they sought clothes produced by Bond Street tailors and continued to fashion themselves—in terms not only of garments but also of identity more broadly—after British models. Fitzgerald characterizes the US during the Jazz Age as a "whole race going hedonistic, deciding on pleasure," which with its newfound prosperity "attempt[ed] to adapt English customs to American conditions" (*The Crack-Up* 15). Claiming that US leaders were not immune to the impulse to associate themselves with the British aristocracy and leisure class, Fitzgerald's double pun parodies the US President (Harding, in this case) as a "Stuffed Shirt" that sat "in a lifelike way . . . upon the throne of the United States." The "throne of the United States" represents a curious emulation of the original "throne of England," serving as a metonymic parody of the monarchy at the height of the British Empire.

Although Fitzgerald's satire operates on multiple levels in this passage, his focus rests at least in part on American postures of class and authority that, ineptly modeled after British manners, rely on materialism at the expense of substance. Critiques of this type, involving in this case the "Stuffed Shirt," appear throughout Fitzgerald's work and almost always are emblematized by gentlemen's clothing, Fitzgerald's symbol for projections of power. In the early short story "May Day" (1920), for example, Fitzgerald gives a "minute examination" of the "shabby" suit of Gordon Sterrett in comparison with the luxurious wardrobe of Phillip Dean, whose "great English travelling bag" produced a "family of silk shirts littered on the chairs amid impressive neckties and soft woolen socks" (*Best Early Stories* 123-24). The contrast between Gordon's and Phillip's modes of dress contributes to a broader picture Fitzgerald paints about the ways in which projections of US identity after World War I became increasingly linked to patterns of consumption. The opening passages of "May Day" foreground the interconnectedness of the American soldiers' victorious return, increased demand for luxury items, the newly created leisure class, and the growth of a culture of consumption:

> There had been a war fought and won and the great city of the conquering people was crossed with triumphal arches and vivid with thrown flowers of white, red, and rose. All through the long spring days the returning soldiers marched up the chief highway behind the strump of drums and the joyous, resonant wind of the brasses, while merchants and clerks left their bickerings and figurings and, crowding to the windows, turned their white-bunched faces gravely upon the passing battalions.
>
> Never had there been such splendor in the great city, for the victorious war had brought plenty in its train, and the merchants had flocked thither from the South and West with their households to taste of all the luscious feasts and witness the lavish entertainments prepared and to buy for their women furs against the next winter and bags of golden mesh and varicolored slippers of silk and silver and rose satin and cloth of gold.

> So gaily and noisily were the peace and prosperity impending hymned by the scribes and poets of the conquering people that more and more spenders had gathered from the provinces to drink the wine of excitement, and faster and faster did the merchants dispose of their trinkets and slippers until they sent up a mighty cry for more trinkets and more slippers in order that they might give in barter what was demanded of them. Some even of them flung up their hands helplessly, shouting:
>
> "Alas! I have no more slippers! and alas! I have no more trinkets! May Heaven help me, for I know not what I shall do!" (*Best Early Stories* 122-23)

Fitzgerald prepares the reader for the critique in the following narrative by starting the story with a preface laced with biting satire: now that "the victorious war had brought plenty in its train," the lack of slippers and trinkets became a cause of grave concern. While images such as the merchants and clerks cramming "their white-bunched faces" against storefront windows to see the passing spectacle might be humorous, they provide US readers an unflattering glimpse of themselves that diminishes the glitter of the newfound splendor. The very title of this story summons visions of the violence of the 1919 May Day Riots, of celebratory parades unable to escape conflicting politics of labor, consumption, and evolving US identities. Fitzgerald explains in "Echoes of the Jazz Age" that economic tensions festered in the social and cultural milieu of this postwar moment, but that because of the relative prosperity, many US citizens shunned politics altogether. During the ten years of the Jazz Age, which spanned from the May Day riots of 1919 to the stock market crash of 1929, Americans became "alienate[d] . . . from the prevailing order," wondering with disillusionment if "maybe we had gone to war for J. P. Morgan's loans after all" (*The Crack-Up* 13). Reasoning that "we were tired of Great Causes," he observes that instead of responding with indignation, Americans channeled all of their "nervous energy stored up and unexpended in the War" into a culture of consumption: "we began to have slices of the national cake and our idealism only flared up when the newspapers made melodrama out of such stories as Harding and the Ohio Gang" (13, 14). Although Fitzgerald claimed in 1931 that the Jazz Age "had no interest in politics at all" (14), he later qualified that statement by recognizing that his own "political subconscious" manifested itself as "an element of irony" in his fiction (79).

Among the ironic portrayals in Fitzgerald's works, the symbolic depictions of gentlemen's clothing provide perhaps the most complex indictments of US materialism during the Jazz Age. These images symbolize a complicated engagement with materialism because they both celebrate and pass judgment on the way people in the US, including Fitzgerald himself, fashioned themselves with cloaks of prosperity, thus reflecting an ambivalent negotiation of wealth and position on an individual and national level. As visible symbols of clothes making the man, Fitzgerald's detailed representations of modes of dress reflect changing US identities after World War I and contribute to the tragic formulation of a distinctly "American dream" that romanticizes both the accumulation of wealth and acts of conquest. With its persistent focus on British fashion, Fitzgerald's fiction depicts the bitter irony of the passage of the "style of man" from Britain to the US: that instead of bringing a new style in vogue, US-Americans, who so fiercely fought for their independence, merely adapted the British imperial model to fit their bigger waistlines.

In this chapter I analyze the political and economic critiques implicit in the images of clothing and fashion in Fitzgerald's oeuvre, particularly those in his most widely read work, *The Great Gatsby* (1925). After tracing the novel's preoccupation with European styles and fashions, the chapter focuses on the famous shirt scene central to the novel in which Daisy weeps over Gatsby's beautiful clothes. Several scholars—including Dan McCall, George Monteiro, and Harold Bloom—have linked this scene to Fitzgerald's favorite poet, Keats, and have claimed that understanding the Keatsian intertexts of the passage are imperative for understanding the ways in which the novel as a whole responds to Keats's conceptualization of beauty and romantic love. These critics claim that the scene's engagement with Keats's poetry—particularly "The Eve of St. Agnes"—provides a sense of the "emotional importance of the [beautiful] moment" (McCall 525), the ironic defeat of the "hero's love-quest" (Monteiro 292), and the "idealized . . . passion . . . profoundly in excess of [Daisy]" (Bloom 2). While I agree with these claims, I argue that the Keatsian echoes signify much more than rewriting of a romantic narrative and that they even more powerfully invoke Keats's preoccupation with materialism and the symbolic force of material objects. The Keatsian intertext of this scene undergirds a commentary on US materialism that is not limited to Gatsby's character, but applicable to the larger culture of consumption developing across the US that both derives from and makes possible the US's superpower. By invoking Keats's poetry in this biting critique, Fitzgerald draws from Keats's engagement with the poetic object to develop a poetic resistance of his own.

Keats, who was marginalized by Byron and many others in the literary establishment for being "shabby-genteel" and "*most* vulgar" in his "*finery*" (Levinson 4), produced a rich tradition of social critique from which Fitzgerald could draw when evaluating his own era. But in addition to his modes of social commentary, there are many other facets of Keats's life and writing that Fitzgerald admired and associated himself with, and these points of identification are important for understanding the reasons why—of all writers—Fitzgerald very self-consciously emulated Keats. Therefore, before demonstrating the significance of Fitzgerald's modeling this most important scene of *The Great Gatsby* on Keats's grand feast in "The Eve of St. Agnes," I will explain more generally the commonalities between Keats's and Fitzgerald's social and literary experiences. In order to understand the depth of Fitzgerald's affinity with Keats, however, one must first have a sense of Fitzgerald's own fraught preoccupations with wealth and class.

## Distrusting the rich, yet working for money with which to share their mobility

Casting himself at various stages of his life as a "poor boy"—"a poor boy in a rich town; a poor boy in a rich boy's school; a poor boy in the rich man's club at Princeton"—Fitzgerald always felt apart from the upper-class circles in which he traveled (Turnbull 150). With his mother's substantial inheritance from her father's grocery profits, Fitzgerald was hardly "poor," but he was acutely aware of the social hierarchy of which he was a part (Bryer 22). He describes the social stratum of St. Paul, Minnesota, where he grew up, by explaining: "There were the two or three enormously rich, nationally known families—outside of them rather than below them the hierarchy began. At the top came those whose grandparents had brought something with them from the East, a vestige of money and culture; then came the families of the big self-made merchants, the 'old settlers' of the sixties and seventies, American-English-Scotch, or German or Irish, looking down somewhat in the order named . . . After this came certain well-to-do 'new people'—mysterious, out of a cloudy past, possibly unsound. Like so many structures, this one did not survive the cataract of money that came tumbling down upon it after the war" (*The Crack-Up* 233). Fitzgerald's mother descended from Irish merchants and thus ranked lower in the social hierarchy than Fitzgerald's father, who had the advantage of east-coast roots: "I am half black Irish and half old American stock with the usual exaggerated ancestral pretensions . . . The black Irish half of the family had the money and looked down upon the Maryland side of the family who had, and really had, that certain series of reticences and obligations that go under the poor old shattered word 'breeding'" (qtd. in Bryer 23-24). Although well bred, Fitzgerald's father suffered a series of business catastrophes that resulted in his financial dependence upon his wife's family. For Fitzgerald, among the most devastating of these failures was his father's losing his job at Proctor & Gamble in 1908: "That morning he had gone out a comparatively young man, full of strength, full of confidence. He came home that evening, an old man, a completely broken man. . . . He was a failure the rest of his days" (qtd. in Bryer 23).

Vowing not to be a failure like his father, Fitzgerald became dedicated to attaining financial success in order to provide for Zelda, whom he metaphorically describes as a "whirlwind": "I was in love with a whirlwind and I must spin a net big enough to catch it out of my head, a head full of trickling nickels and sliding dimes, the incessant music box of the poor" (*The Crack-Up* 86). "For sixteen years," Fitzgerald reveals, "I pretty much lived . . . distrusting the rich, yet working for money with which to share their mobility and the grace that some of them brought into their lives" (*The Crack-Up* 77). Fitzgerald's literary career took off after the stunning debut of his first novel, *This Side of Paradise* (1920), but when his success waned in the 1930s, his contemporaries—most notably Ernest Hemingway—openly mocked his admiration of the rich. Fitzgerald asked Hemingway to "lay off me in print" after Hemingway published this biting reference in the 1936 *Esquire* short story "The Snows of Kilimanjaro": "The rich were dull and they drank too much or they played backgammon. They were dull and they were repetitious. He remembered poor Scott Fitzgerald and his romantic awe of them and how he had started a story once that began, 'The very rich are different from you and me.' And someone had said to Scott, Yes, they have more money. But that was not humorous to Scott. He thought they were a special glamorous race and when he found they weren't it wrecked him just as much as any other thing wrecked him" (*A Life in Letters* 302). Fitzgerald clarified his admiration of the rich to Hemingway by saying that they "have never facinated [*sic*] me, unless combined with the greatest charm or distinction" (*A Life in Letters* 302), but nevertheless it was clear that the rich and their lifestyle had a special appeal for Fitzgerald. Despite his striving to attain their charm and distinction, Fitzgerald ultimately admitted that "I have never been able to forgive the rich for being rich, and it has colored my entire life and works" (qtd. in Turnbull 150).

Complicating Fitzgerald's preoccupation with the rich was his attraction to wealthy girls. In 1915 he began pursuing his first love, the beautiful, wealthy sixteen-year-old Ginerva King. That affair ended early in 1917. Of this relationship, Fitzgerald wrote in his *Ledger*, a yearly chronicle of his life, "poor boys shouldn't think of marrying rich girls" (170). Despite this realization, during the war Fitzgerald "again over-extended [his] flank" in another "one of those tragic loves doomed for lack of money," this time with a girl named Zelda Sayre, the daughter of an Alabama judge, whom he met during military training at Camp Sheridan (*The Crack-Up* 77). Zelda accepted Fitzgerald's engagement ring after an extended courtship, but once she learned that he was a struggling writer she broke off the engagement until he demonstrated that he could support her financially, a blow that must have been doubly hard given his father's history of failing to provide for his family.

In an attempt to win Zelda back, "Fitzgerald plunged into a frenzy of effort. He hammered out stories, hoping to get them into the high-paying *Saturday Evening Post* and revised earlier stories to publish wherever he could" (Roulston and Roulston 26). With the publication of *This Side of Paradise*, Fitzgerald's earnings jumped from $879 in 1919 to $18,850 in 1920 (Bryer 29). Zelda was satisfied, and they were married as soon as the novel's initial success was confirmed, but Fitzgerald indicated that "the man with the jingle of money in his pocket who married the girl a year later would always cherish an abiding distrust, an animosity, towards the leisure class—not the conviction of a revolutionist but the smoldering hatred of a peasant. In the years since then I have never been able to stop thinking that at one time a sort of *droit de seigneur* might have been exercised to give one of them my girl" (*The Crack-Up* 77). The sting of once not being good enough for Zelda—or Ginevra—never fully left Fitzgerald, and its effects are readily observable in his fiction, especially in *The Great Gatsby*. To a friend he explained that "the whole idea of Gatsby is the unfairness of a poor man not being able to marry a girl with money. This theme comes up again and again because I lived it" (qtd. in Turnbull 150).

The theme of not having enough money to marry the girl, a point I will return to later in the chapter, is one that Keats lived, too. Although the pressures that plagued Keats in early nineteenth-century Britain differed from those that Fitzgerald faced in early twentieth-century America, both men had the experience not only of not having enough money, but specifically of not having enough money to wed their sweethearts. Like Fitzgerald, Keats worked hard to overcome formidable social and class barriers in hopes of putting himself in a position where he could marry the woman he loved, Fanny Brawne; he died before he could ever realize that possibility. Keats, who passed up a promising medical career, was not a seeker of wealth, but while committed to his poetry he also wanted to be, in his words, "in the way of acquiring property" (McFarland 177). According to Marjorie Levinson, "Keats was a man whose almost complete lack of control over the social code kept him from living his life. He could not write his poetry in the manner he required, marry the woman he loved, claim his inheritance, hold his family together, or assist his friends" (8). Unlike Fitzgerald, who had the ability to "pass" in high society, Keats was characterized by members of the literary establishment as an ill-bred "Cockney," implying that he was a social climber who "lacked taste and education but was full of 'vulgar' pretension" (Wu 37). Although, as Alan Bewell explains, "Keats was not a spokesman for the working class . . . there is in his poetry an identification . . . with those who lack power and a public, political voice" (229). Similarly, Nicholas Roe argues that "Keats's eloquence [serves] as a representative voice of the most vital sector of contemporary English culture: that is, the culture of dissent in which ideological opposition to and consequent exclusion from the establishment formed the intellectual dynamic of enlightened progress in political, religious, aesthetic, and educational matters" (15). "My name with the literary fashionables," Keats wrote, "is vulgar—I am a mere weaver boy to them." What Keats indicated he wanted was literary success that would "lift [him] out of this mess. And mess it is as far as regards [his] Pockets" (qtd. in McFarland 177).

Both Keats and Fitzgerald were conscious not only of the financial necessity of their literary production, but also of the ways in which the success of their production was tied to images of themselves as authors that existed as products in and of themselves within the literary marketplace. For both writers, these images were tied to upward mobility narratives and projections of class identity. Thomas Pfau cites "Keats's sly allegorical performance as a writer who, fully cognizant of his lack of material resources and cultural accreditation, effectively turns the tables by emulating and thus exposing literariness as a specious good—a commodity as yet unconscious of its commodity status" (335). Although Fitzgerald's work also engages literariness as a commodity, his fiction is read much more often in terms of a semi-autobiographical or confessional performance. As Kirk Curnutt observes, from "the moment that he burst upon the literary scene in 1920 with his debut novel, *This Side of Paradise*, the precocious twenty-three-year-old encouraged audiences to acknowledge the umbilical connection between his life and art" (4). In terms of the "more mundanely mechanical" composition of their works, Fitzgerald, like Keats, "felt compelled *physically*" to escape his respective realities in order to write (Levinson 7). Levinson notes that much of Keats's poetry "was conceived or composed at a number of modest, middle-class . . . resorts," and when he could not afford a resort he sought "a friend's well-furnished living room" (7). Fitzgerald quit his job in New York and went back to his parents' house to work on improving *The Romantic Egoist*, which would later evolve into *This Side of Paradise*. "'Romantic retirement' gains a whole new dimension" with both Keats and Fitzgerald, as Levinson suggests of Keats: "Imagine the solitude of a young man . . . with nothing to do for a set period of time but write the . . . epic which would, literally, *make* him" (7).

In addition to reflecting upon their own negotiations of class, both authors' works invoked representations of themselves that relied upon a melancholia often related to contested relationships with women, but that also involved a deep-seated frustration about the impossibility of material and literary ideals. We can observe this symbolic relationship in their most famous works—in Keats's Odes as well as his romances (e.g., "La Belle Dame sans Merci," "The Eve of St. Agnes," "Lamia," and "Isabella"), and in Fitzgerald's *This Side of Paradise*, *The Beautiful and Damned*, *The Great Gatsby*, *Tender Is the Night*, and many of his short stories. Discussing the importance of this melancholic displacement to Keats's overall body of work, Pfau argues that

> At the heart of Keats's poetry and letters—and defining for the century's subsequent debate concerning the separation of lyric and prosaic writing—we find the axiomatic bond between the public persona of the writer and a culturally motivated hostility toward women. Having found inherited notions of aesthetic purity and authentic poetry to be unattainable, Keats reorganizes his melancholic awareness of that circumstance into a prolific, serial poetic industry. Within the figural order of sonnets and romances, disillusionment is reconstituted as an erotic betrayal, and unattainable ideals resurface as self-imposed illusions. Eventually, the protagonists of Keats's romances must either abandon these illusions or be consumed by them. (377)

Similarly to Keats, Fitzgerald redirected his own melancholic awareness in his novels and short stories, relying upon a "figural order" based on romantic poetic forms—often echoing Keats, as I will discuss in relation to *The Great Gatsby*—to reconstitute disillusionment as romantic betrayal in the serial production of fictional works. In addition to providing a sense of thematic continuity for readers and contributing to the development of the authorial persona, this serialization provides definite financial benefits; as James L. West III explains, the "Serialization of novels was a good way to make literary labor pay twice, once for the magazine run and again for clothbound publication" (53).

Unlike his protagonists, who succumb to their illusions instead of abandoning them, after his "crack-up" in the mid-1930s Fitzgerald sustained a new commitment to seeing himself more clearly, a process that involved understanding his melancholia: "I took a dollar room in a drab little town where I knew no one and sunk all the money I had with me in a stock of potted meat, crackers and apples. But don't let me suggest that the change from a rather overstuffed world to a comparative asceticism was any Research Magnificent—I only wanted absolute quiet to think out why I had developed a sad attitude toward sadness, a melancholy attitude toward melancholy and a tragic attitude toward tragedy—*why I had become identified with the objects of my horror or compassion*" (*The Crack-Up* 80-81). Fitzgerald reasoned during this period of intense self-reflection that he developed these attitudes precisely because he identified himself with the objects about which he wrote. Recognizing the dangers of self-conceptualization through tragic characters consumed by their illusions, Fitzgerald asserts that "identification such as this spells the death of accomplishment." He compares himself unfavorably with Keats, "the Fiery Particle," who "never ceased his struggle against t. b. nor in his last moments relinquished his hope of being among the English poets" (*The Crack-Up* 81). In *Don Juan* (1823), Byron insinuates that Keats, the "fiery particle," died over grief from a poor review of his work: "John Keats, who was killed off by one critique, / Just as he really promised something great, / If not intelligible, without Greek / Contrived to talk about the Gods of late, / Much as they might have been supposed to speak. / Poor fellow! His was an untoward fate: / 'Tis strange the mind, that very fiery particle, / Should let itself be snuffed out by an Article" (11.60).

According to Duncan Wu, in the reception of these verses "Byron's wry skepticism was ignored and the myth embellished" (50). Fitzgerald marvels that Keats, who never attained the type of success that Fitzgerald did in his lifetime, considered himself a great writer though he could speak with neither the authority of failure nor the authority of success. The distinction between the authority of failure and the authority of success is made clear by Fitzgerald's comparison of himself to his contemporary, Ernest Hemingway: in his notebook Fitzgerald wrote: "I talk with the authority of failure—Ernest with the authority of success. We could never sit across the same table again" (*The Crack-Up* 181). Although Keats had neither type of authority, he had a firm confidence in his status as a great author that Fitzgerald could not maintain throughout his career.

In "Pasting It Together" and the other essays of the "The Crack-Up" series, Fitzgerald projects an ironic understanding of the ways in which his authorial persona had become confused on several levels with his actual person, which contributes, I think, to his lack of confidence. Before his literary success, Fitzgerald worked for the New York advertising agency Barron Collier, and even after he left that position he always felt as if he was selling something—a combination of himself and his work. As Curnutt explains, Fitzgerald was haunted by a "remorseful recognition that he never escaped the advertising business . . . the commodity he has sold has merely been himself" (87). With the realization that he had sold out, Fitzgerald relegated the "old dream of being an entire man in the Goethe-Byron-Shaw tradition, with an opulent American touch, a sort of combination of J. P. Morgan, Topham Beauclerk and St. Francis of Assisi . . . to the junk heap of the shoulder pads worn for one day on the Princeton freshman football field and the overseas cap never worn overseas" (*The Crack-Up* 84).

## A place in the line of pioneers

Although Fitzgerald might have discarded his aspiration of being the US-American "entire man," he nevertheless became this type of nationalized author-figure through the distinctively US tenor of his work and the public spectacle of his lifestyle. Fitzgerald says that when he first entered the spotlight, he "was pushed into the position not only of spokesman for the time but of the typical product of the same moment" (*The Crack-Up* 27). At that time, the "uncertainties of 1919 were over—there seemed little doubt about what was going to happen—America was going on the greatest, gaudiest spree in history and there was going to be plenty to tell about it" (*The Crack-Up* 87). Even at the beginning of his career, he was highly attuned to his dual role as seller and product in this "greatest gaudiest spree," and he and his work emblematized American experience. Identifying the author as "intuitively American, and of his age," Larry Phillips suggests that "Fitzgerald always had, as he once said of himself, 'a more than ordinary tendency' to identify with the things outside him. And for a time, it was mutual: the country had the same tendency to identify itself with him as his reputation grew and his books sold in greater numbers" (xv). From Fitzgerald's first appearance in the spotlight, however, Americans identified with him and considered him a national personality. He was, after all, related to and named after the man who wrote "The Star-Spangled Banner," Francis Scott Key.

"When I was your age," Fitzgerald tells his daughter, Scottie, in a 1938 letter, "I lived with a great dream. The dream grew and I learned how to speak of it and make people listen" (*A Life in Letters* 363). Fitzgerald was able to make people listen to his dream—which he presented as a quest for money and love—in part because he projected it as a universal desire to pursue happiness. The preoccupation with the pursuit of happiness carries a distinctively American quality, but in Fitzgerald's estimation it carries a broadly human appeal: "I look out at it—and I think it is the most beautiful history in the world. It is the history of me and my people . . . It is the history of all aspiration—not just the American dream but the human dream and if I came at the end of it that too is a place in the line of pioneers" (Bruccoli xii).

Placing himself "in the line of pioneers," Fitzgerald suggests that he is participating in the process of discovering what the US experience really is, just as the European explorers who first arrived on the North American continent did many years earlier. In the often-quoted conclusion of *The Great Gatsby*, Nick Carraway, the narrator, considers the genealogy of this experience, starting with the sailors who first set eyes on the "fresh, green breast of the new world": "And as the moon rose higher the inessential houses began to melt away until gradually I became aware of the old island here that flowered once for the Dutch sailors' eyes—a fresh, green breast of the new world. Its vanished trees, the trees that had made way for Gatsby's house, had once pandered in whispers to the last and greatest of all human dreams; for a transitory enchanted moment man must have held his breath in the presence of this continent, compelled into an aesthetic contemplation he neither understood nor desired, face to face for the last time in history with something commensurate to his capacity for wonder" (140). Nick frames this "transitory enchanted moment" of European discovery of the new world in the context of "the last and greatest of all human dreams," and one could argue that this moment passed once the first explorers set foot on American soil, the first and last time man was "face to face . . . with something commensurate to his capacity for wonder." But such a reading would ignore the entire book's focus on Gatsby, whose "romantic readiness" served up "an extraordinary gift for hope" with which he pursued a dream he sensed was "so close that he could hardly fail to grasp it" (6, 141). As Nick "brood[ed] on the old unknown world," he immediately "thought of Gatsby's wonder when he first picked out the green light at the end of Daisy's dock" (141). Kenneth Eble notes that when Fitzgerald revised the manuscript of *The Great Gatsby*, he added this reference to the green light in the novel's final paragraphs and also inserted it at the end of the first chapter, making it one of the central motifs in the novel ("The Craft" 83). It originally appeared only in the scene in which Daisy and Gatsby meet, but Fitzgerald edited the manuscript to make it more prominent. The correspondence readers note between the wonder about the "fresh, green breast of the new world" and the green light of Daisy's dock, I argue, is not coincidental, but in fact marks a connection between these two markers of the American dream at different points in time. As objects of wonder, both inspire an "aesthetic contemplation" that is easily understood or desired, but that reflects upon the desire for possession, colonization, and settlement.

Whether or not Lionel Trilling is correct in claiming that the US "is the only nation that prides itself upon a dream and gives its name to one," it is clear that *The Great Gatsby* explicitly emphasizes the national character of its dream and that "Gatsby . . . comes inevitably to stand for America itself" (*Liberal Imagination* 251). Bloom echoes this sentiment, writing not only that "Gatsby's Americanism is so central to him that any other national origin would be impossible for him," but also that Jay Gatsby might very well be "the major literary character of the United States in the twentieth century" ("Afterthought" 233). Three weeks before the publication of *The Great Gatsby,* Fitzgerald, who was on Capri, frantically wired his editor at Scribner's, Maxwell Perkins, with the following message: "CRAZY ABOUT TITLE UNDER THE RED WHITE AND BLUE STOP WHART [*sic*] WOULD DELAY BE" (*Ledger* 31). Perkins advised Fitzgerald against the change of title, and there was not enough time to execute it regardless. But Fitzgerald continued to think that this was the most appropriate title for the book and blamed the book's initial lackluster sales on its title. Fitzgerald's insistence that the title *Under the Red, White, and Blue* was the most appropriate for the novel emphasizes not only the US focus of his novel, but also the importance of symbols and symbolism in relation to that focus.

Scholars and critics have traditionally focused on *The Great Gatsby*'s symbols in their reading of the book as a commentary on the "American dream." James E. Miller has argued that the green light at the end of Daisy's dock is the book's central symbol in its representation of the American dream: "probably no better symbol than the green light could be used for America's restless, reckless pursuit of the 'American Dream'" (35). Others have produced variations on the reading of the green light as a symbol of the American dream. Leslie Chard, for example, suggests that "we can acquire a precise understanding of the nature of Fitzgerald's comment on the American Dream" through the "fruitful analogy [of] Coleridge's 'Dejection: An Ode,'" which also features a green light (189). Arguing that "with a concomitant loss of faith in the American dream itself, a space opened for the fairy tale," Laura Barrett notes that the preponderance of green symbols in *The Great Gatsby*, including the light at the end of the dock, can be read as "smaller and later versions of [Baum's] Emerald City—full of promise and meaning but ultimately deceptive" (151, 161). Regardless of how they situate the green light in the literary tradition or more broadly in popular culture, though, readers tend to see this green light as a representation of the US and what it has to offer.

Another recurring image in the book that functions as a particularly important symbol is the faded billboard advertisement for the oculist Doctor T. J. Eckleburg, which consists of gigantic blue eyes peering out from "a pair of enormous yellow spectacles . . . over a nonexistent nose" that "brood over the solemn dumping ground" of the valley of ashes—"a fantastic farm where ashes grow like wheat into ridges and hills and grotesque gardens" (21). Looming above the dust-covered valley, Doctor Eckleburg gazes over "the waste land" (22), both representing the omnipresence and omnipotence of advertising (which, as Barrett claims, has been equated perversely with divinity [168]) and observing disapprovingly all that goes on below. John Bicknell argues that the valley's "symbols and images of waste, desolation, and futility" are "central to the novel's total effect" and that from the outset "the landscape is charged with symbolic overtones" (68), while Berman observes that the natural landscape is a "backdrop," subordinated to futile, destructive, and ghastly human activity, that provides "a form of silent commentary" (*World of Ideas* 47). Edwin Fussell, who was among the first (1952) to comment on Fitzgerald's symbolism as a type of moral critique, set the groundwork for these and other commentaries that would follow by claiming that his "keenest perception was the universal quality of the patterns he had been tracing, his greatest discovery that there was nothing new about the Lost Generation except its particular symbols. The quest for romantic wonder and the inevitable failure were only the latest in a long series" (293).

## *The Great Gatsby* and "factual imitations" of European models

While maintaining a focus on the newness of the particular symbols in *The Great Gatsby*, my argument complicates the estimation that the patterns of representation themselves "were only the latest in a long series" of manifestations of the American dream. Instead, I argue that Fitzgerald highlights a shift in the evolution of the US experience that began to take place after World War I. US-Americans began to fashion themselves differently once the US truly became a superpower, reflecting the acquisition of "the power that man must hold that passes from race to race" (*The Crack-Up* 15). As Arthur Mizener asserts, Fitzgerald's fictional treatment of this transfer of power was inevitable due to its global import: "The shift of power from Europe to America that took place after the first world war was bound to excite any imagination capable of grasping it all" (103). James Meredith also points out Fitzgerald's preoccupation with the ways in which the war affected US identity, adducing that Fitzgerald deemed it a change for the worse: "In that breaking point Fitzgerald saw profoundly into a tragic inversion. Before World War I, there was the young America. The young America, paradoxically, was the old America, back there in the past when the American world was so young. The post-war new America, however, was no longer the redeemer nation, but was very much part of the old, international, corrupt actuality of history that had eventually burst forth in the sickness of World War I. The new generation that emerged from the war became in Fitzgerald's vision metaphoric material for everything that always had been selfishly irresponsible and greedily self-gratifying in the same old, tired world—and in American life" (166).

As Meredith explains, Fitzgerald's fiction does not highlight a sudden departure after the war from a purely philanthropic, moralistic American dream to a "selfishly irresponsible and greedily self-gratifying" way of life. In fact, Fitzgerald, in a letter to Scottie, lamented the long-standing self-entitlement that has characterized the US: "your generation . . . share[s] with every generation since the Civil War in America the sense of being somehow about to inherit the earth" (*The Crack-Up* 306). Rather, the change Fitzgerald depicts is that the "postwar new America" had a greater tendency to identify with and emulate "the old, international, corrupt actuality" that characterized the great world empires—particularly, as we see in *The Great Gatsby*, the British Empire. For all of *The Great Gatsby*'s focus on time—Ronald Berman claims that there are at least 450 references to time in the short novel—one of the few actual dates it contains is 5 July 1922 (see Wilson's play *5th of July*), the day on which Nick began writing down "on the empty spaces of a time-table the names of [all] those who came to Gatsby's house that summer" (49). Independence Day serves as one of the major frames for temporal references in the text in addition to this specific date. It is the benchmark, for example, when Nick describes the time when he visited Myrtle's apartment: "It was a few days before the Fourth of July" (23). The significance of this particular date evokes America's postindependence negotiation of its contested British legacy with the added temporal dimension of its situation after the First World War. Further, it associates this negotiation with the "endless permutations of class and style and self-chosen character in America" represented by Nick's long list of Gatsby's houseguests (Berman, *Modern Times* 3).

In addition to drawing attention to rapidly changing designations of class and style, *The Great Gatsby* broadly marks the empowered posturing of US citizens and its figurations of global appropriation. Outside of the gaze of Doctor Eckleburg or the view of the New World seen through the "Dutch sailors' eyes," *The Great Gatsby* creates the sense of an American imperial eye by its location of Americanized versions of foreign landmarks on US soil, such as Versailles in Myrtle's cramped New York City apartment (22). *The Great Gatsby* contains several other instances of this type of figurative appropriation. In describing the disjunction between time and space in the novel, Berman identifies many of them:

> The more Nick Carraway tries to locate himself through the named and known quantities of West Egg on Long Island in North America in the Western Hemisphere the more he finds that he is somewhere he scarcely knows at all. We realize the disparities of time and place when we see the Merton College Library on West Egg; or San Francisco somewhere between Denver and Detroit; or Monte Carlo and Versailles on 158th Street on the West Side. Confusions of time and place impose relativity, affect the coordinates of logic as well as geography. We progress (within a very few pages) from New Haven and Westchester and Louisville and Maine and Georgia and Times Square and Oxford and Paris, Venice and Rome, and the Argonne Forest and "Little Montenegro" to the Pisgah view from the Queensboro Bridge, where all of the above are canceled out in order to see the created world for the first time. Very little is simply descriptive: we are asked to see a sidewalk in Louisville become Jacob's Ladder; and to lift our eyes from the Buchanans' lawn—or from the printed page—is to see something and some place that is not there. (*Modern Times* 4)

This transplantation of European markers in the novel's setting is designed to have a comedic effect in addition to that of déjà vu. The sheer comedy of trying to contain Versailles, the ultimate representation of French luxury, in Myrtle's apartment, which consists of "a small living room, a small dining room, a small bedroom and a bath," is not lost on Fitzgerald: "The living room was crowded to the doors with a set of tapestried furniture entirely too large for it so that to move about was to stumble continually over scenes of ladies swinging in the gardens of Versailles" (25). The image of Myrtle's guests stumbling over furniture that her space cannot accommodate can be seen as a metaphor for the US's attempts to fashion itself in the image of Europe as it assumed power after the war. When Fitzgerald compares the US with European colonial powers—"France was a land, England was a people, but America, having about it still that quality of the idea, was harder to utter" (*The Crack-Up* 197)—he points toward the newness and indeterminacy of US national identity that seems antithetical to its increasingly imperial posture. In a testament to its importance, Fitzgerald liked this conception of America as an idea so much that after publishing it in his 1929 story "The Swimmers," he copied it into his notebooks to consider for future projects (Callahan 150).

US citizens were getting, so to speak, a little too big for their britches. This sentiment comes across even more strongly when Tom Buchanan, Daisy's husband and Myrtle's lover, breaks Myrtle's nose: "they stumbled here and there among the crowded furniture with articles of aid, and the despairing figure on the couch bleeding fluently and trying to spread a copy of 'Town Tattle' over the tapestry scenes of Versailles" (32). In this scene, Myrtle, a struggling mechanic's wife, changes clothes—which "stretch tight over her rather wide hips"—three times, going from crêpe-de-chine to muslin to chiffon (23). The failure of her transposition to the leisure class despite her attempts to dress the part is mocked by the spreading of gossip magazines over the tapestry to prevent it from staining. Myrtle, not even fit to say Daisy's name, ultimately becomes a mere "figure" corrupting the idyllic scene of Versailles's ladies.

With the comparisons drawn between Myrtle's gaudy, crowded apartment and the mansions of Gatsby and the Buchanans, Fitzgerald points toward the way that class designations became increasingly tied to various emulations of European styles after the war. Gatsby's mansion, "a colossal affair by any standard," is "a factual imitation of some Hôtel de Ville in Normandy, with a tower on one side, spanking new under a thin beard of raw ivy, and a marble swimming pool and more than forty acres of lawn and garden" (8). Instead of a mere Versailles-inspired upholstery pattern, Gatsby's "huge incoherent failure of a house" reproduces an entire French city hall, despite its stylistic inappropriateness for its setting and its incongruous accoutrements of the swimming pool and tower (140). It is worth noting that Gatsby's mansion was built by a brewer in the 1910s. According to Nick, the original owner "agreed to pay five years' taxes on all the neighboring cottages if the owners would have their roofs thatched with straw." Noting the transmutation of European feudal class structures, Nick concludes that "Americans, while occasionally willing to be serfs, have always been obstinate about being peasantry" (69).

Although the mansion's design attempts to convey a sense of traditional luxury, its "thin beard of raw ivy" betrays its "spanking" newness and Gatsby himself as nouveau riche. Gatsby undoubtedly purchased the mansion to impress Daisy, whose house—which "he was in by a colossal accident" when they met several years earlier—amazed him because "he had never been in such a beautiful house before." At the time, Gatsby's "invisible cloak of his uniform" shielded him from being exposed as "a penniless young man without a past" (116). Gatsby's attempt at winning over Daisy with a house of more striking beauty seems almost parodic considering it has the gaudy, glittery quality of an amusement park, the overstated importance and reach of "the world's fair," and "enough colored lights to make a Christmas tree" (64, 33). Even without its additional adornment, the architectural incongruence of Gatsby's mansion with the surrounding buildings contrasts it with the established residences on East Egg, like the Buchanans' "cheerful red and white Georgian Colonial mansion," that feature more traditional displays of wealth, such as stables and Italian gardens (9, 16, 10).

In contrast to Tom, Gatsby does not own any horses. This lack is made painfully clear when Tom and two of his companions, who have come on horseback to visit Gatsby, insincerely issue a dinner invitation. Gatsby sheepishly explains that "I used to ride in the army, but I've never bought a horse. I'll have to follow you in my car" (80). Before he can get his car—a British-made Rolls Royce—Tom and his friends ride off on horseback, asking Nick to "tell him we couldn't wait" (81). The class difference between Tom and Gatsby highlighted in Tom's equestrian leisure pursuits becomes even more pronounced with the comparison of their abilities to dress the part of the magisterial, Old-World gentleman. When Tom first appears in the novel, he is dressed in British riding clothes that cannot hide the "enormous power" of his body: "he seemed to fill those glistening boots until he strained the top lacing and you could see a great pack of muscle shifting when his shoulder moved under his thin coat" (9). Although Fitzgerald associates the riding clothes with an "effeminate swank," as costumes of the leisure class, they connote a social and political power that complements the "cruel" strength of Tom's body. Even when Tom is not in his riding clothes, his dress conveys an air of power and respectability, one to which Myrtle testifies when she tells Nick about the day that she and Tom met on the train to New York: "He had on a dress suit and patent leather shoes and I couldn't keep my eyes off him but every time he looked at me I had to pretend to be looking at the advertisement over his head. When we came into the station he was next to me and his white shirt front pressed against my arm—and so I told him that I'd have to call a policeman but he knew I lied" (31). Tom's clothes make an impression on Myrtle (literally, in the case of the white shirt), because, ironically, they signal to her that he is a gentleman, someone far different from her husband, who had to borrow the suit he wore for their wedding. As Berman explains, "The phrase 'gentleman' means what Myrtle and many other amateur anthropologists call 'breeding'—that is to say, boots and saddles, English style. Protestant standing, social visibility, and, one hopes, inherited funds. The theme constantly plays against that of classless democracy" (*World of Ideas* 62). The differences between Tom's English-style dress, Myrtle's frequent changes of costume, and Gatsby's "gorgeous pink rag of a suit" (120) expose not only the inaccuracies of the assumption that American democracy is classless, but also the subtle importance of "the style of man" in the distinction of character. Ironically, both Tom and Gatsby try to outfit themselves in a characteristically English style. We can see this in Tom's riding clothes and suits, and, as I will discuss in more detail when analyzing the shirt scene, in Gatsby's wardrobe, purchased in London. "Gatsby aspires to Anglophile leisure," Berman explains, "an idea that comes to him not from the American West but from all of those magazines whose ads swoon over plus fours and British golfing shoes and mackintoshes and the latest tweeds of the Prince of Wales" (*World of Ideas* 121). And in recounting a story from her adolescence, the golfer Jordan Baker (Nick's love interest and Daisy's good friend) specifically mentions that she "had on shoes from England with rubber nobs on the soles that bit into the soft ground" (59).

Gatsby, whose conversation Nick describes as "like skimming hastily through a dozen magazines" and whose appearance Daisy says "resemble[s] the advertisement of the man" (53, 93), knows the importance of images and what they represent, and for this reason he dresses himself in the latest London fashions and presents himself as an Oxford man, even though he only spent a brief amount of time there after the war (100). Tom knows just from looking at Gatsby that it is impossible he could be an Oxford man: "An Oxford man! . . . Like hell he is! He wears a pink suit . . . Oxford, New Mexico . . . or something like that" (95). Nevertheless, Gatsby keeps up the pretense, bringing out a picture taken in Trinity Quad—a thing he always carries as a "souvenir of Oxford days" (53)—for those times he needs categorical validation or material evidence.

Given *The Great Gatsby*'s insistence on the ways in which the material object—whether a pink suit or a picture taken at Oxford or a medal from Montenegro—constitutes the man, one might be inclined to confine the novel's critique to the theme of US materialism. Kermit Moyer, for one, suggests that Fitzgerald's meditation on US history ultimately exposes the "foul dust [which] is the corruptive materialism, like a worm in an apple, at the center of the transcendental [American] dream" (52). In a slight variation on that theme, citing Fitzgerald's putative Marxist theoretical bent (within his notebooks, Fitzgerald claims that D. H. Lawrence is "essential pre-Marxian," just as he himself is "essentially Marxian" [*The Crack-Up* 178]), Scott Donaldson reads *The Great Gatsby* as "a cautionary tale" about capitalism that "uncovers the cracks in the glittering surface" of American society, "the poison eating its way underneath" (210). Henry Dan Piper characterizes the critique as targeting money itself: "From *Gatsby* to *The Last Tycoon*, the morality of money is Fitzgerald's major theme" (299). Robert Ornstein also comes to this conclusion, insisting that contrary to popular opinion, none of *Gatsby*'s characters are materialistic: "The thirst for money is a crucial motive in *Gatsby* as in Fitzgerald's other novels, and yet none of his major characters are materialists, for money is never their final goal" (62). While most scholars and critics agree that material goods or the money used to purchase them represent a darker aspect of the American dream, scholars such as John Bicknell read the novel as a categorical disavowal of that dream, insisting that Fitzgerald "portrayed the beautiful and the rich as essentially damned and . . . implied that the American Dream was, after all, little more than a thinly veiled nightmare" (67). Along those lines, Marius Bewley discredits the assumption that Fitzgerald "approved" of the American dream, claiming instead that "the theme of *Gatsby* is the withering of the American dream" (37). All of these readings have some merit. Certainly *The Great Gatsby*'s critique of US society does not rest specifically on materialism, capitalism, or wealth, but includes all of these themes and more, such as the reestablishment of a European caste system. But, for all of the novel's subtle and overt modes of critique, it does not represent a complete repudiation of the American dream. As Robert Roulston puts it, "despite the jabs, comic or otherwise, at New York's gaudiness and seaminess, the city hardly emerges from the book as H. L. Mencken's third-rate Babylon on the Hudson" (63).

Fitzgerald's genius in his treatment of US-Americanness in *The Great Gatsby* stems from his ability to subtly deconstruct the very makings of the American dream while at the same time paying homage to his countrymen's self-determination. Thus far, I have argued that although Fitzgerald creates a sense of the genealogy of the American dream, he complicates the notion of this dream evolving in isolation from the rest of the world, taking into account the economic, political, and social factors both within and outside of the US at various historical moments that help shape US citizens' notions of who they are and, concurrently, who they want to become. Nick's musings about the Dutch sailors' compulsion toward "aesthetic contemplation" at the end of the novel operates reflexively and constitutively on the novel as a whole, representing Fitzgerald's self-consciousness about *Gatsby*'s being its own aesthetic object and the author's own experience of coming "face to face" with the wondrous possibility that lay before the US at this "time in history," the postwar moment in which the US began to realize its global stature (140). Fitzgerald was among the first to look intently at US-Americanness at a time when the US was becoming the most powerful nation, when nationalism itself began to involve "the generalized production of aesthetic and political effects within a globalizing (if never truly global) capitalist technoculture, the figure for which, mass-produced and inescapable, is America" (Redfield 181). Considering Fitzgerald's background and his role in this "capitalist technoculture," one can understand his ambivalent relation to the American dream and its negotiation of US identity in the wake of the global shift in power.

## Negative capability and the American dream

In describing the US during the Jazz Age, Fitzgerald says both that it "was the greatest nation and there was a gala in the air" and that it "was bloated, gutted, stupid with cake and circuses" (*The Crack-Up* 25, 31). These two statements are representative of the rounded picture he presents of the US postwar experience, highlighting both its glory and its excess without trying to reconcile them and without formulating an essentialist characterization of the US or its people. Suggesting that this ambivalence, in fact, characterizes a superior stance from which to view the US experience or any other experience, Fitzgerald asserts that the ability to realize and accept the complexity of things, to simultaneously believe two opposing thoughts, was an indication of "first-rate intelligence": "the test of a first-rate intelligence is the ability to hold two opposed ideas on the mind at the same time, and still retain the ability to function. One should, for example, be able to see that things are hopeless and yet be determined to make them otherwise" (*The Crack-Up* 69). As indicated earlier, Fitzgerald associates this determination in the face of hopelessness with Keats, "the Fiery Particle," who "never ceased his struggle against t. b. nor in his last moments relinquished his hope of being among the English poets" (*The Crack-Up* 81). Because Keats served as Fitzgerald's "model of creative sensibility," many critics have traced his definition of first-rate intelligence to him. Matthew Bruccoli explains the extent of Keats's influence on Fitzgerald: "Keats became an enduring presence in Fitzgerald's life, providing him with a model of creative sensibility. Like Keats, Fitzgerald was painfully responsive to the mutability of beauty and the evanescence of youth. Both yearned for immortality through art, and Keats's early death imbued Fitzgerald with a sense of urgency. Above all, Fitzgerald identified with the Keatsian archetype—the handsome youth acclaimed for his genius. Literature was a glamorous thing for Fitzgerald. He aspired to early triumph and the fame that went with it . . . [Fitzgerald] knew he had talent; he wondered whether he had the quality of genius to match his ambitions" (73). Because of Fitzgerald's deep identification with "the Keatsian archetype—the handsome youth acclaimed for his genius," he compared himself directly with Keats, whom he considered an "extraordinary genius" who produced "the richest, most sensuous imagery in English, not excepting Shakespeare" (*A Life in Letters* 460). As Sheliah Graham, Fitzgerald's "beloved infidel," states, when he was a student at Princeton, "he had decided he would write prose on the same fine lines as Keats's poetry" (93). Wondering if he, too, "had the quality of genius," Fitzgerald developed a point of comparison from Keats's own letters.

Because of his great admiration for Keats, Fitzgerald was familiar with Keats's poems, letters, and biographies (see especially Sheliah Graham's *The College of One* 93-98) and undoubtedly knew the famous passage in which Keats specifically discusses "Negative Capability" as the principal quality of a man of literary achievement: "Several things dovetailed in my mind, & at once it struck me, what quality went to form a Man of Achievement especially in Literature & which Shakespeare possessed so enormously—I mean *Negative Capability*, that is when man is capable of being in uncertainties, Mysteries, doubts, without any irritable reaching after fact & reason" (*Letters of John Keats* 193). In comparing Fitzgerald's "test of first-rate intelligence" and Keats's marking of "a Man of Achievement," Bloom argues that Fitzgerald's formulation "is quite specifically a personal revision of Keats's hope for negative capability, which Fitzgerald called 'a romantic readiness' and attributed to his Gatsby" (*Fitzgerald*, Introduction 2). While Bloom associates negative capability with Gatsby, Piper attributes it to Fitzgerald himself: "Following the example of Keats, his favorite poet, he had learned how to cultivate a negative capability toward himself and his experience" (236).

Other scholars have considered the semblance between Fitzgerald and his characters to represent a type of negative capability in and of itself—Fitzgerald's unique ability to both personally live and objectively critique the experiences he depicts in his fiction. Curnutt has suggested that Fitzgerald's self-reflexivity sharpened his talent for social critique: "As a social observer, one of his best-appreciated talents was what scholars have called his 'double perspective'—his (and his characters') ability to at once participate in a phenomenon while stepping back to objectively assess its consequences" (123). Robert Morsberger associates the quality that Curnutt terms "double perspective" with "double vision" (a term Cowley coined [Kazin 146]) and contextualizes it within *The Great Gatsby*'s cast of characters: "Here we have at its most effective the double vision of Fitzgerald himself; as he shared Gatsby's dream, winning fortune, Zelda, and fame, so he shared Nick's disillusion and criticism of that life" (129). Donaldson asserts that it "is this double vision that makes *The Great Gatsby* great" (210). Mizener traces Fitzgerald's double vision back to Keats, his literary model, who equates "experienced knowledge" with lived truth: "What [the imagination] does know, however, it knows as experience. Fitzgerald's favorite poet, Keats, felt the importance of this kind of knowledge so strongly that, as he said in a famous letter to Benjamin Bailey, he had 'never yet been able to perceive how anything can be known for truth by consecutive reason.' Because he had never been able to, he cried out for a life of 'Sensations'—that is, the felt understanding of the imagination—rather than 'Thoughts'—the logical conclusions of consecutive reasoning. That is why he said that 'what the imagination seizes as beauty—that is, experienced knowledge—must be true.' Fitzgerald loved Keats as he did because he too had that conviction" (101). In *The Great Gatsby* and his other novels, Fitzgerald depicts his own life through sensation, the "felt understanding" of his imagination, making him, as Bloom claims, "the American Keats" who "sought to affirm a High Romanticism in the accents of a belated counter-tradition" (*Fitzgerald*, Introduction 1).

Fitzgerald was explicit in tracing the development of his writing back to the influence of the British Romantic poets. In his essay "Handle with Care," he reveals that when he was in college, he "took a beating on English poetry," but that once he "got the idea of what it was all about," he "set about learning to write" (*The Crack-Up* 76). When his daughter Scottie—an aspiring writer herself—went to college, based on his own experience he advised her to take English Poetry: "The only sensible course for you at this moment is the one on English Poetry: Blake to Keats . . . Understand me, I think the poetry courses you took in school (and I read the booklets) were utterly sissified drool. But a real grasp of Blake, Keats, etc. will bring you something you haven't dreamed of. And it should come now . . . Poetry is either something that lives like fire inside you—like music to the musician or Marxism to the Communist—or else it is nothing, an empty, formalized bore around which pedants can endlessly drone their notes and explanations" (*A Life in Letters* 457-60). In explaining to Scottie the basis for his own passionate relation to poetry, he turns toward his favorite poet:

> *The Grecian Urn* is unbearably beautiful with every syllable as inevitable as the notes in Beethoven's Ninth Symphony or it's just something you don't understand. It is what it is because an extraordinary genius paused at that point in history and touched it. I suppose I've read it a hundred times. About the tenth time I began to know what it was about, and caught the chime in it and the exquisite inner mechanics. Likewise with *The Nightingale* which I can never read through without tears in my eyes; likewise the *Pot of Basil* with its great stanzas about the two brothers, "Why were they proud, etc."; and *The Eve of St. Agnes*, which has the richest, most sensuous imagery in English, not excepting Shakespeare. And finally his three or four great sonnets, *Bright Star* and the others . . . For awhile after you quit Keats all other poetry seems to be only whistling or humming. (*A Life in Letters* 460-61)

Although Fitzgerald implies that there is something almost magical about the "extraordinary genius" that distinguishes Keats's poetry, he does point to specific qualities that contribute to its brilliance, such as its "chime," its "exquisite inner mechanics," and its "inevitable" rhythmic progression, which seamlessly anticipates "every syllable." He singles out "The Eve of St. Agnes," however, for its imagery, claiming that it "has the richest, most sensuous imagery in English, not excepting Shakespeare" (*A Life in Letters* 460). In the final section of this chapter, I argue that Fitzgerald reproduces the imagery of "The Eve of St. Agnes" in what many critics deem *The Great Gatsby*'s central scene. The Keatsian echoes within the scene not only function to heighten its sensuality and luxuriousness, but also discursively inscribe a materialism of poetic resistance; as Timothy Morton asserts, the "political is found to be inscribed within the minutest particulars of the poetic" (*Poetics* 7). What can be read in this scene as an overinvestment in signs ultimately reflects the fashioning of the American man during the 1920s, when excess could become an occasion for self-definition. As seen in poems like "Ode on a Grecian Urn," Keats's extraordinary genius springs in part from his consideration of beauty to explore the relationship of language—and indeed his own poetry—to time. David Ferris explains the importance of reading "Ode on a Grecian Urn" in relation to representation and time: "As many commentators have rightly noted, the 'Ode on a Grecian Urn' develops out of the sequence of questions that dominates the first verse. In Keats's poem, these questions express less a desire for answers than an exploration of the relation of language to a historical event that, in the terms of this poem, would also include the relation of the poem to the object it views. Keats's presentation of these questions proceeds in such a way that they express an inability to know precisely what is being looked at" (120). Through the examination of overtly commodified beautiful objects, Fitzgerald reframes Keats's poetic exploration within a later "point in history," and in doing so demonstrates "extraordinary genius" of his own.

## Beautiful shirts and the "American" style of man

In his biography of Fitzgerald, *Some Sort of Epic Grandeur*, Bruccoli observes that Fitzgerald's attempts "to become a prose Keats" involved "enriching his own style with lush Keatsian imagery" (73). Various scholars have noted that several of Fitzgerald's works in addition to *The Great Gatsby*, including *Tender Is the Night*, *The Beautiful and Damned*, and *This Side of Paradise*, also contain direct allusions to Keats's poems. John Grube, William Doherty, and Barry Scherr have outlined *Tender Is the Night*'s significant pattern of allusion to "Ode to a Nightingale." Margaret Loftus has noted Keatsian references in *This Side of Paradise* and also has demonstrated correspondences between *The Beautiful and Damned* and Keats's poem "La Belle Dame sans Merci." And Joseph Wagner argues that there are important parallels between *The Great Gatsby* and *Endymion*, while Burroughs focuses on intersections between "Lamia" and *The Beautiful and Damned.*

Fitzgerald demonstrates that his work draws heavily on images from Keats's poetry in a letter to Scottie that teaches her about "the power of the verb in description." Focusing on the fourth stanza of "Ode to a Nightingale," he points out to his daughter not only that the title of his novel *Tender Is the Night* originates here, but also that in "the same stanza is another phrase which I rather guiltily adapted to prose in the 2nd paragraph on p. 115 of *The Great Gatsby*" (*A Life in Letters* 341-42). The fourth stanza of "Ode to a Nightingale" contains the lines which Fitzgerald "rather guiltily adapted" in the following passage: "He lit Daisy's cigarette from a trembling match, and sat down with her on a couch far across the room, where there was no light save what the gleaming floor bounced in from the hall" (74); the lines of the poem read: "But here there is no light, / Save what from heaven is with the breezes blown / Through verdurous glooms and winding mossy / ways" (37-40). Fitzgerald incorporated other of Keats's poems in addition to "Ode to a Nightingale" in *The Great Gatsby*, one of the most notable of which is "The Eve of St. Agnes." As I have already discussed, Fitzgerald considers "The Eve of St. Agnes" to have "the richest, most sensuous imagery in English," but he also claims that it is probably "the finest technical poem in English" (*A Life in Letters* 357). Not surprisingly, he adapted—guiltily or not—phrases, images, and even entire scenes from "The Eve of St. Agnes" in *The Great Gatsby*.

Some of *The Great Gatsby*'s famous lines, in fact, can be traced to "The Eve of St. Agnes." The description of "yellow cocktail music" (34) played by Gatsby's orchestra, for instance, relies on synaesthesia adapted from "The Eve of St. Agnes"—"Music's golden tongue" (20)—to heighten the aura of unreality. The young virgins receive their loves on St. Agnes's Eve in "the honey'd middle of the night" (49), and the "late afternoon sky bloomed . . . like the blue honey of the Mediterranean" when Myrtle receives Tom and guests in her apartment (29). Pairing the romantic quests of Gatsby and Porphyro, Gatsby's "heart was in a constant riot" about Daisy (77), while the thought of Madeline in Porphyro's "painèd heart / Made purple riot" (137-38). Madeline is "Hoodwink'd with faery fancy" (70), and similarly Gatsby relies on "a promise that the rock of the world was founded securely on a fairy's wing" (77). Porphyro promises Madeline, his "lovely bride," that he "will not rob [her] nest" (334, 340), whereas Gatsby asks Kilpspringer to play "The Love Nest" as he tries to enchant Daisy (74). In an ironic twist, Porphyro observes Madeline going to sleep "as though a rose should shut, and be a bud again" (243), but after Gatsby resigns himself to the possibility that he has lost Daisy, according to Nick, coming to the realization that he "paid a high price for living too long with a single dream," he reflects on "what a grotesque thing a rose is" (126).

In addition to phrasing strikingly similar to that of "The Eve of St. Agnes," *The Great Gatsby* incorporates specific images—such as silken chambers, golden objects, silver shrines, women in white supine on couches, and pearl necklaces—from the poem, not only to draw parallels between the similarities of the romantic quests, but also to infuse *The Great Gatsby* with the sense of ancient fantasy. "The Eve of St. Agnes," though composed in the early nineteenth century, tells a tale of "ages long ago" (370) and sets a standard for depictions of sensuous luxury that has withstood the test of time. "No poet," as Trilling asserts, "ever gave so much credence to the idea of pleasure in the sense of 'indulgence of appetites, sensual gratification,' as Keats did, and . . . the complex of pleasure-sensuality-luxury, makes the very fabric of this thought" (*Beyond Culture* 56). Fitzgerald admired Keats's sensuous imagery and his treatment of pleasure more generally, but he read a deeper significance into the sensual luxury that characterized Keats's work. Graham, who studied poetry under Fitzgerald, recounts that he adamantly disagreed with Mathew Arnold's claim in *Essays in Criticism* "that Keats would be remembered because his poetry was 'enchantingly sensuous.'" According to Graham, in "the margin against this, Scott wrote: 'Later ages have entirely disagreed with this. It shows Victorian stiffness and primness in its most unattractive pose'" (98).

Keats's poetry meant more to Fitzgerald than a captivating sensuality because, as Trilling has argued, it ultimately revealed the tension between reality and illusion at the heart of both pleasure and desire. Trilling explains that the Keats's conception of pleasure involves both the principle of reality and the principle of illusion: "The principle of pleasure is for Keats . . . the principle of reality—by it, as Wordsworth said, we *know*. But for Keats it is also the principle of illusion. In 'The Eve of St. Agnes,' to take the most obvious example, the moment of pleasure at the center of the poem, erotic pleasure expressed in the fullest possible imagination of the luxurious, is the very essence of reality: it is all we know on earth and all we need to know. And it is the more real as reality and it is the more comprehensive as knowledge exactly because in the poem it exists surrounded by what on earth denies it, by darkness, cold, and death, which make it transitory, which make the felt and proclaimed reality mere illusion" (*Beyond Culture* 57). Thus, although Keats "may be thought of as the poet who made the boldest affirmation of the principle of pleasure," he may also be considered "the poet who brought the principle of pleasure into the greatest and *sincerest* doubt" (Trilling, *Beyond Culture* 58). Trilling suggests that Keats became of "peculiar cultural interest" for Fitzgerald and others of his generation because at that "point in modern history the principle of pleasure came to be regarded with just such ambivalence" (*Beyond Culture* 58).

The famous shirt scene from *The Great Gatsby* restages the feast in "The Eve of St. Agnes" to depict the ambivalence surrounding the luxury with which Americans cloaked themselves after World War I. Piper claims that another scene from *The Great Gatsby*, "the description of the refreshments at Gatsby's party[,] echoes a well-known stanza from Keats's 'The Eve of St. Agnes'" (313). Piper does not identify the stanza to which he refers, but it is probably one of those that describe the feast Porphyro prepares for Madeline. Although Monteiro posits the shirt scene, which comes "right out of Keats's poem," as "transmuted for the purposes of 1920's realism" (292), the shift of focus from food to clothes more specifically reflects a changing socioeconomic paradigm in its deployment of what Fitzgerald called "the symbol of the power that man must hold that passes from race to race." In describing *Gatsby*'s shirt scene as a "grand passage [that] is an epitome of the novel" and "an apotheosis of Fitzgerald's Keatsian art," Bloom links the novel to "The Eve of St. Agnes," but limits his association to the portrayal of Gatsby as "a version of another passionate lover: Porphyro" (*Gatsby* 2). Although Bloom insists that Gatsby does not represent "a criticism of America" because "his effect upon Nick Carraway, and upon the reader, is so wonderful" (Afterthought 235), he misses the very critique that the Keatsian echoes help inscribe. Gatsby does represent and become an occasion for wonder, a wonder that, like that of the Dutch sailors, reflects upon US-American experience. His characterization is "wonderful," as Bloom suggests; however, this wonder is itself ambivalent, eliciting not only awe and respect for Gatsby's romantic capacity to dream, but also fear and contempt for his materialistic excess and inability to see himself and the world around him clearly. By inscribing the shirt scene with echoes of "The Eve of St. Agnes," Fitzgerald draws on the ambivalence with which Keats engages luxury to present US-Americans with a more accurate picture of the new ways in which they fashion themselves and of how that style projects, for better and worse, a national character.

Like the feast in "The Eve of St. Agnes," the shirt scene in *The Great Gatsby* begins with an illicit collaboration. Gatsby asks Nick, his neighbor and Daisy's cousin, to arrange a rendezvous between him and Daisy (even though she is married and has a child), while in "The Eve of St. Agnes," an "old beldame," Angela, smuggles Porphyro into Madeline's bedroom against the wishes of "hot-blooded lords, / Whose very dogs would execrations howl / Against his lineage" (86-88). Emulating the medieval aura of Keats's poem, Gatsby brings Daisy from Nick's meager house over to his mansion, whose "feudal silhouette" stands in relief against the sky (71). As Gatsby leads Daisy through his house, they pass "period bedrooms swathed in rose and lavender silk" (71) that recall Madeline's "silken, hush'd, chaste chamber" with its "blanchèd linen, smooth, and lavender'd" (185, 263). When Gatsby takes Daisy into his bedroom, he opens "two hulking patent cabinets which held his massed suits and dressing gowns and ties, his shirts piled like bricks in stacks a dozen high" (72). Angela hides Porphyro in a similar "closet, of such privacy / That he might see [Madeline's] beauty unespied, / And win perhaps that night a peerless bride" (165-67). Porphyro's grand gesture designed to win Madeline involves presenting her with a luscious feast that he procures from the closet:

> And still she slept an azure-lidded sleep,
> In blanchèd linen, smooth, and lavender'd,
> While he from forth the closet brought a heap
> Of candied apple, quince, and plum, and gourd;
> With jellies soother than the creamy curd,
> And lucent syrops, tinct with cinnamon;
> Manna and dates, in argosy transferr'd
> From Fez; and spicèd dainties, every one,
> From silken Samarcand to cedar'd Lebanon. (262-70)

Gatsby's presentation to Daisy mirrors Porphyro's offering to Madeline. He explains to Daisy, "I've got a man in England who buys me clothes. He sends over a selection of things at the beginning of each season, spring and fall," and then brings out his own "heap" of precious luxuries: "He took out a pile of shirts and began throwing them one by one before us, shirts of sheer linen and thick silk and fine flannel which lost their folds as they fell and covered the table in many-colored disarray. While we admired he brought more and the soft rich heap mounted higher—shirts with stripes and scrolls and plaids in coral and apple green and lavender and faint orange with monograms of Indian blue. Suddenly with a strained sound Daisy bent her head into the shirts and began to cry stormily. 'They're such beautiful shirts,' she sobbed, her voice muffled in the thick folds. 'It makes me sad because I've never seen such—such beautiful shirts before'" (72-73).

Gatsby's "many-colored disarray" of shirts, although they are clearly not edible, evokes the delicacies of Porphyro's feast with heightened descriptions of colors and textures as well as words like "apple" and "orange." Both passages use the word "heap" to describe the excess of the goods available for consumption, which curiously, are not consumed. As Levinson observes, "the most celebrated scene" in "The Eve of St. Agnes," Porphyro's "midnight banquet," has been rightly described as "a 'love feast,' 'sacrifice,' 'communion'—all symbolic expressions of a subliming digestion," but she rightly maintains that in this scene Keats is constructing "a particular *kind* of fantasy, one that resists its own consummation" (119, 150). "Not only do Madeline and Porphyro not get around to eating," Levinson explains, "but there's no indication that the buffet was ever meant for ingestion. Quite the contrary, the food is used as the dramatic plane for its secondary characteristics (color, form, aroma, texture), on the narrative plane for its enhancement of sexual tension (foreplay), on the discursive plane for its verbal qualities (forepleasure), and on the conceptual plane for the abstention it signifies" (150). Similarly, Morton points out that Keats does not "simplistically present" the foods of the feast; instead, "they are 'antiquated,' becoming the most valuable kind of modern circulating commodity . . . Keats parodies the rhetoric of the commodity by redoubling it, in a traversal of the fantasy" (*Poetics* 170). Thus, Fitzgerald's reframing of Keats's feast scene not only critiques the luxury of excess, but also plays upon the expectations of fantasy in order to parody the language we use to describe commodities and assign them value.

In addition to re-presenting the sensual descriptions of the feast foods in "The Eve of St. Agnes," *The Great Gatsby*'s shirt scene also similarly inscribes a sexual tension underwritten by the abstention from commodity consumption. Several scholars, including Bloom, who notes that Daisy "erotically bends her head into the shirts" (*Gatsby* 2), have read Daisy's reaction to Gatsby's shirts as a representation of the ways in which luxury items operate as objects of eroticized desire. "This 'near orgy of commodity celebration,'" Donaldson suggests, "is too much for Daisy, who sobs into the folds of his beautiful shirts" (201). Posnock calls Daisy's "orgasmic response" to Gatsby's shirts "ironic and absurd," showing that she has "more emotions for Gatsby's possessions than for Gatsby . . . Both desire and commodity fetishism . . . are governed by displacement and mediation and are inherently insatiable, perpetually deferring immediate gratification. In erecting other men's desires as his standard of value, and negating the reality of his own impulses, Gatsby entraps himself in an endless pattern of imitation" (206-08). Similarly, Jeffrey Cox argues that "The Eve of St. Agnes" presents this same "critique of society's mishandling of desire" with an examination of "the erotic as a power of social transformation" (60). As Gatsby indicates to Daisy before presenting her the shirts, his consumption patterns follow a British fashion standard as he tries, like Tom, to dress the part of an English gentleman in hopes of ultimately making himself more desirable.

Although Gatsby's clothes are very different from the ones Tom wears, they are associated with him through the "hulking" cabinets in which they are housed. Tom, whom Fitzgerald deems at the beginning of the novel "a national figure" (8), is himself repeatedly described as "hulking," though he resists the term (13). If Tom as "a great big hulking physical specimen" represents the sheer size and power of the US, then Gatsby's "hulking patent cabinets" suggest the US's increased consumption after the First World War. Mary Balkun associates the cabinets with the novel's broader patterns of "commodities and ownership" (127), and she argues that the "novel itself represents a *Wunderkammer*, or Cabinet of Wonders, that Renaissance invention that was a precursor to the modern museum and one of the earliest examples of commodity fetishism" (128). All of the novel's characters, Balkun explains, are collectors of some sort, exemplifying an increasing relationship between the negotiation of US-American identities and patterns of consumption: "Nick is a souvenir collector, and the novel becomes much like the catalogue for a Cabinet of Wonders, this one containing all the various and sundry mementos of his summer in the East; Gatsby is a fetish collector, gathering objects purely for the work they can do to establish a milieu fit for Daisy, who will be the defining object of his collection; finally, Tom Buchanan is a systematic collector whose primary interest is the acquisition of things, especially women, because they bolster his sense of manhood. Whatever the mode, however, the urge to collect is the logical consequence of a culture that gives objects a central place in the construction of meaning, value, and authenticity. The collection is also the way identity is established, and many characters in the novel are associated with specific items" (131). Fitzgerald illustrates the processes by which his characters seek out and display their possessions as a commentary on the development of an American culture that, fueled by postwar prosperity, "gives objects a central place in the construction of meaning, value, and authenticity." Clothes function as the central symbol in this commentary to represent the role of objects in the fashioning of American postwar identity.

By linking the shirt scene with Porphyro's feast in "The Eve of St. Agnes," however, Fitzgerald does not simply comment on the use of possessions to define identity—the relationship between ownership and identity (as the Dutch sailors illustrate) has been a part of the US experience from the very beginning. Rather, Fitzgerald critiques a postwar US culture that defines status by excessive consumption. In contrast to Myrtle, whose "sheer exhibitionism" during her "three-dress afternoon prefigures what we . . . see in Gatsby's clothes closet" (Donaldson 195), Gatsby does not seem to actually wear the beautiful clothes he has bought—we often see him dressed in his characteristic pink suit. One might wonder, then, why Gatsby has "got a man in England" to buy him clothes if he owns them simply to have around, "piled like bricks in stacks a dozen high." Levinson gestures toward an answer in her reading of Porphyro's untouched feast: while a "luxurious banquet is one thing," a "luxurious banquet not eaten is a lot more luxurious" (120). "The oddly abstract materialism of the poetry," Levinson argues, "its overinvestment in signs—takes on a new look when we remember both Keats's remove from his representational manner and means, and also his want of those real things that help people live their lives" (9). Fitzgerald, too, who throughout his life struggled to find the material means to support himself and a family through his writing, employs an overabundance of representations of luxury in *The Great Gatsby*, over-saturating his text like the sickingly "sensuous" aroma of "overripe" fruits (97).

The shirt scene serves as the defining example of what I call Fitzgerald's materialism of poetic resistance. Fitzgerald's piling of images of excess one on top of the other discursively represents an ethical project, revealing the ridiculousness of the exorbitance seen in Gatsby's "soft rich heap" of shirts, which has been layered itself with allusions to Porphyro's feast and its "heap / Of candied apple, quince, and plum, and gourd." When goods are kept merely for show, as pure representations of excess, they become strictly signs, detached from their utility and material value; they are, in Nick's words, "material without being real" (126). It is worth recalling here that in "The Eve of St. Agnes" when Madeline awakens to find Porphyro and his feast, she is disappointed with the actual experience, which is "pallid, chill, and drear" compared to her dreams of it:

> Her eyes were open, but she still beheld,
> Now wide awake, the vision of her sleep:
> There was a painful change, that nigh expell'd
> The blisses of her dream so pure and deep.
> At which fair Madeline began to weep,
> And moan forth witless words with many a sigh,
> While still her gaze on Porphyro would keep;
> Who knelt, with joinèd hands and piteous eye,
> Fearing to move or speak, she look'd so dreamingly.
>
> 'Ah, Porphyro!' said she, 'but even now
> Thy voice was at sweet tremble in mine ear,
> Made tunable with every sweetest vow;
> And those sad eyes were spiritual and clear:
> How changed thou art! how pallid, chill, and drear! (298-311)

Madeline's disappointment is echoed in the novel. In a commentary on the emptiness of Gatsby's excessive luxury, his shirts—and indeed his entire collection of signs—ultimately "vanished" with the collapse of his dream, "leaving Gatsby—nothing" (117). Stripped of his finery, Gatsby becomes "Mr. Nobody from Nowhere" (101), standing alone in the moonlight "watching over nothing" (114). The preponderance of the words "nothing" and "nobody" toward the end of the novel provide a poignant counterpoint to the rich images and "greatness" of the beginning. This juxtaposition represents what Pyle calls a "poetic passage through negation" that relies upon a Keatsian notion of negative capability: "We are confronted with a poetry whose genuine commitment to a 'system of salvation' demands the poetic passage through a negation, through a potentially endless burning and falling—what Keats famously calls a 'negative capability'—that in the process suspends, even 'obliterates' the very salvation it was to accomplish" (135-36). Generations of readers have sympathized with Gatsby, believing that there was more to Gatsby than his style, something almost magical about his "romantic readiness" and wonder (6). Gatsby made the mistake, however, of valuing his possessions "according to the measure of response it drew from [Daisy's] well-loved eyes" rather than the good they did him

(72). As a national figure, Gatsby holds up a mirror to Americans, who, blinded by power and desensitized to excess, have lost sight of the irony that they fashion themselves after the very imperial presence that their ancestors idealistically renounced long ago, when "the dark fields of the republic rolled on under the night," in "the last and greatest of all human dreams" (141, 140).

# Chapter Five

## The Coleridgean Poetics of *Palace of the Peacock*

Since its publication in 1960, scholars and critics have heralded Wilson Harris's novel *Palace of the Peacock* for its revolutionary language and form. Ashcroft, Griffiths, and Tiffin emphasize the significance of Harris's innovation, claiming that his collective works "compromise the most radical experiment in post-colonial cultures of any revolutionary rewriting, through fiction, of the concepts of 'language' and 'history'" (151). Anthony Boxill explains that what makes *Palace of the Peacock*, Harris's first and most famous novel, so revolutionary is its poetics. He deems the novel a seminal work for contemporary West Indian literature because it added "a new kind of novel . . . to the repertoire of West Indian fiction—the poetical novel" (380). Observing that the "language has a lyrical quality which frequently suggests to the reader that it is more than mere prose" (381), Boxill suggests that the language use in *Palace of the Peacock* marks the advent of a new type of novel in the West Indian literary tradition. Although Boxill notes that Harris's "radical 'formal experimentation'" in *Palace of the Peacock* is so important "because of the strong limiting influence of English literature upon West Indian literature" (386), he does not closely examine what, exactly, this "radical 'formal experimentation'" is, how it responds to or breaks from this "strong limiting influence of English literature," or what such a formal departure might represent in a contemporary Caribbean context.

To address these questions, we might begin by looking to Harris himself, who has discussed his desire for a "new conceptual language" with which to address the "living landscapes" that we have neglected due to our "illiteracies of the imagination" (*Selected Essays* 61, 58). Harris reveals that although it is necessary to draw on resources of literary tradition, he is "uneasy about the traditional novel," an "unease" that he says "became profound when I became a topological and hydrographic surveyor and began my work in the interior" of Guyana (*Selected Essays* 1, 2). He asserts that in order to engage with our "living landscapes" and draw on "the numinous and unsuspected resources available to the imagination within the abyss of our late twentieth-century age," the novelist must develop "a counterpoint between originality and tradition unlike the models we possess" (*Selected Essays* 250).

With *Palace of the Peacock* Harris develops such a model, which, despite its unconventional composition, draws from a vast network of literary and cultural resources to give rise to what Harris terms a "cross-cultural imagination" that expands worldview and establishes an ecological frame of reference. Tracing this imagination through varied routes, past scholarship has discussed ways in which the novel incorporates elements from sources as diverse as modernism and Vodun iconography (see Drake and Toliver). In this chapter I take a different approach, examining *Palace*'s engagement with British Romantic poetry, the tradition that I argue most influences the novel's reconceptualization of language itself. My analysis singles out Samuel Taylor Coleridge, the Romantic writer from whom Harris's revolutionary project extends. It is fitting that the Romantic poet most preoccupied with the workings of the imagination would play a definitive role in shaping Harris's cross-cultural imaginative vision. Although the novel does engage with issues relating to Coleridge's philosophical speculations about the imagination and creative genius, this chapter focuses on what *Palace*'s engagement with Coleridge's poetry contributes to the novel's figuration of language and how this engagement ultimately proposes a model for postcolonial discourse. In *Palace,* Harris explicitly highlights problems of language and address, problems that he explores in his reimaginations of Coleridge's poem "The Rime of the Ancient Mariner." This chapter argues not only that Harris invokes Coleridge's work to illustrate how colonialism inscribes and operates through distinct registers of language in its acts of naming, claiming, and calling, but also that his adaptations of Coleridge's poems gesture toward an alternative dialogue for postcolonial societies that is itself articulated through poetic language.

## Looking into the sources of tradition

Before directly examining *Palace*'s Coleridgean poetics, however, I would like to discuss how Harris's cultivation of a "cross-cultural imagination" relates to his broader postcolonial vision in order to contextualize the import of his engagement with Coleridge's work. Harris asserts that "the imaginative arts, the roots of tradition," provide resources for cross-cultural imagination as they interact with one another in "complex dialogue" (*Selected Essays* 77). Ashcroft, Griffiths, and Tiffin observe in *The Empire Writes Back* that "Harris has a profound belief in the possibilities of . . . regeneration through . . . the transforming powers of the imagination," which enable the recuperation of that which "appears to have [been] irretrievably lost" (148). They explain that "Harris sees language as the key to these transformations" in which "language must be altered, its power to lock in fixed beliefs and attitudes must be exposed, and words and concepts 'freed' to associate in new ways" (149). Asserting that language does in fact have the power to effect change, Harris says that we must develop a new conception of, and relation to, language itself. We have grown, Harris insists, illiterate—not in the sense that we cannot read words on a page, but in the sense that our capacity for engaging with what we read is very limited. Claiming that we have learned "to read and write in a mechanical way," Harris contends that we have lost sight of "the very sources of tradition, the very sources of the imagination" that facilitate meaningful engagement with our past and present states, as well as our ability to conceive of what could be a better future (*Selected Essays* 76).

According to Harris, it is the responsibility of the "imaginative writer" to address this problem with the way in which we read and interpret the world around us. The solution, he maintains, "is a complex one for which one has to look very, very deeply into the resources of one's civilization [and] has to ask oneself questions about the very nature of tradition." For a colonial or postcolonial subject, these questions of tradition can be fraught with a sense of forced inheritance and feelings of loss, disempowerment, or mimicry, but Harris suggests that colonialism, despite the destruction it incurs, does by the nature of its enterprise expand the range of resources from which the creative artist may draw. "There is an enigma to tradition" for writers who discount works they associate with colonial presence, Harris observes: "basically, the cross-cultural roots which may lie in Shakespeare or Dante have apparently vanished" (*Selected Essays* 76). As a native of Guyana, Harris himself was a British colonial subject before Guyana achieved independence from the United Kingdom in 1966 (six years after *Palace* was published). He insists that it is not only acceptable, but also necessary for a writer from his colonial background to engage with "American and English writers of genius [who] were profoundly aware of the dimensionalities of allegory within the modern world" (*Selected Essays* 248).

In an interview with Fred D'Aguair, Harris explains that in addition to the "ravages" that imperialism leaves in its wake, it also confers valuable cultural legacies that themselves provide the postcolonial artist with new opportunities for negotiating relations and approaches to dialogue: "There are all sorts of ways of looking at it . . . we see there the burden of an entire civilization which picks up the impact of the imperial age which, despite the ravages it brought, also brought that seed of value. But on the other hand, the cultures that were devastated also possessed a seed of value. In short, we cannot, I think, establish a genuine morality if we live in a world which compartmentalizes cultures and people. There must be this profound dialogue and to trace that dialogue in creative terms requires us to see frail connections; there are no massive connections" (qtd. in D'Aguair 38-39). Harris describes the legacies of both colonial and precolonial civilizations as offering "seed[s] of value," a metaphor that sheds light onto his organic conception of the broader "nature of tradition." On one level, the seed figure represents concentrated potential for growth and reproduction that is buried and may appear latent, but, when exposed to elements that will nurture its growth, can metamorphose into a much more substantial form and can take on a totally different shape, transforming the (imaginative or collective literary) landscape. The seed metaphor also conveys Harris's ecological view of relation, which considers not only the human, but also the nonhuman characteristics of place. In calling for a moral understanding that takes into account the importance of subtle or "frail" connections, Harris suggests that we should not underestimate the complexity of relationships in a way that "compartmentalizes cultures or people," but should instead place them in dialogue to tap into the fertile richness of our common ground.

In his own fiction, Harris draws from the diverse traditions of his Amerindian, European, and African heritage—claiming that he would do so "even if they were not in [his] biological fold"—and he asserts that these heritages surface in the English language: "English is my native language now, a changing, subtle medium of imageries and numinous resource, a living possession or gesture of psyche after centuries and generations of conflict in the Americas" (*Selected Essays* 220). Harris observes that one can locate within the English language traces of past American civilizations: "there exist the voices of . . . pre-Columbian tongues that have been eclipsed" and "when these ancient tongues come into play they affect the rhythm of the English language." Harris evokes these voices in his novel to map a primordial dimension of the cross-cultural imagination that allows for placing British colonialism within the broader historical context of American conquest and displacement.

Scholars and critics such as Sandra Drake have been quick to discuss the influences of ancient Amerindian and African traditions on Harris's work, but they have, on the whole, been more reluctant to focus on European influences. In *Caribbean Poetics*, Silvio Torres-Saillant exemplifies this resistance to tracing European connections, asserting that "West Indians . . . will achieve their sense of self-recognition effectively when, free from Eurocentric vision, they are able to tell their story themselves" (91). Although Torres-Saillant argues that negotiations of West Indian identity should involve a break or departure from European modes of thinking, the self-recognition he urges necessarily involves consideration of the ways in which the West Indian experience has been affected (and continues to be affected) by European colonialism. Harris himself suggests that the vision itself should not—and indeed could not—be Eurocentric, but that it should incorporate reflection upon the devastation as well as the "seed[s] of value" that European presence conferred on the West Indies. Furthermore, West Indian stories, though told by West Indians, respond to and appropriate European languages and literatures. To understand what makes these stories postcolonial, readers must consider how these texts de-center European worldviews, a process that involves identifying and analyzing intertexts with European canonical works.

Asserting that "the only useful approach to Caribbean literature is an intertextual one" (*The Other America* 20), J. Michael Dash writes that its diverse range of cultural influence is the defining characteristic of Caribbean literature. But as Caribbean writer and theorist Edouard Glissant makes clear, in characterizing the pattern of influence associated with the region, "we are not referring to a circuit, a line of energy curved back onto itself. Trajectory, even bent or inflected, no longer applies." Instead, what is at work is a "poetics of Relation [that] interweaves and no longer projects, that . . . inscribes itself in a circularity" (*Poetics* 32). The poetics of relation, according to Glissant, is not a "'forced' poetics or counterpoetics, which does not spring to life from a fertile past, but, on the contrary, builds its 'wall of sticks' against fated destruction, negation, confinement" (*Caribbean Discourse* 132). A reactionary "forced" poetics "will become worn out if it does not develop into a natural, free, open, cross-cultural poetics" (*Caribbean Discourse* 132). Glissant's conception of "cross-cultural poetics" can be seen to operate within what Harris terms the "cross-cultural imagination." In fact, Sam Durant directly compares the two Caribbean figures, observing that, like Glissant, Harris "seeks to make the 'void' of Caribbean history the basis for a new cross-cultural humanism. In place of the subject-centered politics of reclamation that characterize so many theories of multiculturalism, Harris offers us an other-oriented politics—and poetics—of relation" (54). Similarly, D'Aguiar notes that Harris shuns "being identified purely as a Caribbean or South American writer." In addition to the fact that he has lived in England for most of his adult life, Harris reminded D'Aguiar during an interview that his "first literary influence was Homer, and his central concern is all mankind in time and space" (33).

Harris's other-oriented poetics of relation can be traced through his cross-cultural imagination of the Romantics. As Gregory Shaw has pointed out, Harris's imaginative vision places him "in the tradition of the Romantic artist." Shaw observes that, like many Romantic poems, Harris's "fictional constructs primarily derive . . . from an inner vision of the shapes, contours, topography of mind and that shimmering frontier where mind meets the world" ("The Novelist" 149). Shaw explains that the "dialectical" basis of Harris's fiction can be traced to Romantic conceptions of the imagination: "Harris has been writing dialectical novels whose logic . . . is in fact to be found in the idealist/romanticist notions of nineteenth-century German philosophy" ("Metamorphoses" 158). Like Coleridge before him, who introduced tenets of German Romanticism to British literary circles, Harris adapts Romantic conceptions of the imagination in his own creative work to develop a poetics that is not only dialectical, but more overtly dialogic as well. In emphasizing the dialogic nature of Harris's writing, I call into question Michael Gilkes's assessment of Harris's fiction in which he claims that "the purpose of [Harris's] work is to convey the conjunction of disparate elements which contribute to his complex vision of reality as a 'oneness' in which both Man and Nature . . . participate" (*Wilson Harris* 3). Gilkes likens Harris's "universe" to William Blake's because it is "composed of contraries," but he is quick to claim that "this is not . . . the Romantic Vision: the 'wise passiveness' of a Wordsworth or the 'negative capability' of a Keats; but primarily an existential position in which the artist's own creative leap is a pre-requisite" (*Wilson Harris* 3). Instead of conjoining "disparate elements" and collapsing them into a singular "vision of reality" characterized by its "one-ness," as Gilkes claims, I argue that Harris purposefully emphasizes the separateness of individual entities, particularly "Man and Nature," in order to explore the possibilities for—and barriers to—dialogue.

*Palace of the Peacock* explicitly poses questions of language and address and tests the limits of the creative power of the writer and of language itself by probing failures of language and breakdowns of communication that inform Harris's imagination of the poetics of relation. In the section that follows, I analyze how *Palace* invokes Coleridge's poem "Rime of the Ancient Mariner" (and, to a lesser degree, "Kubla Khan") as it explores the significance of these issues and ways in which the writer can respond to them. Harris, who studied Coleridge's work at Queen's College in Guyana (see "An Autobiographical Essay" xxiv), extends Coleridge's radical Romantic vision as he assumes the task "of the imaginative genius" that he has inherited. For Harris, this task involves using the "unsuspected sources available to the Imagination" to transform barriers that seemingly prevent relation in order to create new opportunities for communication (*Selected Essays* 250). Coleridge provides a model both for Harris's mobilization of the cross-cultural imagination and his transformative vision; as John Beer has noted, Coleridge is well known for "devouring and assimilating the work of previous poets and writers" whose "language can be seen behind his, evidencing a series of poetic relationships, some intimately detailed, others strong but general, which call for further examination" ("The Languages" 225). In the tradition of Coleridge, Harris's work is characterized by its poetic relationships with other great works, including the poems of Coleridge himself. Reading the rearticulations of Coleridge's works in *Palace* reveals not only Harris's application of Coleridge's synthetic mode of composition, but also his own radical reimagination of the possibilities for dialogue through poetic language.

## "Is it a mystery of language and address?"

Harris prefaces *Palace of the Peacock* with two epigraphs. The first he attributes to William Blake: "It ceases to be history and becomes . . . / fabricated for pleasure, as moderns say, / but I say by Inspiration" (16). This excerpt comes from one of Blake's annotations to *An Apology for the Bible*: "If Moses did not write the history of his acts, it takes away the authority altogether it ceases to be history & becomes a Poem of probable impossibilities fabricated for pleasure as moderns say but I say by Inspiration" (*The Complete Blake* 616). By prefacing his novel with this quotation, Harris places his entire narrative within the context of the British Romantic poetic tradition while gesturing toward the novel's own revisions of history and its evocation of a larger spiritual imagination. Harris's quotation of Bible passages is revealing in that it, too, "takes away" the focus on "authority" and that it leaves out what the writing becomes when it ceases to be history, "a Poem of probable impossibilities." Since Harris published poetry before writing *Palace of the Peacock*, prefacing the novel with this particular quotation but omitting the portion of the quotation that discusses the transformation of the word from history to poetry is significant. This omission signals from the very beginning of the novel the importance of reading between the lines of the narrative and actively seeking out the gaps in the text, of contemplating that which remains unsaid. The novel itself can be read as "a Poem of probable impossibilities" that considers the capabilities and limits of language itself. These themes are reinforced in the second epigraph, taken from the Bible's Book of Kings: "And after the earthquake a fire; but the / Lord was not in the fire: and after the / fire a still small voice" (I Kings 19:12). Like the passage from the Book of Kings, *Palace* explores what it means to have a voice, how voice relates to presence, and why listening for a voice matters, especially in the wake of destruction. As it reimagines voice, in fact, one of *Palace*'s most revolutionary "probable impossibilities" is conceiving of a possible dialogue with those who lack the power of speech.

By inscribing the presence of "the folk," *Palace* collectively represents people who have—via colonialism or some other mode of subordination—historically been denied a voice. The entire novel follows the journey of a crew, led by a conquistadorial figure named Donne, through the rivers of Guyana in search of the folk, whom Donne wants to labor on his plantation. Mark Williams and Graham Huggan have analyzed the correspondences between the searches for the folk in *Palace* and in Joseph Conrad's *Heart of Darkness*; while this particular intertextual connection works on one level, it fails to account for some of the unconventional characteristics of Harris's poetic narration, such as its nonlinearity, its refusal to develop characters, its departure from chronology, its supernaturalism, and its simultaneous settings in different historical frames of reference. The conscious break of the imagination from the absolute codes of realism manifests itself in several different ways in *Palace*. One such deviation can be seen in Harris's depiction of *Palace*'s characters. As Mark McWatt has pointed out, although Harris differentiates the members of the crew who embark on *Palace*'s journey, they do not emerge as normal literary characters who may be understood through "traditional symbols or archetypes"; instead, "Harris's characters function more like diagrams of processes within the creative imagination, what he himself has called 'agents of possibility' as opposed to 'Sovereign principles'" (34).

Another one of *Palace*'s agents, its departure from chronology, resembles that of Coleridge's "Rime of the Ancient Mariner." As Jerome McGann has argued, the layering of language from different historical periods contributes to the "transhistorical significance" of the "Rime": "In general, Coleridge means us to understand that the ballad narrative dates from the sixteenth century, that the gloss is a late seventeenth-century addition, and, of course, that Coleridge, at the turn of the nineteenth century, has provided yet another (and controlling) perspective upon the poetic material. Indeed, Coleridge certainly intended his more perspicuous readers—that is, those read in the theory and practice of the new historical criticism—to see that the 'Rime' was an imaginative presentation of a work comprising textual layers of the most primitive, even pre-Christian, sort" (54, 50-51). About *Palace*'s transhistoricism, M. Keith Booker and Dubravka Juraga have noted that although it is "anachronistic that the boat has a motor . . . this merging of the seventeenth and twentieth centuries is typical of the book's depiction of Guyanese history as muddled and confused. It also suggests that the rapacious impulses of seventeenth-century colonial expansion are still alive and well in the present day. Indeed, such links between the present and past run throughout the text, which often contains vague hints that all the events that occur have somehow happened before" (155). Thus, while

Harris responds to and complicates some of the larger themes about colonization and racialization at the center of *Heart of Darkness*, more significant conceptual correspondences can be found with Coleridge's " Rime of the Ancient Mariner," which displays the departures from conventions of time, place, and narration seen in *Palace*.

In addition to highlighting these common elements, reading *Palace* alongside "The Rime of the Ancient Mariner" draws attention to the novel's preoccupation with failures of language and address. This preoccupation first becomes explicit in a conversation in which Donne and *Palace*'s dreaming narrator discuss the crew's pursuit of the folk. Donne, rejecting the folk's claim to the land, muses: "Who would believe that these devils have title to the savannahs and to the region? A stupid legacy—aboriginal business and all of that nonsense: but there it is. I've managed so far to make a place for myself—spread out myself amply as it were—and in a couple of years I shall have firm prescriptive title myself." With these musings, Donne raises questions about the relationship between titles, and language more generally, to possession, place, and identity in a postcolonial context. By stating, "I'm as native as they," and pointing to his "dark racial skin," Donne relates identification and belonging to geographical place to inhabiting a cultural space, claiming, "in fact I belong already" to "the family" (51). Responding to Donne's claims, the narrator suggests that Donne has confused ownership with belonging, and that no matter how much he "spread[s] out" into the novel, the unspoken claims of the folk will remain indelible within the narrative. "We're all outside of the folk," the narrator says, "Nobody belongs yet" (52). When Donne "quickly and mockingly" asks the narrator: "Is it a mystery of language and address?," the narrator takes the question seriously, and his failure to communicate ironically demonstrates the very failures of language and address he associates with Donne's dealings with the folk:

> "Language, address?" I found it hard to comprehend what he meant. "There is one dreaming language I know of. . . ." I rebuked him . . . "which is the same for every man . . . No it's not language. It's . . . it's" . . . I searched for words with a sudden terrible rage at the difficulty I experienced . . . "it's an inapprehension of substance," I blurted out, "an actual fear . . . fear of life . . . fear of the substance of life, fear of the substance of the folk, a cannibal blind fear in oneself. Put it how you like," I cried, "it's fear of acknowledging the true substance of life. Yes, fear I tell you . . . And somebody," I declared, "must demonstrate the unity of being, and *show*. . . ." I had grown violent and emphatic . . . "that fear is nothing but dream and an appearance . . . even death. . . ." I stopped abruptly.
>
> Donne was not listening to my labour and expression and difficulty. He already knew by heart my unpredictable outbursts and attacks and inmost frenzy. Old Schomburgh and the Arawak woman stood at his side.
>
> "What does she say?" he demanded. "You know the blasted Buck talk." (52)

All of the exchanges in this scene—the narrator's rambling, Donne's ignoring what he says, Donne's inability to understand the language spoken by the Arawak woman—represent on some level failures of language and address. Although the narrator's statements are disjointed, they collectively point toward the impossibility of achieving a "unity of being" through language—there is no language that is "the same for every man." The narrator lacks the words with which to describe the "it" that he envisions acting as a universalizing force, and instead of defining the "dreaming language" he evokes, he leaves the reader with a series of questions about language: how does his outburst respond to the claims of Donne that precede it? What happens when there are failures of communication? Why does he link the act of interpretation to dreaming? And how is violence linked to frustrated articulation? By examining impossibilities of address and failures of language, this scene introduces questions to which *Palace* returns in its reimaginations of Coleridge's work.

## Literal and linguistic crossings

When looking for a model of intractable language, Harris might have very well sought out Coleridge's prose instead of his poetry. In describing Coleridge's prose and critical writings, Jerome Christensen observes that "he is eccentric, even peripheral, his texts a circle whose center is nowhere and whose circumference is everywhere . . . Coleridge's prose . . . will not stay put, strays beyond the garden walls into the forest of error" and figures "the writer as a displaced person, wanderer in a language he can never fully express or entirely escape" (27). Concluding that "Coleridge's prose charts the daunting itinerary that awaits the post-enlightenment man of letters," Christensen suggests that by examining Coleridge's marginal method, we can gain new insight into his rhetorical and philosophical innovations (*Blessed Machine* 16). Christensen identifies the rhetorical figure that most distinguishes Coleridge's work as the chiasmus, "the blessed machine of Coleridge's language" (27):

> Though a Romantic, Coleridge is also a figure in his own right. And I will argue that a particular figure marks the oscillation of his optimistic advance from and anguished return to the catastrophe of his prose. That figure is the chiasmus, representative of true method and link between absolute principle and moral discourse. In Coleridge the chiasmus is where extremes meet. But that encounter is not, as the author would have it, the methodological envoy of a dialectical empire. Instead the chiasmus figures the promise of dialectic as merely the enabling presupposition of a rhetorical practice; its elegant mechanics render the concord of identity and opposite, proposition and inverse, as a marginal yet indelible sophistication of metaphysical truth. Eddy rather than bridge, the chiasmus in Coleridge's text tropes method as the indefinitely reproducible, always liminal traverse between consciousness and unconsciousness, will and willfulness, writer and text. (26-27)

The chiasmus, figuring the imagined encounter of opposites that moves beyond fixed binaries of opposition, provides a rhetorical prototype for the type of dialogue that Harris's narrator attempts to evoke in his discussion of "dreaming language." The inverted parallelism of the chiasmus itself structurally represents a cross, which, as

Christensen suggests, can represent a wide range of crossings through the medium of language, such as the "liminal traverse between consciousness and unconsciousness" that might constitute a dreaming language.

In Coleridge's poetry, the liminal traverse between consciousness and unconsciousness or waking and dreaming states most explicitly emerges in "Kubla Khan"—one can read it within the story of composition of the poem told in the preface, in the transition between the preface and the actual poem, and within the poetic fragment itself. *Palace*, too, plays with a fluid notion of consciousness with its "dreaming narrator," ambiguity surrounding whether the narration is actually happening or in dream, and articulation of a "dream-speak." But the crossing of consciousness through language inscribed in Coleridge's prose does not carry with it the "promise of dialectic" when it becomes manifest in Coleridge's poems. The failure of this transfer is particularly evident in the "Rime." Tim Fulford observes that whereas other of Coleridge's poems "discover and reflect upon a language of renewed social unity, 'The Ancient Mariner,' in striving towards a similar goal, discovers an unprecedented language of social and personal isolation. In so doing it develops out of their thesis; their attempts to make the language of intimacy bear the burden of religious and social unity load that language until collapse becomes a constant threat. 'The Ancient Mariner' is courageous enough to imagine that threat becoming real, and destroying not only unity with God and society, but unity with friend, brother and self" (*Figurative Language* 72).

Coleridge symbolically renders the destruction of unity to which Fulford refers through the death of the Albatross, which the Mariner kills with a cross-bow after it crosses into the world of man. On a purely symbolic level, the fate of the Albatross represents the impossibility of, or at the very least dangers associated with, linguistic crossing. James McKusick suggests that the Albatross's "act of 'crossing' the boundary between nature and civilization indicates a possible resolution" for the Mariner ("Coleridge" 385), but since the cross-bow is to blame for the Albatross's death, one might wonder, as does Barbara Johnson, if "the politics of violence [are] already encoded in rhetorical figures as such" (184). In terms of Coleridge's work, one might wonder if Christensen has been overly optimistic about the promise of dialogue inscribed within the chiasmus.

## Inscribing "foundations of care within the vessel of place"

In Harris's rewriting of the "Rime," Coleridge's "blessed machine of language," the chiasmus, haunts the narrative as an ideal but impossible poetic reconciliation of opposites. This haunting is actually figured into Coleridge's own 1798 version of the poem, which, as Michael Macovski observes, "Coleridge took pains to introduce . . . as a dialogue with definite 'other'" using "the following parallelism": "Never sadder tale was told / To a man of woman born . . . // Never sadder tale was heard / By a man of woman born" (71, 366-67, 370-71). This parallelism, instead of inscribing the promise of dialectical relation via the chiasmus's inversion, actually emphasizes the separateness of the tale's teller and listener. Macovski argues that in the "Rime," Coleridge "represents poetic address that ultimately fails to enable understanding," but that "the incorporation of the Romantic addressee as a metonymic listener within the text sets up the formal configuration of 'co-respondence'—the structure, at least, of a communication" (39, 11). Noting that "the Hermit's inability to expiate the Mariner resembles the Guest's failure to comprehend him," Macovski notes that "Coleridge's poetics become the paradigm for agnostic dialogue. The auditors represented in his poems provide the most explicit model of the poetic agon" (39). In choosing "Rime" as the intertext for *Palace*'s climactic scene that stages the problems of address and communication, Harris draws upon Coleridge's poetics for agnostic dialogue to highlight problems bound up with interpretation and to propose another rhetorical figure associated with the Romantic tradition—apostrophe—as initiating a dialogic, as opposed to a simply dialectic, mode of communication. Macovski deems "Romantic apostrophe" the "rhetorical synecdoche or figure for dialogue—even if its forms remain vestigial or unspoken" (11). Harris explores the possibility of giving this form a voice. By invoking a revolutionarily new apostrophe, which—in prose rather than poetry—"trop[es] not on the meaning of a word, but on the circuit of communication itself" (Culler 135), Harris critiques the colonial impulse to name and narrativize while literally and figuratively calling West Indians to reconsider the landscapes they inhabit as they negotiate their postcolonial identities.

Apostrophe, which derives from the Greek root meaning "turning away," poetically represents an address to an absent other. In his influential essay on apostrophe, Jonathan Culler claims that apostrophe can be seen as "the figure of all that is most radical, embarrassing, pretentious, and mystificatory in the lyric" (137). Culler explains that because the poet pretends to be talking to himself or to someone or something else other than his audience when performing apostrophe, apostrophic gestures put the reader or listener in a position of overhearing, rather than hearing, the lyric. He suggests that this self-conscious poetic declaration, which is not directed toward the audience but presented to it, draws attention to the issue that is really at stake in apostrophe—"the power of poetry to make something happen" (140). Douglas Kneale argues that the "central problem" associated with Culler's understanding of apostrophe "lies in his failure to distinguish, on either historical or theoretical grounds, between apostrophe and address" (142). Emphasizing that apostrophe represents a "movement of voice" and a "'diversion' of speech," Kneale describes it as a "carrying over of address" (143, 147). In his reimagination of apostrophe, Harris himself blurs the distinction between apostrophe and address to "manipulat[e] the I/thou structure of direct address in an indirect, fictionalized way" (Johnson 185). Harris does not imagine apostrophe in the same way as Johnson, as a "form of ventriloquism through which the speaker throws voice, life, and human form into the addressee, turning its silence into mute responsiveness," thereby making the "absent, dead, or inanimate entity . . . present, animate, and anthropomorphic" (185). Instead, he envisions it as enabling an antiphonal form of call and response that gives postcolonial peoples a sense of the land that they have lost and, as a consequence, of themselves. To Harris, apostrophe represents "more than merely a poetic device"—it is, in the words of Helena Feder, "a practice of awareness that emphasizes the processes of human perception, the interconnectedness of all things, and the subjecthood of Earth and its inhabitants." Feder traces this practice specifically to Coleridge (and "The Eolian Harp") and suggests that it serves "to call our attention to the poet's interaction and connection with the natural world and the understanding that interconnectedness is itself a form of reciprocity" (43).

In conceiving of his own apostrophic discourse, Harris draws on Coleridge's tradition to emphasize the interconnectedness between people and their landscape. In *Caribbean Discourse*, Glissant claims that for writers of the Americas "the inescapable *shaping force* in our production of literature is what I would call the language of landscape" (145), and for Harris this language of landscape manifests itself through revisionary apostrophe. With its focus on distinct but disconnected voices, Coleridge's "Rime" provides a rich intertext with which Harris can explore the possibilities for call and response through apostrophe. Susan Eilenberg observes that "The 'Rime,' one of the most deeply and elaborately anonymous poems ever written, comes to speech through the medium of an alien voice—archaic, inhuman, uncanny—in response to an impossible demand. 'What manner of man art thou?'" (45). Further, Eilenberg suggests that, "divided from himself as from other men, inhabiting a world of baffling disjunction, and speaking a language neither whose motive force nor whose meaning is apparent, the Mariner is in no position to tell who he is . . . In a world where identity fails to coincide with character, where motivations are external and apparently autonomous, the difficulty of naming himself would be enormous. Perhaps the 'Rime' really is the shortest answer to the Hermit's question, demonstrating the difficulty of saying 'I am' in one's own voice" (68).

Eilenberg argues that "the 'Rime, ' like the Mariner, is obsessed with its need to talk about itself and its relation to speech but never quite manages to name its subject. The poem is filled with emblems and allegories of its history and constitution: the Mariner possessed by his 'strange power of speech' and the dead crew whose bodies house the spirits that sometimes sing and sometimes sail are working through aspects of inspiration, influence, and intertextuality" (67). The poem's obsession with "talk[ing] about itself and its relation to speech" manifests itself in Coleridge's revisions with the addition of another voice in the gloss, which, as McGann suggests, both "serves to emphasize the remoteness of the story and its teller" and "calls attention to the multiple points of view that are embedded in the work" (41). Jack Stillinger agrees, noting that the addition of "the voice of the theologically minded, scholarly annotator who supplies commentary in the margins" makes the poem "much more complex" in expanding the wide range of voices (181). Harris can be seen to similarly expand *Palace*'s range of voices with his preface to the revised version of the *Guyana Quartet*.

As Eilenberg's reading suggests, one of the most striking aspects about the poem is the disjunction between the Mariner and his voice compelled to repeat his tale of woe, a disconnection that is mirrored in the sixth part of the poem in dialogue presented by disembodied first and second voices. The perceived distance between the Mariner's character and his own voice points toward the more important dislocation of dialogue between the Mariner and the Wedding Guest with whom he shares his story, who "cannot choose but hear" him (38). As the Mariner relates his compulsion to tell the tale, he reveals that his focus rests solely on telling, not on dialogue or genuine engagement with another person: "I pass, like night, from land to land; / I have a strange power of speech; / That moment that his face I see, / I know the man that must hear me: / To him my tale I teach" (586-90). With his rewriting of the "Rime" in *Palace*, Harris complicates the compulsion to tell the story by making the story itself and the mode of telling center on dialogue. Thus instead of demonstrating the difficulty of saying "I am," Harris is concerned with the difficulty of engaging "you" and conceptualizing "we." The Mariner's "strange power of speech" in the "Rime" is transformed in *Palace* into "the partial rehabilitation of a tradition of empty names and dead letters" (80), which directs us to rethink what is actually at stake in naming as well as the ways in which we address others and call ourselves.

In the passage of the novel that immediately precedes the maiming of the bird, the crew members have the "monstrous thought . . . that they had been shattered and were reflected again in each other at the bottom of the stream," which generates an "unceasing reflection of themselves in each other" and makes "them see themselves everywhere save where they thought they stood" (80). This passage about the shattered image of the crew reflected in the stream serves as a counterpoint to the passage from Coleridge's poem, "The Picture" in the preface to "Kubla Khan." Of particular interest are the following lines: "The stream will soon renew its smoothness, soon / The visions will return! And lo, he stays, / And soon the fragments dim of lovely forms / Come trembling back, unite, and now once more / The pool becomes a mirror" (40-44). Since the apostrophe ultimately "dramatize[s] or constitute[s] an image of self" (Culler 142), Harris's use of apostrophe in *Palace* ultimately gestures toward a reimagination of postcolonial identity which is emblematized in the "shattered" reflection and is achieved by a conscious rethinking of the relationship between language and place. That which Harris calls, that which is "absent," the "natural" world, is not really absent at all, but Harris addresses it as lost, in the terms of apostrophe, to reflect that modern societies have lost sight of the land and their relation to it, lost sight of the dialogic relationship between imagination and place, and lost sight of the things nature can teach about building human communities.

In a 1990 interview, Harris describes this importance of reconnecting with the landscape and the writer's role in this process: "The landscape is alive, it is a text in itself, it is a living text. And the question is, how can one find, as an imaginative writer, another kind of living text which corresponds to that living text. There is a dialogue there between one's internal being, one's psyche, and the nature of place, the landscape. There has to be some sort of connection, some sort of bridge, which allows one to sense all sorts of relationships which one tends to eclipse, which one tends not to see at all" (qtd. in Gilkes 33). Written texts allow Harris to construct this "bridge," which, like Coleridge's chiasmus, conveys the relationships he envisions between the psyche and the land to his audience: "Language," Harris explains, "possesses resources which one has to sense as coming not only from within oneself, but from outside, from the land itself, from the rivers, from the forests[, a]nd also from those persons and those cultures that existed in the landscape and have left their trace" (qtd. in Gilkes 33). The apostrophe provides figurative space that allows for the illumination of these resources in language; restated with Harris's terminology, apostrophe is the living text that constitutes the bridge between his fiction and the landscape.

By revising Coleridge's "Rime," Harris is able to tap not only into the poem's crossings that connect the worlds of nature and man, but also more broadly into Coleridge's ecological poetics, which figure the landscaping of the natural world. As McKusick explains, this landscaping involved the creation of an entirely new poetic language: "Coleridge largely succeeded in creating a uniquely ecological idiom, an *ecolect* that reflects local environmental conditions and expresses his own distinctive way of perceiving and responding to the natural world" ("Coleridge" 384). McKusick notes that Coleridge's "ecolect" includes a wide range of words used to describe specific aspects of the natural environment; he in fact coined the terms "waterslide" and "greenery," to name a few ("Coleridge" 384). According to Helena Feder, "of all the romantic poets, Coleridge was the most holistic thinker, acutely aware of the interconnectedness of human and nonhuman nature" (48). Regardless of whether we agree with Feder's claim, it is clear that Coleridge's work has revolutionized the way in which writers relate to the natural world and the way that they map this relationship in their literary landscapes.

In *Palace*, Harris develops his own representation of this interconnectedness with the figure of Mariella, who at once represents the landscape, the mission on which the folk live, the goal of the crew, the folk themselves, and Donne's Amerindian lover: "On the obvious level," Drake observes, "the 'Mission of Mariella' refers simply to one of the numerous Christian missions that dot the banks of the Guyanese rivers. But its other grammatically possible meaning is . . . a special task for which one is destined" (66-67). Drake concludes that in a destiny of interconnectedness, "Mariella symbolizes Nature, the Americas, the Amerindians, the land itself" (67). Shona Jackson explains that Mariella is a "figure *that extends beyond the space of the text* to reveal the tensions surrounding the folk, herself, and the land because of how the intersection of race and sex at different historical junctures objectively positions figures like hers" (94). Harris, like other Caribbean writers about whom Braziel has written, rethinks "the material, political consequences of colonialism in relation to the vital critiques of natural spoilage offered by ecocriticsm" and "position[s] the violence of genocide and ecoside as intertwined . . . unravel[ling] the interwoven genres of marked bodies and marked territories" ("Caribbean Genesis" 112). Thus, in depicting Donne and his crew chasing after Mariella, which is at once a place, a people, a person, and the "mission" or act of conquest itself, Harris is able both to illustrate the ways in which bodies are linked to landscapes through language and to demonstrate the arbitrariness and universalizing tendencies that characterize colonial modes of address.

In addition to figuring the land, Mariella, as one with the displaced and marginalized folk, Harris is able to further explore the ways in which colonialism is bound up with landscape by invoking Coleridge's "Rime." The "Rime" serves as a particularly rich intertext within which Harris can inscribe his postcolonial apostrophe because the "Rime" shares *Palace*'s concern with, and uncomfortable relation to, colonialism. As has been noted, the mission of Donne's crew in *Palace* is to enslave the folk, and, although it is not explicit in the poem, critics have argued that the "Rime" should be interpreted as a critique of slavery when read in the contexts of "Coleridge's material concerns with travel, colonialism, and the slave trade" (Lee 676). Patrick Keane asserts that "the simile of the ocean 'Still as a Slave before his lord'" invites such an interpretation (169); McKusick claims that the Albatross represents "an emblematic representation of all the innocent lives destroyed by European conquest" (*Coleridge's Philosophy* 106); and Debbie Lee concludes that the Mariner and members of the crew serve as allegories with which Coleridge "explain[s] how by way of disease the slave trade destroyed the British national body by destroying individual bodies" (685). As these interpretations suggest, contemporary audiences are likely to read a critique of the slave trade and colonialism more generally within the "Rime," and thus, Harris's rewriting of the poem can be seen as an attempt to grapple with these same issues, but from a postcolonial (as opposed to a colonial) narrative frame of reference.

## *Palace* and "the partial rehabilitation of a tradition"

Because it stages failures of address that result from intersections of the natural and human worlds, Coleridge's "Rime" provides a particularly fitting pretext through which Harris could envision the dialogic possibilities of apostrophe within the postcolonial landscape. In Harris's rewriting, a member of the crew senselessly wounds a bird that—conveying a good omen—approaches the ship, as in Coleridge's poem. More subtle connections also exist between the two works, such as their presentation of "a ghastly crew" ("Rime" 340) comprised of members who appear to have died on the journey but, defying reason, return to continue on the mission. In *Palace*, the crew members' "living names matched the names of a famous dead crew that had sunk in the rapids and been drowned to a man . . . But this in no way interfered with their lifelike appearance and spirit and energy" (26), while in the "Rime" it "had been strange, even in a dream, / To have seen those dead men rise" when "a troop of spirits blest" came "to their cor[p]ses" (333-34, 349, 348). Although the principle elements are the same in the two episodes, there are a few notable differences. In contrast to the "Rime," in *Palace* added emphases are placed on failed communication as the cause of the violence of two of the crew members, daSilva and Cameron, as well as on the collective implications of their acts of aggression.

The scene involving the bird can be seen as the turning point in *Palace* not only because in it the crew for the first time considers its collective consciousness, but also because it is the moment when the crew members realize that "the past would always catch up with them"—that, like the Mariner—"they were the pursuers and now had become the pursued" (84). Harris suggests that this past, the pursuit, and the "horrifying exchange of soul" the crew undergoes as a result of this encounter with the bird are all bound somehow to a misuse of language, which he characterizes as a "tradition of empty names and dead letters" (80). Noting at the beginning of the chapter that "none dared say anything yet knowing their common speech was . . . debased coinage and currency," Harris brings the reader's attention to the characters' speech and foreshadows the valuable lesson the crew will learn about language in the drama that follows (75). In the context of this knowledge, "silence seem[s] golden" to the crew, whose "broken speech," "in the old manner of distortion and debasement," "die[s] awhile on their lips" (75-6). daSilva breaks this silence with his nonsensical dream-speak, which eventually takes the form of "'Water start dream, rock and stone start dream, tree trunk and root dreaming, bird and beast dreaming'" (87). This dream-speak, which mirrors the earlier monologue of the dreaming narrator, stands out from the surrounding text because of its "impossibil[ity]," its personification of nature, and its broken, awkward constructions (87). Isolated from the surrounding narration, daSilva's utterance is a re-visionary apostrophe, especially because it is something he "spoke to himself" while literally and figuratively "turning helplessly to the old Arawak woman . . . to face the truth which lay farther and deeper than he dreamed" (76).

DaSilva's frustrated call for truth mirrors the misdirected pursuit of the folk he calls into question while it ruptures the story's flow, suggesting that both language and the journey of the crew are placed into a different perspective in the context of this dream-speak. Connecting the "truth" daSilva seeks to his speech act, Harris dramatizes what is at stake in language during the fight between Cameron and daSilva, which essentially enacts the war of words that brings it about. The war of words hinges broadly on naming and specifically on the flying bird that the Arawak woman, whom Donne has captured and held hostage to guide the crew's pursuit of the folk, points out to the crew. The ensuing disagreement between Cameron and daSilva arises because they call this bird, which very quickly assumes symbolic import, different names: daSilva first identifies it as a parrot, and then Cameron calls it a vulture. Although this simple disagreement over the identification of the bird might appear to be paltry grounds for murder, it allegorizes the larger issues that are at stake (as symbolized by the ring on the bird's foot) in this dramatization: the importance of naming and address for making dialogue possible.

In depicting the breakdown of communication between Cameron and daSilva, Harris not only emphasizes the arbitrariness of categories into which we—in the colonial tradition—classify things and people, but also scrutinizes the larger problem of the crew's misperception of the natural world. The importance of this perspective and its relevance to language becomes increasingly obvious to the reader each time Cameron reiterates that he cannot see what daSilva is talking about, although he ironically notes that daSilva "never speak a truer word than when [he] say [he] got everything mix up in [his] head" (89). DaSilva's visionary dream-speak not only eludes Cameron, but is also disconcerting and cryptic for the reader, who works to understand exactly what daSilva is trying to say: "Speaking to himself as if he had forgotten Cameron's presence," it is as if daSilva is addressing nature itself without regard to an audience within or outside the text, performing apostrophe to initiate an "impossible" correspondence with the natural world through which he can "lose [his] own image and time" and reconceive of his identity (87). This act of apostrophe allows daSilva to conceptually free himself from the crew's boat and "lose [his] own image and time" because apostrophe inscribes both its speaker and the other in a timeless present. Because apostrophe constitutes a poetic image of self, its referentiality is circumscribed within the poetic consciousness where it exists independent of historical narrative, providing the subject imaginative space to break from "the tradition of empty names and dead letters" that underwrites the crew's pursuit of the folk (80).

DaSilva's dream-speak teaches him something about the empty significance of all the things he "kn[e]w all of [his] life to be something," but because this empty significance is registered in language, he cannot articulate, he cannot name what it is that he has learned: "He stopped at a dead loss for words open mouthed and astonished as if he had been assaulted by the madness and innocence of the stream" (87). After this failure of language, daSilva reverts to his normal speech and reasserts himself with terms of ownership, declaring to the crew that the bird in the sky "is me . . . is mine" because he thinks it belongs to his mistress (88). Donne notes that this is "good news" not only because he sees the bird as "daSilva's promissory ring" that guarantees finding the folk, but also because he is relieved that daSilva has returned to the language of ownership and appropriation that the crew is accustomed to hearing and can understand (88).

After Donne equates the bird with "good news," it comes to represent the crew's successful tracking of the folk and takes on the symbolic weight of Coleridge's Albatross. Gilkes suggests that "when . . . Cameron wounds one of the birds with a stone, the action assumes (like the Ancient Mariner's killing of the Albatross) a moral significance" (*Wilson Harris* 43). It might seem inevitable, given this connection, that Cameron or some other ill-fated crew member would launch a stone that would maim the bird, producing a bloody wound that, as Donne notes, violently marks the crew's presence in the natural landscape: "'Oh well,' said Donne speaking without conviction, 'the bird may return bleeding with a mark upon it. The folk may take it in their heart now to start hunting us. We can never outwit them now. Our strength is gone . . . No ammunition. Nothing remaining. Everything overboard. We can only throw imaginary stones into the air to frighten and alarm ourselves and make imaginary rings in the water'" (89). Donne, whose voice earlier in the chapter "was so terrible and full of suppressed turbulence and demonic authority" and had "an air of aristocratic fury beyond words" (79), now speaks "without conviction," alternatively implying both a wavering of his beliefs (might Donne's exploitation now be done?) and a deferral of guilt. Although Donne speaks without conviction, what he says is significant because his words reiterate two important revelations from the chapter: "they were the pursuers and now had become the pursued" (84; "The folk may take it in their heart now to start hunting us") and daSilva's lesson that "nothing I know of all me life to be something" in fact "really was there" (87, "Nothing remaining"). The wounding of the bird demoralizes Donne. He is beginning to understand that his previous maneuvers to "outwit" the folk were empty gestures and that the only thing he can do on this journey is to establish an "imaginary" connection with the surrounding environment.

While Donne might have been trivializing the work of the imagination when he talks about "mak[ing] imaginary rings," the ring itself can be seen to represent the "O" of apostrophe which Harris traces throughout the dialogue that follows the maiming of the bird. In the two pages of dialogue that follow, there are seven inscriptions of the letter "O" (89-90). Staring at the crew "with a glassy eye" evocative of the Mariner's "glistening eye," Donne says, "O it's a hellish business and a trial and responsibility I never foresaw. If one of us . . . gets across he'll carry the mark of a beast or a bird I tell you. It's a wounding dream and task . . . Let's hope there'll be someone there to meet us and heal us in the end whatever we are. It's all that counts" (90). In this statement Donne not only gestures toward apostrophe by starting out with its signature "O," but he also moves toward a penance that differs from that of the Mariner (who is likewise burdened with the "mark" of the bird) with the prospect of a true dialogue that begins with a crossing over and ends with an encounter with "someone there to meet us."

The bird soars away from the crew's view after it recovers from Cameron's attack, and it continues to provide a grim, but hopeful presence within the narrative after it crosses back over into the natural world. Fulfilling Donne's prophecy, an apparition of the bird and its bloody mark haunts both the text and the crew, which "gave a sudden answering cry" at the sight of the bird's flesh being cut by the stone (89). This "cry" can be seen as a collective apostrophe that calls for reconciliation between man and nature when the crew sees the mark of this rupture brought about by the wounding of the bird. Echoes and precursors to the crew's apostrophe, such as daSilva's dream-speak, circulate throughout *Palace* and return the reader to this site of trauma within the text while invoking the lost state of the natural world and resurrecting an image of landscape before man left his mark upon it. The narrative, with its nonlinear progression, restages and reenvisions this traumatic rupture in radically different contexts to suggest that this rupture is not an isolated incident in the text, but rather a pattern of behavior that can be traced through—and is inscribed within—language. In the most dramatic reenactment of this rupture, which closes the chapter on the wounded bird, daSilva reprimands Cameron for pelting the bird and conflates man and animal into one image, insisting that, "'when you pelt she you pelt me'" (90). Here again the reader witnesses a breakdown in communication; while Cameron says that daSilva is "bewitched," daSilva hears Cameron calling the bird "a witch" and, to avenge her name, he kills Cameron. As this tragic scene draws to a close, the Arawak woman again points to the sky, this time to a "blue ring of pentecostal fire" that not only reinscribes the rupture which daSilva, ironically, tried to seal, but also illuminates apostrophe's signature "O," gesturing toward the possibility that still remains for initiating a dialogue with the silent other.

By replaying these unnatural violations in the text, Harris not only dramatizes our defilement of the environment, but also rehearses the recuperation that *Palace* gestures toward in its imagined correspondences with nature. These correspondences literally appear in the novel as Harris gives speech to the landscape. In extending Coleridge's poetics and reframing his "parable of ecological transgression" (McKusick, "Coleridge" 385), Harris relies on a dialectical dialogue with nature. In this dialogue, when the crew calls for reconciliation, nature answers—not with words, for the voice Harris gives nature is inarticulate—but with a speech-act that mirrors the apostrophe that solicited a response. Guyana's "land of waters" literally does not say anything, but nonetheless it responds to the crew throughout the journey through subtle changes in tone; for example, "the voice of the roaring water" differs from the "sigh [that] swept out . . . of the trees," and while "the whole forest quivered and sighed . . . in a throaty clamour of waters," "whispering trees" cast "a moving spell in the tropical undergrowth" (28).

The existence of this call-and-response pattern between the natural world and the crew suggests to the reader that nature is not an "absent" other, but merely one that has been overlooked in our modern world-view. Johnson's observation about Shelley's "Ode to the West Wind" applies to Harris's work as well: "The voices of the wind are not created by the lyric apostrophe; they rather initiate the need for one" (190). Harris explains that we fail to hear the nonhuman voices around us because our ecological perspective has been obscured and overwritten by biased consumer interests: "By and large a great deal of what is written today is heavily biased. It's biased in favour of certain vested interests. It's biased in favour of, perhaps, the conquistadorial cultures that go in and want to get treasure or wealth out of the landscape. These biases have grown up across centuries and generations, and language tends to correspond to that. So much literature that deals with landscape is a one-sided discourse, something imposed on the landscape. It's not even a discourse in any real sense. It's a one-sided thing, when something is imposed on the landscape. To break out of that one has to discover links and connections that open the language to resources which one has forgotten one possesses" (qtd. in Gilkes 34).

Harris's use of apostrophe in *Palace* reminds the reader that there are resources in language with which one can connect with the environment. This connection, as the novel's call-and-response demonstrates, is not "one-sided," but rather embodies a dialectical connection that provides the imaginative context for discourse. Harris reveals the dangers of one-sided discourses that correspond to and perpetuate the conquistadorial impulse and shows that this limiting perversion of language is implicated not only in our relationship to the land, but also in our relationships with other people. Harris suggests that imagining a dialectical correspondence with the landscape leads people to adopt a different worldview and, in turn, to imagine themselves differently. He links this transformation of consciousness to liberation of language when he describes the journey of *Palace*'s crew: "The connections are there if these people [the crew members] could sense that there must be some way in which they can free themselves from a certain restriction, in which they would approach themselves in a different way, the landscape around them, the living text of the landscape around them. The language which comes in imaginative art has deep intuitive roots. It is not something totally man made" (qtd. in Gilkes 38). As the crew members realize the importance of reading this "living text," of "reading the river's mysterious book" (*Palace* 25), they internalize its possibility for dialogic discourse that "has deep intuitive roots" in the poetical imagination. Once this imaginative capacity is tapped, it flows freely and liberates them from their preconceived notions, allowing them to "approach themselves in a different way."

Because the crew represents the diverse demography of postcolonial Guyana, negotiation of the crew members' identities has particular significance for West Indian society. Gilkes suggests that *Palace*'s engagement with the "impulse [of] the Romantic movemen[t], with [its] insistence on imagination as an associative impulse," makes the West Indian "'search for identity' . . . deeper [and] more meaningful . . . by examining [its] relationship to the environment [and] to the natural and historical condition of the West Indies" (*Wilson Harris* xvi). In personal testament to the significance of grounding the quest for West Indian identity in the landscape, Harris has described the effect Guyana's environment has had on him and his postcolonial thinking in his 1995 interview with Charles Rowell: "The rainforest made an enormous impact on me," he said, explaining that "I learned that one should not attempt to—indeed one cannot—colonize the unconscious" (qtd. in Rowell 192). In "Tradition and the West Indian Novel," Harris applies this lesson he has learned from the landscape to the West Indian author's exploration of postcolonial identity. Explaining that "the environment of the Caribbean is steeped . . . in . . . misconceptions of the residue and meaning of conquest," Harris suggests that the West Indian novel provides a particularly liberating discursive space in which the author can create images of the environment that expose these misconceptions and the colonial "tradition of empty names and dead letters" that support them (*Palace* 80).

Harris creates such a discursive space in *Palace*, which not only undoes this "meaning of conquest" by enacting a dialogic exchange with nature through antiphonal apostrophe, but also further explores how terms of conquest are literally and figuratively mapped onto the landscape and internalized by its people. The dreaming narrator tells us that "[t]he names Brazil and Guyana were colonial conventions that [he] had known from childhood" that "were close to [him] as [his] ribs, the rivers and flatland, the mountains and the heartland [he] intimately saw" (24). Although the narrator knows that the map's arbitrary borders and names denote a "dream" of conquest, he "could not help cherishing [his] symbolic map" in which he "[sees] this kingdom of man turned into a colony and battleground of spirit, a priceless tempting jewel [he] dreamed [he] possessed" (24). Harris calls the authenticity of the symbolic map into question by juxtaposing the names "Brazil" and "Guyana," which represent the terminology of possession that underwrites the colonial enterprise, with the "nameless" landscape which the countries supposedly contain (75, 79). It is worth noting that in the seventeen-page chapter on the wounding of the bird, there are at least ten uses of the words "nameless" or "name." Even Donne, "the last landlord" who "fight[s] everything in nature" and has had "a bad name in the savannahs," tells the dreaming narrator that "every boundary line is a myth. No-man's land" (20, 38). As Drake has pointed out, by admitting that the map is a fiction, that the land "intrinsically belongs to no one," Donne undermines his own colonial project of subjugating the folk to work the land for his profit (85).

Shaw notes that we "can clearly trace a process whereby the empirical map, the scientific plotting, is gradually replaced by that dream-map of the interior which in *Palace of the Peacock* supplies the basic plot and guide to the surreal journey into the interior" ("The Novelist" 149). The transition from the empirical to the dream-map is facilitated by language, Shaw asserts: "In this context language becomes a fluid medium translating the objects of perception, through an inner dialectic of subjectivity, into an inner realm of images" ("The Novelist" 149). Language's ability to open this dialectic of subjectivity becomes evident when Donne is unable to communicate his motto—"rule the land . . . and you rule the world" (23)—to the crew members, who instead remain rooted in the landscape: "He started suddenly addressing the company in the lurid storm but it was as if he spoke only to himself. The whole crew were blasted and rooted in the soil of Mariella like imprisoned dead trees . . . Words came as from a frightened spiritual medium and translation. Meaning was petrified and congealed and then flashing and clear upon his rigid face and brow hanging in his own ultimatum and light" (49). Immediately after his failed address, Donne, recognizing the futility of his polemic, begins to reflect on the human costs of his conquistadorial habit: "I have treated the folk badly . . . I am beginning to lose all my imagination save that sometimes I feel I'm involved in the most frightful material slavery . . . Perhaps there's a ghost of a chance that I can find a different relationship with the folk, who knows? Nothing to lose anyway by trying. I suppose it's what I've always really wanted" (50-51). To forge this different relationship with the folk, Donne, "the only one in their midst who carried on his sleeve the affection of a rich first name," must address the folk in terms other than "economic names to command and choose from (as one chose to order one's labouring folk around)" and "signs of address from a past dead investment and history with its vague pioneering memories" (69, 70). "There was nothing he appeared to have that commended him," the dreaming narrator tells us, "[s]ave the nameless kinship of spirit older . . . than every material mask and label and economic form and solipsism" (70). As the dreaming narrator tries to tell Donne when they discuss the "mystery of language and address," this nameless kinship of spirit needs to take linguistic form in a "dreaming language" that can be addressed to "everyman" (52).

*Palace*'s dreaming language evolves from the collective apostrophe that reconnects the crew with nature, using a song "that [breaks] every spell" (103). Harris casts Carroll, the youngest member of the crew, who is "nameless out of shame and yet named with a new distant name . . . to forge for their descendents new mythical far-flung relationships" (69), as this musical presence in the text. Carroll frees the crew from colonialism's spell and its pattern of naming by giving life to an apostrophic call that reclaims both the people and the land: "Carroll had begun laughing and the fresh ringing sound of his voice made everyone forget himself and turn in involuntary surprise. The laugh struck them as the slyest music coming clear out of the stream . . . It was an ingenious sound like the homely crackle of gossiping parrots or of inspired branches in the leaves, or the slicing ecstasy and abandonment of the laughing wood when the hunter loses and finds his game in the footmark he has himself left and made . . . Something had freed them and lifted them up out of the deeps, a blessing and a curse, a reverberating clap of thunder and still music and song. The sound was jubilant and obscure and tremulous in their ear like a dreaming sword that had cut them from the womb" (54-55).

Carroll's laugh embodies the imagined possibility for words of poetry to collapse into pure sound, not signifying or naming or even limiting discourse by language or dialect, but instead circulating a harmonious call that connects caroler with listener, writer with reader, and man with the land. These connections, Harris insists, have particular importance today as postcolonial subjects negotiate their places in the modern world: "When we breathe we are not only breathing out through our lungs but through the lungs of the globe. The lungs of the globe look out on the stars, they have connections with the stars. So you have that thread running right through; all these links and connections running right through and those links and connections are pertinent to language. If we simply bottle ourselves up in what appears to be a kind of journalistic prose we are lost . . . language has to bring *all* the connections in if one is to find the beginnings of some kind of reverence for what we are, for the world in which we live, for a world that is endangered. And yet a world that is mysteriously potent and alive" (qtd. in Gilkes 38). In *Palace of the Peacock*, Harris highlights possibilities for making these connections through Romantic poetics. With its reimagination of "The Rime of the Ancient Mariner," the novel proposes an ecocritical mode of apostrophe for addressing our endangered world, which even now remains "mysteriously potent and alive."

# Conclusion

## British Legacy in the Americas

In the previous chapters I examine where and how twentieth-century novels from former British colonies in the Americas have appropriated and adapted British Romantic poetry. One conclusion we can draw from these examinations is that Romantic poetry continues to make an impression on postcolonial America. The use of these Romantic texts demonstrates the lasting impact of England on its colonies, their educational systems, and their literary production. As I have shown, some of the novelists have explicitly discussed studying British Romantic poetry, suggesting that since they had to memorize the words of Romantic poets, they decided to use them. Internalizing the words of these poems allowed the words to become a part of themselves and their works. In Atwood's words, the Romantic poems influenced their conceptions of who they are—"what we are or ought to be like," how to write—"what constitutes good writing," and what writing should do—"what social functions writing fulfills, or ought to fulfill" (*Negotiating* 5).

All of the novels examined in this study refigure Romantic poetry to illustrate the legacy of British imperialism in the Americas. Mimicking the appropriation of Romantic poetry by colonial educators, the authors and their works I examine adapt Romantic poetics for their own purposes. While other scholars have noted connections between British Romanticism and colonial or postcolonial writing, I focus on Romantic works not typically examined in a postcolonial context to show that Romantic poetry as a body of work has something to offer postcolonial writers. My analyses suggest that reframing Romantic poetry allegorically landscapes a confrontation with empire, revealing how subjectivity is shaped by considerations of place and power. Although the Romantics' impact can be seen in all of the novels analyzed, the way in which Romantic poetry shaped these works differed because the novelists had different experiences with the poems themselves and the country and culture they represent. Having a broad range of novels allowed for an examination of how British influence differs based on place, particularly from which former colony the writer hails. For example, in Kincaid's *Lucy,* the protagonist reacts against the daffodil that represents Wordsworth's lyric because it seems to be a foreign entity forced upon her; the poem and its images are out of place, transplanted in a nonsustainable, hostile native setting. Kincaid draws attention to the foreign nature of the daffodil and makes it reappear in the novel unexpectedly—standing out each time like a sore thumb—to emphasize the contrast between her world and that of Wordsworth. Fitzgerald, on the other hand, emulates Keats consciously and reframes his famous feast scene to identify with Keats's critique of the excess of empire. Fitzgerald appropriates Keats's feast scene, transforming only the luxury goods, so that it takes an astute reader to recognize the semblance. In comparing Kincaid's intertexts to Fitzgerald's, we can see the difference in the degree to which each work identified with British Romanticism. Given the similarities between the US and Britain, it might come as no surprise that Fitzgerald is able to reframe Keats's lines to convey a similar critique in a US context. Kincaid, however, must establish the "daffodil gap" that her protagonist, who is from an unnamed Caribbean island, faces even if she herself matches Wordsworth's lyricism.

Romantic poetry operates on many different levels in *Lucy*. While Kincaid, the author, produces passages about Lucy's experiences with the daffodils in a lyric style comparable to that of Wordsworth, Lucy, her character, vows to "erase from [her] mind, line by line, every word" of Wordsworth's famous lyric poem "I wandered lonely as a Cloud" (18). It is not a coincidence, I argue, that Lucy shares the name of the woman famously denied a voice in Wordsworth's Lucy Poems. Lucy's antagonism toward Wordsworth's lyric and its image of the daffodil resurfaces throughout the narrative with several after-images of the daffodil, which haunt the novel as well as Lucy. The recurrence of the daffodil image throughout the text suggests that Wordsworth's poetry is not only important in terms of Lucy's educational experiences, but also in the telling of her life's story. For *Lucy* itself is a bildungsroman, much like Wordsworth's epic poem *The Prelude*: both recount a type of journey that results in the growth of the writer's mind. Wordsworth's words obviously shape the way in which Lucy sees the world and her own development as a writer. The same could be said for Kincaid, who has indicated that she has adapted the Romantic poetry she learned in school for her own literary production.

Atwood, too, has explained the importance of Romantic poetry for her development as a writer. As shown in chapter 2, Romantic intertexts appear prominently in her fiction, particularly her short story "Death by Landscape" and her novel *The Handmaid's Tale*. By revealing how Atwood rewrites the fate of Wordsworth's Lucy within "Death by Landscape," I hope not only to have demonstrated that Atwood incorporates Romantic intertexts in her work, but also to have illustrated how Atwood uses Romantic poetics to critique empire through the figure of landscape. She achieves this in *The Handmaid's Tale* to show how place affects subjectivity. Offred, marked by Gilead's tattoo, is confined physically within the Gileadean empire, but this inscription within the regime also indelibly marks her psyche, as the Romantic intertexts reveal. Professor Pieixoto's description of the Handmaid's tale as having "a whiff of emotion recollected, if not in tranquillity, at least *post facto*" references Wordsworth's Preface to *Lyrical Ballads* (303). In this failed attempt at humor, the professor contrasts the Handmaid's ability to recount her experiences with that of the poet, who is able to configure his relation to the world around him in both the past and present in a way the Handmaid cannot. Despite—or perhaps because of—the stifling conditions she endures, the Handmaid invokes Coleridge's phrase "I AM" to remind herself of the capacity of her imagination to shape her reality. By adopting "I AM" as a mantra, she attempts to save herself from fading into the Gileadean landscape. Atwood uses these Romantic intertexts not only to warn us about the dangers of empire, but also to emphasize the importance of writers for challenging tyranny and identifying injustice: "The writer functions in his or her society as a kind of soothsayer, a truth teller . . . Writing is not mere self-expression but a view of society and the world at large" (*Second Words* 353). The Romantic intertexts in *The Handmaid's Tale* illustrate how crucial it is for writers to have this view.

In *Blood Meridian* McCarthy uses Romantic poetry to dispel a view of the world, in this case, revising Byron's perceptions of the American Arcadia presented in *Don Juan*. Byron had great influence within the US and also shaped how the rest of the world viewed in the US. The inscription on the judge's gun, *Et in Arcadia Ego*, serves to parody idyllic representations of the US West seen in Byron's works. In addition to contrasting the images of Arcadia seen in Byron's poetry, McCarthy adapts scenes from Byron's lyric poem "Darkness" to project his own apocalyptic vision of life on the plains. The kid, like Childe Harold, embarks on a pilgrimage, but his quest is one of mindless violence. The kid's scalp hunting reveals the inner workings of Manifest Destiny, the rhetoric of empire adapted for an American setting.

In *The Great Gatsby* Fitzgerald portrays life in the US after World War I, when the nation was emerging as the world's superpower. Jay Gatsby represents both the potential the US had to create its own identity and the dangers it faced of falling into patterns of consumption that would betray its roots. Gatsby, with his gaudy mansion, Rolls Royce, and his pink rag of a suit, draws attention to the fact that he is nouveau riche. After the war, many in the US fell into a similar pattern of conspicuous consumption fashioned from British luxury icons like the Rolls Royce. Fitzgerald uses men's clothing to symbolize the passage of power from Great Britain to the US, and he adapts Keats's famous feast scene from "The Eve of St. Agnes" with shirts bought in London to mock the excesses of US empire.

More revolutionary than the other novels, Harris's *Palace of the Peacock* asks us to reconsider language, both how we use it and what the words we utter say about us. Harris rewrites Coleridge's "Rime of the Ancient Mariner" to demonstrate how colonization affects our naming of people and places and the way we address others. The "Rime," with its symbolism, elements of storytelling, and forms of address, adapts to *Palace*'s setting in Guyana, which still bears the mark of British colonialism. In his recasting of the "Rime," Harris offers a new conceptual language that invokes apostrophe to emphasize the connection between people and their landscape. By changing the way we address the world around us, Harris suggests, we can "generate foundations of care within the vessel of place" ("A Note" 9).

All of these novels use Romantic intertexts to show the continued influence of the legacy of the British Empire on its former colonies in the Americas. But in addition to charting the connections to Great Britain, the Romantic intertexts of *Lucy* explore relationships between other British former colonies in the Americas and the US. Kincaid characterizes the superiority complex of those in the US who elide other of these former colonies into a monolithic other. Mariah's friend Dinah, for instance, identifies Lucy as being from "the islands," without specifying which one she is from. Emphasizing that each island has its own unique history and culture, Lucy muses, "Which islands exactly do you mean?" (56). Further distancing the natives of the Caribbean from those in the US is Kincaid's likening of Mariah and her family members to the poet's daffodils (12). Since the daffodils function as a symbol of British colonial influence within the novel, the depiction of Mariah and her family as daffodils suggests that they are the new generation of colonizers.

I argue that like *Lucy* other works in this study suggest that the US has come to resemble Great Britain's imperial power much more closely than its other former American colonies do. In "Death by Landscape," Atwood draws clear distinctions between Lois, the Canadian girl, and Lucy, who is from the US, in part to characterize the difference between Canadian and US attitudes and behavior, and Atwood sets the dystopia of *The Handmaid's Tale* in the US because she "couldn't fly it in Canada" (*Conversations* 223). McCarthy reveals the realities of Manifest Destiny to upend the mythology of a US Arcadia in *Blood Meridian,* suggesting that as the US grew in the 1800s, its actions more closely resembled that of the most powerful empire of the time, Great Britain. And in *The Great Gatsby*, Fitzgerald depicts the US as the new world superpower that models its culture of consumption from its imperial parent. Although the US might represent the most powerful outgrowth of the British Empire in the Americas, *Palace of the Peacock* suggests that all former colonies betray a use of language, of address, that inscribes colonization. This mode of address is personified by Donne, himself a namesake of the British poet. With Donne, Harris shows how the terms of conquest are literally and figuratively mapped onto the landscape and internalized by its people.

*Palace* and the other novels analyzed here suggest that the legacy of British colonialism in postcolonial America can be traced through language use. The poems of the British Romantics provide postcolonial writers with particularly rich material because they involve the assertion of subjectivity at the height of the British Empire. Over time, the words of these poets have been used to both justify and undermine imperial power, but these novels collectively use Romantic poetics to offer a critique of British imperial legacy and the US's emergence as a new imperial power. These intertexts change our conceptualization of America by showing that imperial roots run deep, that British colonization in the Americas continues to affect how we see ourselves even though we are now part of postcolonial societies. Ultimately, these intertexts give us a better understanding of the postcolonial condition—suggesting that the colonial mindset might not be as far in the past as we are inclined to think.

# Epilogue

## Angels in America Guard and Guide

In the previous chapters and conclusion of *Romantic Revisions in Novels from the Americas*, I discuss how twentieth-century novels from across the Americas invoke British Romantic poetry to highlight the imprints of British colonialism that continue to shape American sociopolitical landscapes. Returning to British Romantic poetry allows these authors to extend Romantic poetics of landscape that traditionally considered the British subject's relation to place within contemporary American frames of reference. By recasting British poetics of landscape in the Americas, these writers show how negotiations of identity and power in former British colonies in the Americas are defined by the legacies of British imperialism, illustrating that these nations, their peoples, and their works of art are truly postcolonial. To depict the politics of location that emerge in the wake of colonialism, they employ figures adapted from British Romantic poetry to landscape the impact of British influence within their respective American contexts. Kincaid relies on the repeated image of the daffodil, Atwood displaces Lucy in the landscape, McCarthy counters the Romantic projection of the American arcadia, Fitzgerald heaps Keatsian images of luxury as excess, and Harris transforms the albatross.

This epilogue aims to explain why tracing the circulation of Romantic poetics of landscape furthers an understanding of politics of resistance within contemporary American societies. While discussing the significance of mapping poetics of landscape, I hope to illustrate how these poetics participate in calls for revolution in media of popular culture and show why they have such powerful revisionary capacity. For this case study I turn to William Blake, the most radical of the Romantic poets, and in particular his poem *America: A Prophecy* (1793). Reading poetics of landscape in Blake's work requires, as Mitchell proposes in *Landscape and Power*, that we "decode landscape as a body of determinate signs" (1). Blake's illuminated books demonstrate landscape poetics because they rely on image and text to map negotiations of power within a conceptual place. In the case of *America: A Prophecy*, this place is the geographical US and the predominant figure that the prophecy repeatedly—and in multiple manifestations—maps onto this national space is that of the angel. This association of angels with the US has remained strong within the collective imagination, and I suggest that contemporary artists working in a variety of media have seized upon Blake's apocalyptic vision, defiance of empire, and prophetic mapping of angels onto the US in order to further movements for political resistance within—and outside of—the US.

Despite being more than 200 years old, Blake's illuminated works generate a political power that allows his visionary landscapes to take on a life of their own when appropriated by other prophets. As David Erdman asserts, "The action of the poem-picture is larger and more complex than would be indicated by the pictures or the words taken separately, for these point not at each other . . . but beyond themselves. The artifact only opens the sensory doors to mental theater" ("*America*: New Expanses" 92-93). Analyzing the concomitant mapping of angels and revolution onto *America* helps explain why such a wide range of prophetic works dramatize the American angel to stage the next cultural revolution.

## A prophecy

When Blake began work on *America*, his first prophetic book, in 1792, the poem focused on the American War for Independence. However, W. H. Stevenson points out that as Blake's vision evolved, angelic figures took center stage: "in the first version of *America*, we have the historical struggle between the British government and the American colonies (not between two heavenly powers). In the final version, although the scene is the same, the heroes and tyrants of earth are little more than accessories to the battle, whose full fury rages above them" (497). One might speculate that Blake's focus shifted to a higher realm because he wanted not only to reflect upon the American War for Independence, but also to explore the phenomenon of revolution more generally. Stevenson is typical in arguing that Blake was writing "at a time [in which] such interpretations of temporal events in universal terms would be valuable" (503). The events that preoccupied the minds of Blake and his contemporaries in the early 1790s involved the French Revolution, a topic on which Blake had tried to write directly but abandoned under threat of retaliation. William Richey notes that Blake's "first revolutionary narrative, *The French Revolution*, had been withheld from publication in 1791" and that "the proclamation against seditious writings in May 1792 made it dangerous for radical writers to express their opinions openly" (196). Richey maintains that *America* functions as Blake's rebuttal to Burke's "prophecies of chaos and catastrophe" in which he "attempts to shift the blame for the mounting bloodshed in France to the forces of counter-revolution" (196). Although *America* responds to the politics within and outside of England during the French Revolution, by restricting their readings of the prophecy to the politics of the war in France literary critics have lost sight of two of the defining aspects of the poem: its American setting and its insistence on prophecy.

While "America itself the place," might serve as "a crucial organizing reference point for the radical struggle in London" as Saree Makdisi suggests (*Impossible*

*History* 14), the vision that Blake maps in *America* carries significance for the projection of the imaginary of the US as a nation that is distinct from both its colonial parent and revolutionary France. *America*, which consists of eighteen illuminated plates, opens with a frontispiece that depicts a large winged figure—which many readers have interpreted as Orc, the personification of revolution associated with the US in the poem. This figure is crouched with his head on his knees and chained within a gap in a crumbling wall, surrounded by mortar casings and a forlorn woman and child (plate 1; 82; all quotations from *America: A Prophecy* refer to Copy H, held by the British Museum. The pagination corresponds to the reprinting in *The Continental Prophecies*). With this first image, *America* introduces its prophecy with the promise of liberation: that the great, chained angel will soon break his fetters and soar over the ravaged landscape. In the Preludium to the Prophecy, this promise is realized when Orc frees himself, seizes the shadowy woman who fed him in captivity, and enters into her "Canadian wilds" and "American plains" (plates 3 and 4; 85, 86). The woman recognizes Orc as the one who "art fall'n to give me life in regions of dark death." Brought in touch with a newfound sense of place and rootedness through Orc, she now feels "the struggling afflictions" affecting the extremities of her American body:

> On my American plains I feel the struggling afflictions
> Endur'd by roots that writhe their arms into the nether deep:
> I see a serpent in Canada, who courts me to his love;
> In Mexico an Eagle, and a Lion in Peru;
> I see a Whale in the South-sea, drinking my soul away.
> O what limb rending pains I feel. thy fire & my frost
> Mingle in howling pains, in furrows by thy lightnings rent;
> This is eternal death; and this the torment long foretold. (plate 4; 86)

As we consider the implications of Orc's entering the woman, we should, according to Mitchell, consider geographic and spatial terms: Blake's poetry "affirms the power of the human imagination to create and organize time in its own image, and his painting affirms the centrality of the human body as the structural principle of space. The essential unity of his arts, then, is to be seen in the parallel engagements of imagination and body with their respective media, and in their convergence in the more comprehensive idea of the 'Human Form Divine'" ("Blake's Composite Art" 69). The woman's address to Orc, which closes the Preludium, maps the US in terms of its own revolutionary battles and growing pains in relation to political struggles for and with neighboring lands. But it also prefaces the prophecy itself that follows with the apocalyptic vision of "eternal death," the "torment long foretold." As an examination of the Prophecy will show, Blake reconciles the impossible coexistence of revolutionary liberation and apocalyptic destruction in America by projecting the process of negotiation onto competing angelic figures who vie for the power either to cripple America and what it stands for or to salvage this "portion of the infinite" (plate 16; 110). Meanwhile, on the ground, the common people labor under "Angels & weak men" and revolutionary fires smolder (plate 18; 114).

The Prophecy, announced by angelic figures carrying chains and flames, begins with fires of the "Guardian Prince of Albion" traveling across the Atlantic and "Piercing the souls of warlike men, who rise in the silent night, / Washington, Franklin, Paine & Warren, Gates, Hancock & Green; / Meet on the coast glowing with the blood from Albions fiery Prince" (plate 5; 89). The focus on actual historical figures and events is one characteristic distinguishing *America: A Prophecy* from *Europe: A Prophecy* (1794). The first few lines of *America: A Prophecy* establish the important transatlantic connection between the England and its colonial American sons (soon to become founding fathers), who, although they rise up in rebellion, still share the same "blood" as "Albions fiery Prince," his same "warlike" nature. Then Washington stirs his fellow compatriots with a speech that elicits Albion's dragon-like wrath: "Friends of America look over the Atlantic sea; / A bended bow is lifted in heaven, & a heavy iron chain / Descends link by link from Albions cliffs across the sea to bind / Brothers & sons of America, till our faces pale and yellow; / Heads deprest, voices weak, eyes downcast, hands work-bruis'd. / Feet bleeding on the sultry sands, and the furrows of the whip / Descend to generations that in future times forget" (plate 5; 89).

Images Washington invokes in this speech, those of the male body worn down by physical labor, recall the pains the woman describes in the Preludium and remind us of the work that both incites and is necessary for revolution. Makdisi suggests that those recognized for the work might not be those primarily responsible for it:

> The most striking thing about Blake's American rebels is that they are crushed by the hardships of physical labor, battered and torn by their work. Chains and whips, work-bruised hands and furrowed scars, bleeding feet on hot sands—these are not the images that one typically associates with the genteel work or the political struggles of Washington and Benjamin Franklin and Horatio Gates and Joseph Warren. These are images of the hardship of physical labor, and of slave-labor in particular. We are, then, not only *not* dealing here with the work performed by Washington and Thomas Jefferson and company, but on the contrary with the work performed by the slaves *owned* by them and the other leaders of the American war. (*Impossible History* 33)

Although he might underestimate the physical involvement of Washington and other leaders of the revolution, Makdisi rightly points out that unsung heroes contributed to the effort.

Churning "vast wheels of blood," the workings of the American Revolution give rise to "a Wonder o'er the Atlantic sea; / Intense! Naked! a Human fire fierce glowing, as the wedge / Of iron heated in the furnace; his terrible limbs were fire . . . heat but not light went thro' the murky atmo / sphere" (plate 6; 90). Blake depicts the revolution as powerful, as having a great deal of potential, but that energy produced by labor is manifested only in heat, not in light. However, the Prophecy suggests that the moment of illumination is not far away. We get our first glimpse of "Albions Angel" and then witness Orc, the "terror like a comet, or more like the / planet red" streak across the sky and with these words usher in the new dawn:

> The morning comes, the night decays, the watchmen leave their stations;
>
> . . .
>
> Let the slave grinding at the mill, run out into the field:
> Let him look up at the heavens & laugh in the bright air;
> Let the inchained soul shut up in darkness and sighing,
> Whose face has never seen a smile in thirty weary years;
> Rise and look out, his chains are loose, his dungeon doors are open
>
> . . .
>
> For Empire is no more, and now the Lion & Wolf shall cease. (plate 8; 94)

Orc's declaration, which echoes"A Song of Liberty" from *The Marriage of Heaven and Hell* (45), proclaims an end to the British Empire in America, whose "times," he says, "are ended" (plate 10; 98). On the contrary, what Orc's presence actually brings about is not an end of American empire, but a battle among America's warring angels. It is worth noting here that the negative characterization of Albion's Angel in *America* recasts the figuration of angels in both Blake's *The Marriage of Heaven and Hell* and Milton's *Paradise Lost*. More generally, the battle between Orc (US) and Albion (England) mirrors that of Satan (like Orc, a fallen angel) and the angels of heaven in *Paradise Lost*. In Blake's *America*, Albion's Angel twice sounds the alarm, summoning the "eternal Wolf" and "eternal Lion" to the epic battle over the fate of the Anglo-American empire (plate 11; 101). Albion's Angel fails in his attempts to rally his "Thirteen Angels," who have been resting on Atlantis, "On those vast shady hills between America & Albions shore; / Now barr'd out by the Atlantic sea" where they can "pass to the Golden world / An ancient palace, archetype of mighty Emperies" (plate 12; 102). Blake's placement of the Thirteen Angels on Atlantis, in the hidden, liminal space between England and the US, not only reflects the divided loyalties of the American colonies, but also contextualizes this epic battle within the broader history of empire itself. Because Atlantis recalls the "Golden" ages of past empires, staging this encounter there encourages reflection on British—and future US—imperialism.

In response to the summons of Albion's Angel, the Thirteen Angels emerge shrouded in the fires of Orc and led by "Bostons Angel," demanding "who commanded this, what God, what Angel? . . . What God is he, writes laws of peace & clothes him in a tempest / What pitying Angel lusts for tears, and fans himself with sighs / What crawling villain preaches abstinence & wraps himself / In fat of lambs? no more I follow, no more obedience pay" (plate 13; 105). Although the Thirteen Angels remove their imperial robes and strike down their commanding scepters, they cannot prevent all of Albion's angels in America—who number "forty million[]" strong and are "Arm'd with diseases of the earth to cast upon the Abyss"—from unleashing their plagues upon the country (plate 15, 109). Faced with "Fury! rage! [and] madness!" from above, revolutionary American colonists band together and tap into Orc's fighting spirit:

> And the red flames of Orc that folded roaring fierce around
> The angry shore, and the fierce rushing of th' inhabitants together;
> The citizens of New-York close their books & lock their chests;

> The mariners of Boston drop their anchors and unlade;
> The scribe of Pensylvania casts his pen upon the earth;
> The builder in Virginia throws down his hammer in fear.
> Then had America been lost, o'erwhelmed by the Atlantic,
> And Earth had lost another portion of the infinite!
> But all rush together in the night in wrath and raging fire
> The red fires rag'd! the plagues recoil'd! then rolld they back with fury
> On Albions Angels: then the Pestilence began in streaks of red
> Across the limbs of Albions Guardian, the spotted plague smote Bristols
> And the Leprosy Londons Spirit, sickening all their bands." (plates 16 & 17; 110, 113)

This "fierce rushing of th' inhabitants together" represents some sort of transformation of the community in response to Albion's pestilence, but one wonders, other than dropping everything and banding together to combat terror, how the national community has really changed. Apparently, in an act of retribution, Americans have deflected the plague back to its source, to infect the English public body. Erdman claims that a "new humanity, a new human form of society, is the vision Blake wants us to see *beyond* the revolutionary drama presented on this split stage of the American and British shores of the Atlantic" ("*America*: New Expanses" 110). What form of postcolonial society might this be? Steve Clark and David Worrall, responding to Erdman's seminal work *Blake: Prophet Against Empire*, suggest that Blake "may be seen as a prophet not for or against nation and empire, but as necessarily envisioning their growth, dissemination, and eventual demise in order to attempt to imagine a future outside and beyond them" (17). But, again, what future comes after and operates outside of imperial rule? Orc's fires are so hot at the end of the prophecy that they melt the "bolts and hinges" of "the five gates" of perception, making it impossible to sense and therefore represent the rebuilding that takes place after the fire, or to ascertain if any life remains (plate 18; 114).

In *America*, the people, not their angels, change the course of history and lay the groundwork for future societies. As Makdisi has observes, "the only revolutionary 'action' that can properly be said to take place in *America* is carried out . . . by ordinary citizens" (*Impossible History* 34). Makdisi gives what might be seen as a hopeful reading of the rallying public, claiming that "it is only 'the fierce rushing of th'inhabitants together,' who 'all rush together in the night in wrath and in raging fire,' and not the frozen and almost comical posturing of the revolution's 'real' leaders (who never come to power in Blake's prophecy), that apparently could keep Earth from 'losing another portion of the infinite'" (35). Furthermore, Makdisi suggests that *America*'s "affirmation—however conspiratorially secretive it might have been—of the insurrectionary politics of the multitude takes on new meaning and has added significance in [the] dangerous and unstable context" arising from "the illuminated book[s' operation] as an open network of verbal and visual texts" whose "meaning cannot be figured independently" (*Impossible History* 7, 52). Thus, the ending of *America* refuses to project the ultimate future of the American people or their relation to empire and leaves the reader with many questions about the poem's prophecy.

Has the US already been lost as a "portion of the infinite"? Where is it that "Angels & weak men . . . govern o'er the strong"? Why do the Americans look to angels, and what angels are inspiring, guarding, and guiding the US now? Do we need angels from both of Blake's camps to drive the forces of revolution forward, or, restated in Rilkean terms, if our devils leave us, will our angels take flight as well? Although many questions about the future remain unanswered, the one point the poem clearly prophesies is that now that they have touched down, we will be "unable to stem the fires of Orc" (plate 18; 114).

Revolutionary flames have been blazing in the US from its beginnings, and the contemporary works that I turn to next represent attempts to locate and steer those fires within political and cultural frameworks by evoking the angels of America. In tracing the circulation of revolutionary (or counter-revolutionary) angels within the American cultural imagination, I am not suggesting that these artists are rewriting Blake's *America*, but rather that they participate in the circulation and evolution of the poetics of landscape that he helped create. The narrator of Blake's "Proverbs of Hell" claims that "the sayings used in a nation . . . mark its character" (35). My analysis extends this notion to the visual realm to include images—in this case, those of the angel—projected onto the nationscape. This is not to say that the US is itself angelic, but instead that its artists use the image of the angel because, in signifying both revolution and revelation, it forces Americans to consider the politics of location. Mike Goode has argued that "Blake's proverblike poetry reads, among other things, as a canny attempt to evade the lethal power the law wielded against the era's radicals, while [both] simultaneously eroding the forms of sociopolitical individuation the law underwrote" and creating "enduring forms of political collectivity that would never need to become conscious themselves as such in order for them to undermine systems tactically" (776). Blake's American angels can be seen to wield a similar subversive power. As Goode notes of the proverbs, they serve as "a medium that is its own heterogeneous message, and that message, like the 'rhizomatic' forms that Gilles Deleuze and Félix Guattari celebrate . . . becomes senderless and receiverless over time, directed toward everybody by everyone" (772). Tracing the flight of the American angel—although it might seem to be strictly a religious symbol—back to Blake provides historical, literary, and political contexts that suggest why the image of the angel resonates so powerfully with Americans today.

## Blake on stage, on screen, on radio, and in your Home Box Office

Given the commercial success and popular appeal of Blakean adaptations and appropriations in recent years, it comes as no surprise that even academics are riding the wave of popularity. In a 2007 collection entitled *Blake, Modernity, and Popular Culture*, Mark Lussier observes that "when measured within a very different and enriched textual environment (advertising, cinema, comic books, nonfiction prose, pulp fiction and dedicated websites), Blake's influence ripples well beyond academic confines to circulate in a vortex of semiotic (in)formation in the dense core of postmodernity" (153). Although one could certainly argue that Blake's work has influenced the creation of texts long before the postmodern period, Lussier identifies a distinct timeliness that has made Blakean representations particularly significant for contemporary audiences. Lussier claims that "such images and evocations indicate that Blakean influence has crept from a counterculture presence to become embedded in consumer culture, or rather that the counterculture has become the consumer culture of postmodernity" (157). In focusing on the Blakean adaptations within postmodern consumer culture, however, Lussier loses sight of the broader political forces that are driving the Blakean renaissance and motivate those from across the ideological spectrum who are inspired by his work. As Goode points out, usurpations of Blake's works like the Proverbs of Hell painted on the walls of Donald Trump's "Library Dining Room" raise "more than a few academic eyebrows," but nonetheless when "the historical scholars stop laughing," they need to ask why Blake's work is being used in this way and "what it means" as a sociopolitical phenomenon (769-70).

Because Blake has long stood as a Romantic figure of rebellion, visionary artists have looked to his illuminated works for inspired political commentary. Even Blake's prophecies, with their universalizing figures and projections for the future, "were intended, on one level at least, to have something of the immediacy of political cartoons" (Erdman, *Prophet* 202). The angels of *America: A Prophecy*, like other symbolic figures in Blake's work, circulate within Blake's corpus and outside of it, not contained by the plates on which they were engraved or the political contexts into which they were first embedded. Mitchell reminds us that "imagination is not simply a product for Blake, a fixed body of well-defined forms; it is the *process* by which any symbolic form comes into being" ("Blake's Composite Art" 72). American artists of varied sorts tap into the Blakean imagination and take on his "infernal method" in different media (39), continuing the process of these figures' emergence.

One might think of the character of Francis Dolarhyde in Brett Ratner's 2002 movie *Red Dragon* (which was adapted from Thomas Harris's 1981 novel) as a recent personification of a Blakean "great becoming." Dolarhyde represents what Mitchell would call the emergence of the "Dangerous Blake," but there have been a great many films that have drawn from the "Radical Blake" to convey social and political commentary. Shirley Dent and Jason Whittaker have singled out Jim Jarmusch's 1995 film *Dead Man*, which stars a character named William Blake, as the prime example "of the ways in which American literature and art has attempted to reconcile a Blakean dilemma between vision and materialism, that the imaginative perception of the world is the first step to its transformation" (118).

Most striking about Blake's influence on popular culture is the widely divergent manner in which artists who adapt Blake's work both perceive the world and try to transform it. Goode argues that the "radical political work" of Blake's proverbs "depends on their semantic availability to multiple and incompatible interpretations and on their formal availability to a reading that is itself tactical" (783). To a degree, the radical politics of this "semantic availability" holds true for the contemporary adaptation of his symbols as well. Blake's symbols themselves, as we have seen with the figures of American angels, open themselves up to multiple readings, and so, too, do many of the adaptations that map angels onto America. Lift To Experience's song "To Guard and To Guide You" (2001) serves as a case in point:

> Angels we have heard on high, sweetly singing o'er the plains.
> And the mountains in reply echo back their joyous strains.
> Marching on towards Zion, marching on towards Zion.
> Under the X in Texas is where you'll find me, it's where I'll be,
> Singing out the songs, warnin' the world of the perils to come.
> With a cloud by day and a fire by night, forced out of the garden of earthly delights.
> And one by one the states will know, as they crumble like Jericho,
> From Canada to Mexico, Texas is the rock.
> To lift you up when your worlds collide,
> With the angels to guard, and the angels to guide.
> Upon this truth you can rely, so take two steps toward Texas tonight.
> For the sheep shall flock to the call of that mighty Texas rock, singing:
> Angel of God, my guardian dear,
> To whom God's love commits me here.
> Ever this day, be at my side, to light to rule, to guard and to guide.
> Angel dons the metaphor, swings open wide those prison doors.
> There's going to be a war to end all war.
> When your heart hears the call, feels the weight of the fall,
> And the gravity of life's circumstance pulls you down, follow your fate to the Lone Star State. Join us as we sing along.
>
> . . .
>
> If you survive the coming rains, the crash and the tide of the latter days,
> You can secure your slot, and fall in rank with the crippled and the faint.
> As the saints go marching on toward Zion, with guns in hand.
>
> . . .
>
> Angels we have heard on high, sweetly singing o'er the plains.
> And the mountains in reply, echoing their joyous strains,
> To teach the world to sing, in perfect harmony.
> As for me and my house, we will not go gently.
> Now the time has come when you must decide
> To take two steps toward Texas tonight.
> So follow the Lone Star in the sky, and beg for the angels to guard and to guide.

On the back cover of *The Texas-Jerusalem Crossroads*, Lift To Experience (members Josh T. Pearson, Andy Young, and Josh Browning) provides a context for the album: "THIS IS THE STORY OF THREE TEXAS BOYS BUSY MINDING THEIR OWN BIDNIS WHEN THE ANGEL OF THE LORD APPEARED UNTO THEM." As the album title suggests, the collection also corresponds to Blake's epic poem *Jerusalem* (1804-1820). Prophesying the coming of the "latter days," the angel, shocked that "YOU BOYS [DON'T] KNOW NOTHIN,'" informs them that "THE USA IS THE CENTRE OF JERUSALEM." The way in which this proclamation is presented is noteworthy: The capitalized letters U, S, and A within JERUSALEM are colored blue, white, and red, respectively, while the rest of the text is either yellow or white and the background is black. Pearson, the band's lead singer and songwriter, provides a bit of an explanation for this focus, saying that *The Texas-*

*Jerusalem Crossroads* is "a concept album about the end of the world where Texas is the Promised Land" ("Lift To Experience").

All of the songs on the album build on this theme, but "To Guard and To Guide You" has particular significance for this epilogue because the revelatory poetics espoused by the angel are literally echoed by the American landscape: "Angels we have heard on high, sweetly singing o'er the plains. / And the mountains in reply echo back their joyous strains." The first two lines of "To Guard and To Guide You" can be traced to the Christian Christmas carol "Angels We Have Heard on High," which has the refrain "*Gloria in excelsis Deo.*" Lift To Experience's gesture toward apocalypse provides a stark contrast to the carol's celebration of the baby Jesus's birth. The melody of "To Guard and to Guide You" also differs greatly from the carol, obscuring the connection between the two works. In addition to sharing a focus on the angelic figures whose "worlds collide," the song (as well as the Christian carol) shares with *America* both the futurity of prophecy and the warnings of apocalypse. Whereas Albion's Angel sounds the alarm, the angel of God warns of "crash and the tide of the latter days," and unlike the Thirteen Angels, who throw down their scepters, in this case the saints actually take up arms and follow suit. When thinking of the political implications of "To Guard and To Guide You," the call to bear arms and the positioning of Texas as the "rock" are reflective of the state of US politics at the time of the album's release, 2001 (pre-11 September). With George W. Bush—a Texan and born-again Christian—in the White House, an ongoing debate over gun control laws infringing on the right to bear arms, and rhetoric of nation building as foreign policy strategy, the song's assertions that "there is going to be a war to end all war" and that "we will not go gently" take on new meaning. People have speculated that the song parodies Bush's rhetoric, but the accounts of Pearson's conception of the album on the website of the band's label seem to belie that presumption:

> Josh pieced together his opus, The Texas Jerusalem Crossroads, in solitude, every word, note, wash of feedback carefully choreographed. He gathered two dear friends, passionately gifted musicians, and laid his sacred communication down on tape. They called themselves Lift To Experience, and took to the road, every night discovering new truths within their symphonic sprawl. The feedback rose, fierce and tapering like a flame, Josh's voice keening, close to holy, picking out an apocalyptic parable cross-pollinating . . . mythologies. Gentle melodies shimmered in the air, the Leslie-speaker coating the guitar with a heat-haze, the cymbals struck so hard they sprayed the drummer's own blood and sweat. The volume soaring, until it infested you, until it felt like you might suffocate without it, gospel ringing in every gap, a call for salvation, a call to arms. The Leslie spontaneously bursting aflame, as French boys crooned sweetly, we will be free, we will be free. ("Lift To Experience")

The image of Pearson's guitar, the Leslie, bursting into flames projects the intensity of Blake's "fires of Orc" onto "To Guard and To Guide You." Although in his review of the album Matthew Moyer compares Pearson's visions to Blake—saying that "they put William Blake to shame"—he subsumes their importance to the beauty of the music. Matthew Moyer writes, "The music is more important to me than the visions (which admittedly, might even put William Blake to shame), and [is] more thrilling than any ideology" ("Lift To Experience"). But the insistence of the lyrics on freedom and resistance brings the focus, no matter how captivating and cataclysmic the melody, back to inspired revolution, to the "Angel [who] dons the metaphor [and] swings open wide those prison doors" in the tradition of Blake's Orc, who makes possible a world where "dungeon doors are open."

Ridley Scott's 1982 science-fiction thriller *Blade Runner* (adapted from Philip K. Dick's 1968 *Do Androids Dream of Electric Sheep?*) projects an entirely different apocalyptic vision than "To Guard and to Guide You," but, likewise, finds inspiration in Blake's *America: A Prophecy*. In the dystopian vision of this cyberpunk cult classic set in 2019, humanoid replicants that serve on an off-world colony have escaped, come back to earth, and landed in the city Los Angeles to demand that their life spans be extended. Owing to their bloody mutiny, these replicants are to be terminated, and the job of blade runners, like Rick Deckard (Harrison Ford), is to retire them before they wreak any havoc. Roy Batty (Rutger Hauer), the replicant programmed as a combat model who leads the renegade crew, echoes Blake's *America: A Prophecy* when he self-reflexively proclaims: "Fiery the angels fell, deep thunder rolled around their shores, burning with the fires of Orc"; *America* reads: when "Fiery the Angels rose, & as they rose deep thunder roll'd / Around their shores; indignant burning with the fires of Orc" (plate 13; 105). Batty's lines resemble Blake's words, but significantly, Batty describes the angels as falling rather than rising, linking Batty and his fellow fallen angels to the Orc of *America*'s Preludium, who has "fall'n to give . . . life in regions of dark death." Given the purposeful misquotation of *America*, Alexis Harley has speculated about why "the poem's influence on *Blade Runner* is generally ignored." She claims that it "is a symptom of the way *Blade Runner* itself tends to be discussed either for its myth-making properties and its interest in metaphysical questions, or for its political critique and its pessimistic depiction of the futures of capitalism, scientism, and America." The failure to connect the two works in light of these critiques is, as Harley argues, ironic, since *Blade Runner* engages with *America* precisely because the poem's "political meaning is also mythic meaning, an exemplary precedent for their mingling" (62). Mythic associations in no way obscure the movie's political message, with its graphic critiques of the histories of US imperialism—including slavery—and environmental devastation.

*Blade Runner* reframes *America*'s visionary transatlantic revolution by expanding the frame of reference so that the realms of the heavens and earth are not divided and so that super-humans must interact with humans. The film dramatizes Blake's proverb "What is now proved was once only imagin'd" by depicting the world through the eyes of Batty, who has "seen things you people wouldn't believe" (36). This expanded context allows for the projection of the future of US empire, which now extends into outer space. In *Blade Runner*'s dystopia, instead of finding a society outside of the imperial mode, Americans have begun to colonize places off the map and have created a whole new race of colonized subjects for labor and entertainment. While *Blade Runner* paints a dismal picture of the future of the US, I disagree with Harley's assessment that "the world *Blade Runner* depicts is everything Blake would have abhorred, a Romantic dystopia" (74). True, the outlook remains dreadfully bleak, but through Batty's rebellion, the film inscribes the transformative struggle for revolution that Blake deemed vital for societies to thrive. Batty, designed with superior intelligence and strength, ultimately wants only one thing. As he tells Eldon Tyrell, the replicants' creator, "I want more life, father!" Defying the imperial system to further life "in regions of dark death," Batty ultimately proves himself to be an avatar of Blakean revolution.

"More Life" is the prophecy and final blessing that Tony Kushner's award-winning and critically acclaimed play *Angels in America* (1992) bestows upon the audience (*Perestroika* 146). Divided into two parts, *Millennium Approaches* and *Perestroika*, the play is set in New York and relies on the arrival of the Angel of America to jumpstart activism—the beginning of "The Great Work"—in much the same way as Albion's Angel incites "the fierce rushing of th' inhabitants together" in *America: A Prophecy*. Subtitled "A Gay Fantasia on National Themes," the play examines US politics of the late 1980s and questions what it means to be a US citizen in a time of discrimination based on sexual orientation and HIV status. The Angel singles out Prior Walter as a prophet, he thinks, because he is HIV-positive. Because he is immunocompromised, he appears to be susceptible to the Angel's message: "On you in you in your blood we have written: STASIS! The END" (*Perestroika* 46). Prior refuses to stop moving, to give up, to refuse life; he asserts that "I've got no resistance left. Except to run" (*Perestroika* 48). The Angel projects an apocalyptic end—"The slow dissolving of the Great Design, / The spiraling apart of the Work of Eternity, / The World and its beautiful particle logic / All collapsed. All dead forever . . . Oh who asks of the Orders Blessing / With Apocalypse Descending? / Who demands: More Life?" (*Perestroika* 132)—but Prior demands more life because he sees the necessity of undoing the "Great Design" and questioning the "particle logic." Throughout the play, Kushner uses the human body like Blake does in *America* as a representation of the social body, with all of its collective ills and threats to the health of its constitution. At the conclusion of *Perestroika*, before he gives the blessing, Prior maps an expanded conception of US citizenship onto the diseased body struggling for more life: "This disease will be the end of many of us, but not nearly all, and the dead will be commemorated and will struggle on with the living, and we are not going away. We won't die secret deaths anymore. The world only spins forward. We will be citizens. The time has come" (146).

When Kushner first staged *Angels in America*, the play created an uproar, but the response was overwhelmingly positive at a time when many more in the US were opposed to gay rights than are today. One might ask, as Deborah Geis and Steven Kruger have, "Why, among all the plays, novels, and poems written out of the current moment of gay and lesbian activism, and out of the experience of the AIDS crisis, has Kushner's work particularly struck a chord of response?" (3). One reason why is that this is truly an exceptional play. As John Lahr states, "Not since Williams has a playwright announced his poetic vision with such authority on the Broadway stage" (113). Another reason for the play's ability to open up discussions about homosexuality has to do with its ability to equate the gay rights movement with more (and better) life, and to contextualize that struggle in a long line of American revolutions using angel imagery. Kushner said in an interview that "I think the subtitle *A Gay Fantasia on National Themes* may be one of the most important things about the play, because it announces immediately that it has immense ambition. Of course it's pretentious, and of course it's grandiose, but that's part of the fun of it. It's reclaiming something American" (qtd. in Jonas 161). While the "something American" to which Kushner is referring is, on one level, grandiosity itself, it also represents the wrestling with angels that has come to define American revolution.

Through a line of antecedents, Kushner has associated the Angel of America in his play tangentially with Blake. When discussing the "mix-upedness of the angel," Kushner comments: "I like that she is so Luddite and so terrified by progress. I'd like to explore her. My great antecedent in that is James Merrill's *The Changing Light and Sandover* . . . it's a constantly opening series of doors into ever deeper and deeper chambers of the sublime. That's a fun, sort of Blakean thing" (qtd. in Kinzer, Richards, Galati, Bommer 209-10). Arguing that the Blakean connection is not all fun and games, Thomas Whitaker insists that "Prior's Angel is quite Blakean in ancestry": "When she says, 'I I I I am Your Released Female Essence Ascendant,' she is talking like one of Blake's fallen Emanations in *Jerusalem*. But the meaning of the angelic incursion, which remains in doubt throughout *Millennium Approaches*, is disclosed in *Perestroika* to be a call to stasis, to immobility, to the end of creative life—which is very much like the passivity that Blake considers angelic in *The Marriage of Heaven and Hell*, in which the angel's 'Reason' or 'Good' is at odds with the creative 'Energy' called 'Evil'" (272). While I agree with Whitaker's claims, I am less interested in establishing a genealogy that traces Kushner's Angel back to Blake than in describing the Blakean poetics of landscape in which the figure participates, one in which the angel represents American revolution.

In an article on *Angels in America*, David Savran has commented on the semblance of Kushner's angel to that of another famous writer, Walter Benjamin, and asks "What is the linkage between the two primary sources for the play's theory of history and utopia—Walter Benjamin and Mormonism? And what does this linkage suggest about the constitution of the nation?" (208). As an answer to the first of his questions, one might imagine this linkage culminating in the projection of the American Angel, who like Benjamin's angel of history, faces backward and wants to thwart the storm of progress, but who, like Mormonism, comes from the US, remains wedded to the geographical space, and believes in divine authority as written in the book. Responding to the second question, Kushner's Angel of America provides a bitter commentary about the ways in which US written laws and social codes—underlined by practices of discrimination—have deviated from the national constitution. In the play, Louis links these patterns of discrimination to those in Britain, but he suggests that the US, in its process of becoming a postcolonial nation, has "real hope of change" through political activism (*Millennium* 90-91). Kushner has admitted that he has a "dangerously romantic reading of American history," but he nonetheless claims that "there is an advantage to not being burdened by history the way Europe is. . . . Movements that capture the imagination of people [in the US] are movements that deny racism and exclusion. The country is too mongrel to do otherwise" (qtd. in Szentgyörgyi 16-17). What the US's melting pot—"prisoners and criminals and religiously persecuted and the oppressed and the slaves"—gives rise to is "a radical possibility in this country that's unique" (qtd. in Szentgyörgyi 17). As dramatized in *Angels in America*, the concomitant mapping of angels and revolution within the national imaginary represents the struggle to tap into this radical potential.

Ron Scapp writes that "*Angels in America* is an attempt to extend the political imagination of Americans through fantasy" (93). The same can be said for "To Guard and To Guide You" and *Blade Runner*, works that strike a chord because of their timely messages. As I write this epilogue, the US is at war, fighting terror within and without, and faces an economic recession under President Barack Obama, who offers visions of hope and change. At this crucial time, these revolutionary fantasies have a newfound relevance for US politics. And for the changing times, the forms of these works have also changed. All three have been reformulated and recirculated in the past decade. In addition to the "Final Cut" of *Blade Runner* being released in 2007 and more recent live recordings of Lift To Experience's "To Guard and To Guide You," in 2003 HBO produced a television production of *Angels in America* with a star-studded cast. At the time of its release, Gretchen Minton and Ray Schultz noted that "the irony of this movie's coming out now is that the US is not in an entirely different situation from the time that Kushner wrote and published his play . . . we have another Bush in the White House, another Iraq war, and a fear of terrorism that could potentially lead to McCarthy-like hunting of suspected criminals" (39). Despite the déjà vu, Terry McCabe poses a valid question in asking, "Does the enshrinement of Angels in a big-guns TV version spread the revolution, or certify that it's over?" But if imagination, as Mitchell claims, is a process, then the television adaptation will only expand its reach and involve more people in "The Great Work." And the stage productions of *Angels in America* retain their ability to bring the script to life in a unique performance every time the curtain rises.

At a time when "we've lost our way so profoundly, [when] we're in such a complete miasma, theoretically and politically," Kushner insists that we "have to reinvent ourselves" (qtd. in Szentgyörgyi 16; qtd. in Jones 28). This process of reinvention must involve transforming the national imagination of both the US as a country and its conception of citizenship. Kushner has convinced audiences to reconsider these modes of self-definition in part by invoking the Angel of America as a guard and a guide: "The spiritual has to be examined in a new way," Kushner claims, in order to shift political thinking (qtd. in Rose 49). With *Angels in America*, Kushner has succeeded in envisioning a new emanation of the American Angel who, in her insistence on stasis, keeps us moving forward. Part of the process of revelation involves the actual enacting of this national fantasy onstage "to hook into a great political energy" (qtd. in Rose 45):

> You're going to be left alone, and you can be in this kind of semitrance state with a bunch of other people who will be sharing a vision that you're watching. That's the deal. What we get to do, since you've agreed to come and pay your money and sit in the dark, is enact scenes of pity and terror that you really wouldn't want to be in the middle of in daily life. Because you're safe, you're willing to watch them. You'll control your anxieties. We're presenting them to you in metaphors, in aesthetic forms, in vessels that make them watchable. And then it's up to you to decide whether you forget the dream when you wake up or when the lights come up, or whether you remember it . . . I believe that everybody in a room together having the same experience creates something. It creates an energy. It creates a community. It creates a phenomenon that didn't exist before, and that in almost a mystical way creates good in the world, and it also empowers people and makes it more likely that they will act. (qtd. in Kinzer, Richards, Galati, and Bommer 207-08)

The theatrical medium, with its endless possibility for recreating a communally shared vision, serves as a particularly effective vehicle for transforming the Blakean poetics inscribed on plates with image and text for a contemporary US audience. Asked about his playwriting, Kushner maintains that "it is not an art of narrative and it's not an art of image. It's an art of dialectic. And it's an art of argument" (qtd. in Kinzer, Richards, Galati, and Bommer 210). Like Blake, Kushner landscapes a political argument onto the national imagination by producing art that surpasses both image and text, making an impression on the ways in which people conceive of themselves in relation to place. By enacting the resistance Blake prophesied in *America*, Kushner continues Blake's great work.

# Works Cited


Ashcroft, Bill, Gareth Griffiths, and Helen Tiffin, eds. *The Empire Writes Back: Theory and Practice in Post-Colonial Literatures*. New York: Routledge, 2002.

Atwood, Margaret. *Bodily Harm*. 1981. New York: Anchor, 1998.

Atwood, Margaret. *The Circle Game*. 1966. Toronto: House of Anansi, 1970.

Atwood, Margaret. "Death by Landscape." *Harper's* August 1990: 49-57.

Atwood, Margaret. *The Handmaid's Tale*. 1985. New York: Anchor, 1998.

Atwood, Margaret. *Negotiating with the Dead: A Writer on Writing*. Cambridge: Cambridge UP, 2002.

Atwood, Margaret. *Oryx and Crake*. 2003. New York: Anchor, 2004.

Atwood, Margaret. *Second Words*. Boston: Beacon, 1984.

Atwood, Margaret. *Surfacing*. New York: Bantam, 1972.

Atwood, Margaret. *Survival*. Toronto: House of Anansi, 1972.

Atwood, Margaret. *True Stories*. New York: Simon and Schuster, 1981.

Atwood, Margaret. "Writing Susanna." *Patsy Moore*. (2007): <http://www.patsy-moore.com/bohemians/ANatwood.pdf>.

Bahri, Deepika. *Native Intelligence: Aesthetics, Politics, and Postcolonial Literature*. Minneapolis: U of Minnesota P, 2003.

Bailey, Charles. "The Last Stage of the Hero's Evolution: Cormac McCarthy's *Cities of the Plain*." *Myth, Legend, Dust: Critical Responses to Cormac McCarthy*. Ed. Rick Wallach. Manchester: Manchester UP, 2000. 293-301.

Balkun, Mary McAleer. *The American Counterfeit: Authenticity and Identity in American Literature and Culture*. Tuscaloosa: U of Alabama P, 2006.

Barrett, Laura. "From Wonderland to Wasteland: *The Wonderful Wizard of Oz, The Great Gatsby*, and the New American Fairy Tale." *Papers on Language & Literature* 42.2 (2006): 150-80.

Bassnett, Susan, and Harish Trivedi, eds. *Post-Colonial Translation: Theory and Practice*. New York: Routledge, 1999.

Beer, John. "The Languages of *Kubla Khan*." *Coleridge's Imagination*. Ed. Richard Gravil, Lucy Newlyn, and Nicholas Roe. Cambridge: Cambridge UP, 1985. 218-62.

Beer, John. *Romanticism, Revolution and Language: The Fate of the Word from Samuel Johnson to George Eliot*. Cambridge: Cambridge UP, 2009. <http://dx.doi.org/10.1017/CBO9780511720055>.

Begley, Sharon. "What's in a Word?" *Newsweek* (20 July 2009): 31.

Bell, Vereen M. *The Achievement of Cormac McCarthy*. Baton Rouge: Louisiana State UP, 1988.

Berman, Ronald. "Fitzgerald's Intellectual Context." *A Historical Guide to F. Scott Fitzgerald*. Ed. Kirk Curnutt. Oxford: Oxford UP, 2004. 69-84.

Berman, Ronald. *The Great Gatsby and Fitzgerald's World of Ideas*. Tuscaloosa: U of Alabama P, 1997.

Berman, Ronald. *The Great Gatsby and Modern Times*. Chicago: U of Illinois P, 1994.

Berman, Ronald. *Wordsworth and the Enlightenment: Nature, Man and Society in the Experimental Poetry*. New Haven: Yale UP, 1989.

Bewell, Alan J. "The Political Implication of Keats's Classicist Aesthetics." *Studies in Romanticism* 25.2 (1986): 220-29. <http://dx.doi.org/10.2307/25600594>.

Bewley, Marius. "Scott Fitzgerald's Criticism of America." *Twentieth-Century Interpretations of The Great Gatsby*. Ed. Ernest Lockridge. Englewood Cliffs: Prentice-Hall, 1968. 37-53.

Bhabha, Homi. "DissemiNation: Time, Narrative, and the Margins of the Modern Nation." *Nation and Narration*. Ed. Homi Bhabha. New York: Routledge, 1990. 291-322.

Bhabha, Homi. "Representation and the Colonial Text: A Critical Exploration of Some Forms of Mimeticism." *The Theory of Reading*. Ed. Frank Gloversmith. New York: Barnes & Noble, 1984. 93-122.

Bicknell, John W. "The Waste Land of F. Scott Fitzgerald." *F. Scott Fitzgerald*. Ed. Kenneth Eble. New York: McGraw-Hill, 1973. 67-80.

*Blade Runner*. Dir. Ridley Scott. 1982. Hollywood: Warner Brothers, 2007.

Blake, William. *The Complete Poetry and Prose of William Blake*. Ed. David V. Erdman. Berkeley: U of California P, 1982.

Blake, William. *The Continental Prophecies*. Ed. D. W. Dörrbecker. London: Tate Gallery, 1995.

Bloom, Harold. "Afterthought." *F. Scott Fitzgerald*. Ed. Harold Bloom. New York: Chelsea House, 2006. 233-37.

Bloom, Harold. Introduction. *Blood Meridian, or, The Evening Redness in the West*. By Cormac McCarthy. 1985. New York: Modern Library, 2001. v-xiii.

Bloom, Harold. Introduction. *F. Scott Fitzgerald*. Ed. Harold Bloom. New York: Chelsea House, 2006. 1-5.

Bloom, Harold. Introduction. *F. Scott Fitzgerald's* The Great Gatsby. Ed. Harold Bloom. New York: Chelsea House, 1986. 1-4.

Bonetti, Kay. Interview with Jamaica Kincaid. *The Missouri Review* (1992-93): 124-32.

Booker, M. Keith, and Dubravka Juraga. *The Caribbean Novel in English*. Portsmouth: Heinemann, 2001.

Bouson, J. Brooks. *Brutal Choreographies: Oppositional Strategies and Narrative Design in the Novels of Margaret Atwood*. Amherst: U of Massachusetts P, 1993.

Bouson, J. Brooks. *Jamaica Kincaid: Writing Memory, Writing Back to the Mother*. Albany: State U of New York P, 2005.

Boxill, Anthony. "Wilson Harris's *Palace of the Peacock*: A New Dimension in West Indian Fiction." *College Language Association Journal* 14 (1971): 380-86.

Braziel, Jana Evans. *Caribbean Genesis: Jamaica Kincaid and the Writing of New Worlds*. Albany: State U of New York P, 2009.

Braziel, Jana Evans. "Caribbean Genesis: Language, Gardens, Worlds." *Caribbean Literature and the Environment: Between Nature and Culture*. Ed. Elizabeth DeLoughrey, Renée K. Gosson, and George B. Handley. Charlottesville: U of Virginia P, 2005. 110-26.

Braziel, Jana Evans. "Daffodils, Rhizomes, Migrations: Narrative Coming of Age in the Diasporic Writings of Edwidge Danticat and Jamaica Kincaid." *Meridians: Feminism, Race, Transnationalism* 3.2 (2003): 110-31.

Brownley, Martine Watson. *Deferrals of Domain: Contemporary Women Novelists and the State*. New York: St. Martin's, 2000.

Bruccoli, Matthew J. *Some Sort of Epic Grandeur: The Life of F. Scott Fitzgerald*. New York: Harcourt Brace Jovanovich, 1981.

Bruhn, Mark J. "Margaret Atwood's Lucy Poem: The Postmodern Art of Otherness in 'Death by Landscape.'" *European Romantic Review* 15.3 (2004): 449-61. <http://dx.doi.org/10.1080/1050958042000240352>.

Brydon, Diana. "Beyond Violent Dualities: Atwood in Postcolonial Contexts." *Teaching Atwood's* The Handmaid's Tale *and Other Works*. Ed. Sharon R. Wilson, Thomas B. Friedman, and Shannon Hengen. New York: Modern Language Association of America, 1996. 49-54.

Bryer, Jackson R. "F. Scott Fitzgerald, 1896-1940: A Brief Biography." *A Historical Guide to F. Scott Fitzgerald*. Ed. Kirk Curnutt. Oxford: Oxford UP, 2004. 21-46.

Burroughs, Catherine. "Keats's Lamian Legacy: Romance and the Performance of Gender in *The Beautiful and Damned*." *F. Scott Fitzgerald: New Perspectives*. Ed. Jackson R. Bryer, Alan Margolies, and Ruth Prigozy. Athens: U of Georgia P, 2000. 51-62.

Byron, George Gordon. *The Complete Poetical Works*. Ed. Jerome J. McGann. 7 vols. Oxford: Clarendon, 1980-1993.

Callahan, John F. "F. Scott Fitzgerald's Evolving American Dream: The 'Pursuit of Happiness' in *Gatsby, Tender Is the Night*, and *The Last Tycoon*." *F. Scott Fitzgerald*. Ed. Harold Bloom. New York: Chelsea House, 2006. 141-62.

Campbell, Neil. "Liberty Beyond its Proper Bounds: Cormac McCarthy's History of the West in *Blood Meridian*." *Myth, Legend, Dust: Critical Responses to Cormac McCarthy*. Ed. Rick Wallach. Manchester: Manchester UP, 2000. 217-26.

Casteel, Sarah Phillips. *Second Arrivals: Landscape and Belonging in Contemporary Writing of the Americas*. Charlottesville: U of Virginia P, 2007.

Césaire, Aimé. *Discourse on Colonialism*. 1955. Trans. Joan Pinkham. New York: Monthly Review, 2000.

Césaire, Aimé. *A Tempest*. 1969. Trans. Richard Miller. New York: TCG, 1992.

Chard, Leslie F. "Outward Forms and the Inner Life: Coleridge and Gatsby." *Fitzgerald/Hemingway Annual* (1973): 189-94.

Chick, Nancy. "The Broken Clock: Time, Identity, and Autobiography in Jamaica Kincaid's *Lucy*." *CLA Journal* 40.1 (1996): 90-103.

Christensen, Jerome. *Coleridge's Blessed Machine of Language*. Ithaca: Cornell UP, 1981.

Clark, Steve, and David Worrall. Introduction. *Blake, Nation and Empire*. Ed. Steve Clark and David Worrall. New York: Palgrave, 2006. 1-19.

Clubbe, John. *Byron, Sully, and the Power of Portraiture*. Burlington: Ashgate, 2005.

Clubbe, John. *Byron's Natural Man: Daniel Boone & Kentucky*. Lexington: King's Library, 1980.

Cochran, Peter. Introduction. *Lord Byron's Life in Italy*. By Teresa Guiccioli. Ed. Peter Cochran. Trans. Michael Rees. Newark: U of Delaware P, 2005. 1-51.

Coleridge, Samuel Taylor. *The Complete Poetical Works of Samuel Taylor Coleridge*. Ed. Ernest Hartley Coleridge. Oxford: Oxford UP, 1912.

Coleridge, Samuel Taylor. *The Major Works*. Ed. H. J. Jackson. Oxford: Oxford UP, 2000.

Conrad, Joseph. *Heart of Darkness*. 1902. Ed. Paul B. Armstrong. New York: Norton, 2005.

Cox, Jeffery N. "*Lamia*, *Isabella*, and *The Eve of St. Agnes*: Eros and 'Romance'." *The Cambridge Companion to Keats*. Ed. Susan J. Wolfson. Cambridge: Cambridge UP, 2001. 53-68. <http://dx.doi.org/10.1017/CCOL0521651263.004>.

Culler, Jonathan. *The Pursuit of Signs: Semiotics, Literature, Deconstruction*. Ithaca: Cornell UP, 1981.

Curnutt, Kirk. "Fitzgerald's Consumer World." *A Historical Guide to F. Scott Fitzgerald*. Ed. Kirk Curnutt. Oxford: Oxford UP, 2004. 85-128.

Curnutt, Kirk. Introduction. *A Historical Guide to F. Scott Fitzgerald*. Ed. Kirk Curnutt. Oxford: Oxford UP, 2004. 3-19.

D'Aguiar, Fred. "Interview with Wilson Harris." *Writing Across Worlds: Contemporary Writers Talk*. Ed. Susheila Nasta. New York: Routledge, 2004. 33-44.

Damrosch, David. "World Literature in a Postcolonial, Hypercanonical Age." *Comparative Literature in an Age of Globalization*. Ed. Haun Saussy. Baltimore: Johns Hopkins UP, 2006. 43-53.

Dash, J. Michael. *The Other America: Caribbean Literature in a New World Context*. Charlottesville: U of Virginia P, 1998.

Davidson, Arnold. "Making History in *The Handmaid's Tale*." *Margaret Atwood: Vision and Forms*. Ed. Kathryn VanSpanckeren and Jan Garden Castro. Carbondale: Southern Illinois UP, 1988. 113-21.

de Man, Paul. *The Rhetoric of Romanticism*. New York: Columbia UP, 1984.

*Dead Man*. Dir. Jim Jarmusch. West Palm Beach: 12 Gauge, 1995.

Deer, Glenn. "*The Handmaid's Tale*: Dystopia and Paradoxes of Power." *Margaret Atwood's The Handmaid's Tale*. Ed. Harold Bloom. Philadelphia: Chelsea House, 2001. 93-112.

Deloria, Philip J. *Playing Indian*. New Haven: Yale UP, 1998.

Dent, Shirley, and Jason Whittaker. *Radical Blake: Influence and Afterlife from 1827*. New York: Palgrave, 2002.

Dick, Philip K. *Do Androids Dream of Electric Sheep?* 1968. New York: Random House, 1996.

Dingly, R. J. "'I had a Dream . . .': Byron's Darkness." *Byron Journal* 9 (1981): 20-33.

Doherty, William E. "*Tender Is the Night* and the 'Ode to a Nightingale.'" *F. Scott Fitzgerald*. Ed. Kenneth Eble. New York: McGraw-Hill, 1973. 112-26.

Donaldson, Scott. "Possessions in *The Great Gatsby*." *Southern Review* 37.2 (2001): 187-210.

Dowd, Gregory Evans. *War under Heaven: Pontiac, the Indian Nations, & the British Empire*. Baltimore: Johns Hopkins UP, 2002.

Doyle, Jacqueline. "Developing Negatives: Jamaica Kincaid's *Lucy*." *The Immigrant Experience in North American Literature: Carving Out a Niche*. Ed. Katherine Payant and Toby Rose. Westport: Greenwood, 1999. 59-72.

Doyle, Laura. "The Racial Sublime." *Romanticism, Race, and Imperial Culture, 1780-1834*. Ed. Alan Richardson and Sonia Hofkosh. Bloomington: Indiana UP, 1996. 15-39.

Drake, Sandra. *Wilson Harris and the Modern Tradition: A New Architecture of the World*. New York: Greenwood, 1986.

Durrant, Sam. *Postcolonial Narrative and the Work of Mourning*. Albany: State U of New York P, 2004.

Dvorak, Marta. "'What is Real/Reel.' Margaret Atwood's 'Rearrangement of Shapes on a Flat Surface,' or Narrative as Collage." *Margaret Atwood's The Handmaid's Tale*. Ed. Harold Bloom. Philadelphia: Chelsea House, 2001. 141-53.

Eaton, Mark A. "Dis(re)membered Bodies: Cormac McCarty's Border Fiction." *Modern Fiction Studies* 49.1 (2003): 155-80. <http://dx.doi.org/10.1353/mfs.2003.0003>.

Eble, Kenneth. "The Craft of Revision: *The Great Gatsby*." *F. Scott Fitzgerald*. Ed. Kenneth Eble. New York: McGraw-Hill, 1973. 81-92.

Eble, Kenneth. "*The Great Gatsby* and the Great American Novel." *New Essays on The Great Gatsby*. Ed. Matthew J. Bruccoli. Cambridge: Cambridge UP, 1985. 79-100.

Edmondson, Belinda. *Making Men: Gender, Literary Authority, and Women's Writing in Caribbean Narrative*. Durham: Duke UP, 1999.

Eilenberg, Susan. "Voice and Ventriloquy in *The Rime of the Ancient Mariner*." *Coleridge, Keats, and Shelley*. Ed. Peter J. Kitson. London: Macmillan, 1996. 45-73.

Emery, Mary Lou. "Refiguring the Postcolonial Imagination: Tropes of Visuality in Writing by Rhys, Kincaid, and Cliff." *Tulsa Studies in Womens Literature* 16.2 (1997): 259-80. <http://dx.doi.org/10.2307/464362>.

Erdman, David V. "*America*: New Expanses." *Blake's Visionary Forms Dramatic*. Ed. David V. Erdman and John E. Grant. Princeton: Princeton UP, 1970. 92-114.

Erdman, David V. *Blake: Prophet Against Empire*. Princeton: Princeton UP, 1977.

Fanon, Frantz. *Black Skin, White Masks*. Trans. Charles Lam Markmann. New York: Grove, 1991.

Fanon, Frantz. *The Wretched of the Earth*. Trans. Constance Farrington. New York: Grove, 1963.

Faragher, John Mack. *Daniel Boone: The Life and Legend of an American Pioneer*. New York: Holt, 1992.

Feder, Helena. "Ecocriticism, New Historicism, and Romantic Apostrophe." *The Greening of Literary Scholarship: Literature, Theory, and the Environment*. Iowa City: U of Iowa P, 2002. 42-58.

Ferguson, Frances. *Wordsworth: Language as Counter-Spirit*. New Haven: Yale UP, 1977.

Ferguson, Moira. Interview with Jamaica Kincaid. "A Lot of Memory." *Kenyon Review* 16.1 (1994): 163-88.

Ferguson, Moira. *Jamaica Kincaid: Where the Land Meets the Body*. Charlottesville: U of Virginia P, 1994.

Ferguson, Moira. "*Lucy* and the Mark of the Colonizer." *Modern Fiction Studies* 39.2 (1993): 237-59. <http://dx.doi.org/10.1353/mfs.0.0804>.

Ferris, David. "Keats and the Aesthetics of Critical Knowledge; or, The Ideology of Studying Romanticism at the Present Time." *Lessons of Romanticism: A Critical Companion*. Ed. Thomas Pfau and Robert F. Gleckner. Durham: Duke UP, 1998. 103-25.

Fielder, Adrian V. "Historical Representation and the Scriptural Economy of Imperialism: Assia Djebar's *L'Amour, la fantasia* and Cormac McCarty's *Blood Meridian*." *Comparative Literature Studies* 37.1 (2000): 18-44. <http://dx.doi.org/10.1353/cls.2000.0002>.

Fitzgerald, F. Scott. *The Beautiful and Damned*. 1922. New York: Penguin, 1998.

Fitzgerald, F. Scott. *The Best Early Stories of F. Scott Fitzgerald*. Ed. Bryant Mangum. New York: Modern Library, 2005.

Fitzgerald, F. Scott. *The Crack-Up*. Ed. Edmund Wilson. New York: New Directions, 1945.

Fitzgerald, F. Scott. *F. Scott Fitzgerald's Ledger: A Facsimile*. Ed. Matthew J. Bruccoli. Washington: Bruccoli Clark/NCR, 1973.

Fitzgerald, F. Scott. *The Great Gatsby*. 1925. Ed. Matthew J. Bruccoli. Cambridge: Cambridge UP, 1991.

Fitzgerald, F. Scott. *A Life in Letters*. Ed. Matthew J. Bruccoli. New York: Scribner's, 1994.

Fitzgerald, F. Scott. *The Short Stories of F. Scott Fitzgerald*. Ed. Matthew J. Bruccoli. New York: Scribner's, 1989.

Fitzgerald, F. Scott. *Tender Is the Night*. 1933. New York: Scribner's, 1951.

Fitzgerald, F. Scott. *This Side of Paradise*. New York: Scribner's, 1920.

Fleming, Anne. *Byron the Maker: Liberty, Poetry and Love*. Sussex: Book Guild Publishing, 2009.

François, Irline. "The Daffodil Gap: Jamaica Kincaid's *Lucy*." *MaComère* 4 (2001): 84-100.

Freibert, Lucy M. "Control and Creativity: The Politics of Risk in Margaret Atwood's *The Handmaid's Tale*." *Critical Essays on Margaret Atwood*. Ed. Judith McCombs. Boston: G. K. Hall, 1988.

Fulford, Tim. *Coleridge's Figurative Language*. London: Macmillan, 1991.

Fulford, Tim, and Peter Kitson, eds. *Romanticism and Colonialism*. Cambridge: Cambridge UP, 1998. <http://dx.doi.org/10.1017/CBO9780511519017>.

Fussell, Edwin S. "Fitzgerald's Brave New World." *English Literary History* 19.4 (1952): 291-306. <http://dx.doi.org/10.2307/2871901>.

Gandhi, Leela. *Postcolonial Theory: A Critical Introduction*. New York: Columbia UP, 1998.

Garis, Leslie. "Through West Indian Eyes." *New York Times Magazine* (4 October 1990): 42.

Geis, Deborah R., and Steven F. Kruger. Introduction. *Approaching the Millennium: Essays on Angels in America*. Ed. Deborah R. Geis and Steven F. Kruger. Ann Arbor: U of Michigan P, 1997. 1-10.

Gilbert, Helen, and Joanne Tompkins. *Post-Colonial Drama: Theory, Practice, Politics*. New York: Routledge, 1996. <http://dx.doi.org/10.4324/9780203421062>.

Gilkes, Michael. Interview with Wilson Harris. "The Landscape of Dreams." *Wilson Harris: The Uncompromising Imagination*. Ed. Hena Maes-Jelinek. Sydney: Dangaroo, 1991. 31-38.

Gilkes, Michael, ed. *The Literate Imagination: Essays on the Novels of Wilson Harris*. London: Macmillan, 1989.

Gilkes, Michael. *Wilson Harris and the Caribbean Novel*. London: Longman, 1975.

Gillin, Edward. "Telling Truth Slant in the 'Crack-up' Essays." *F. Scott Fitzgerald Review* 1.1 (2002): 158-76. <http://dx.doi.org/10.1111/j.1755-6333.2002.tb00064.x>.

Glissant, Edouard. *Caribbean Discourse: Selected Essays*. Trans. J. Michael Dash. Charlottesville: U of Virginia P, 1989.

Glissant, Edouard. *Poetics of Relation*. Trans. Betsy Wing. Ann Arbor: U of Michigan P, 1997.

Goldstein, Laurence. *Ruins and Empire: The Evolution of a Theme in Augustan and Romantic Literature*. Pittsburgh: U of Pittsburgh P, 1977.

Goode, Mike. "Blakespotting." *Publications of the Modern Language Association of America* 121.3 (2006): 769-86. <http://dx.doi.org/10.1632/003081206X142878>.

Grace, Dominick M. "*The Handmaid's Tale*: 'Historical Notes' and Documentary Subversion." *Margaret Atwood's* The Handmaid's Tale. Ed. Harold Bloom. Philadelphia: Chelsea House, 2001. 155-66.

Graham, Peter W. *Lord Byron*. New York: Twayne Publishers, 1998.

Graham, Sheliah. *College of One*. New York: Viking, 1967.

Grosz, Elizabeth. *Volatile Bodies: Toward a Corporeal Feminism*. Bloomington: Indiana UP, 1994.

Grube, John. "*Tender Is the Night*: Keats and Scott Fitzgerald." *Dalhousie Review* 44 (1964): 433-41.

Hancock, Geoff. Interview with Margaret Atwood. "Tightrope-Walking over Niagara Falls." 1986. *Margaret Atwood: Conversations*. Ed. Earl G. Ingersoll. Princeton: Ontario Review, 1990. 191-220.

Harley, Alexis. "*America, A Prophecy*: When Blake Meets *Blade Runner*." *Sydney Studies in English* 31 (2005): 61-75.

Harris, Thomas. *Red Dragon*. 1981. New York: Random House, 2000.

Harris, Wilson. "An Autobiographical Essay." *Exploring the Palace of the Peacock: Essays on Wilson Harris*. Ed. Irving Adler. Kingston: U of the West Indies P, 2003. viii-xxxiv.

Harris, Wilson. "A Note on the Genesis of The Guyana Quartet." *The Guyana Quartet*. London: Faber and Faber, 1985. 7-14.

Harris, Wilson. *Palace of the Peacock*. 1960. London: Faber, 1985. *The Guyana Quartet*. London: Faber and Faber, 1985.

Harris, Wilson. *Selected Essays of Wilson Harris: The Unfinished Genesis of the Imagination*. Ed. A. J. M. Bundy. New York: Routledge, 1999.

Harris, Wilson. *Tradition the Writer and Society: Critical Essays*. London: New Beacon, 1967.

Hartman, Geoffrey H. *Wordsworth's Poetry 1787-1814*. New Haven: Yale UP, 1964.

Hatch, Ronald B. "Margaret Atwood, the Land, and Ecology." *Margaret Atwood: Works and Impact*. Ed. Reingard M. Nischik. Rochester: Camden House, 2000. 180-201.

Hickey, Alison. "Dark Characters, Native Grounds: Wordsworth's Imagination of Imperialism." *Romanticism, Race, and Imperial Culture, 1780-1834*. Ed. Alan Richardson and Sonia Hofkosh. Bloomington: Indiana UP, 1996. 283-310.

Hogsette, David S. "Margaret Atwood's Rhetorical Epilogue in *The Handmaid's Tale*: The Reader's Role in Empowering Offred's Speech Act." *Critique* 38.4 (1997): 262-78.

Holcomb, Gary E. "Travels of a Transnational Slut: Sexual Migration in Kincaid's *Lucy*." *Critique* 44.3 (2003): 295-312.

Holloway, David. "'A False Book is No Book at All': The Ideology of Representation in *Blood Meridian* and the Border Trilogy." *Myth, Legend, Dust: Critical Responses to Cormac McCarthy*. Ed. Rick Wallach. Manchester: Manchester UP, 2000. 185-200.

Huggan, Graham. "Anxieties of Influence: Conrad in the Caribbean." *Commonwealth Essays and Studies* 11.1 (1988): 1-12.

Hulme, Peter. "The Profit of Language: George Lamming and the Postcolonial Novel." *Recasting the World: Writing after Colonialism*. Ed. Jonathan White. Baltimore: Johns Hopkins UP, 1993. 120-36.

Hutchings, Kevin. "'The Nobleness of the Hunter's Deeds': British Romanticism, Christianity and Ojibwa Culture in George Copway's *Recollections of a Forest Life*." *Native Americans and Anglo-American Culture, 1750-1850*. Ed. Tim Fulford and Kevin Hutchings. Cambridge: Cambridge UP, 2009.

Ingersoll, Earl G. *Margaret Atwood: Conversations*. Princeton: Ontario Review, 1990.

Irvine, Lorna. "The Here and Now of *Bodily Harm*." *Margaret Atwood: Vision and Forms*. Ed. Kathryn VanSpanckeren and Jan Garden Castro. Carbondale: Southern Illinois UP, 1988. 85-100.

Jackson, Shona N. "Subjection and Resistance in the Transformation of Guyana's Mytho-Colonial Landscape." *Caribbean Literature and the Environment: Between Nature and Culture*. Ed. Elizabeth DeLoughrey, Renée K. Gosson, and George B. Handley. Charlottesville: U of Virginia P, 2005. 85-98.

James, David, and Philip Tew. "Introduction: Reenvisioning Pastoral." *New Versions of Pastoral: Post-Romantic, Modern, and Contemporary Responses to the Tradition*. Ed. David James and Philip Tew. Madison: Fairleigh Dickinson UP, 2009. 13-28.

Jarrett, Robert L. *Cormac McCarthy*. New York: Twayne Publishers, 1997.

Johnson, Barbara. *A World of Difference*. Baltimore: Johns Hopkins UP, 1987.

Jonas, Susan. "Tony Kushner's *Angels*." 1997. *Tony Kushner in Conversation*. Ed. Robert Vorlicky. Ann Arbor: U of Michigan P, 1998. 157-69.

Jones, Adam Mars. "Tony Kushner at the Royal National Theatre of Great Britain." 1992. *Tony Kushner in Conversation*. Ed. Robert Vorlicky. Ann Arbor: U of Michigan P, 1998. 18-29.

Jones, Alun R. *Wordsworth's Poems of 1807*. London: Macmillan, 1987.

Jones, Mark. *The Lucy Poems: A Case Study in Literary Knowledge*. Toronto: U of Toronto P, 1995.

Joseph, Betty. "Gendering Time in Globalization: The Belatedness of the Other Woman and Jamaica Kincaid's *Lucy*." *Tulsa Studies in Womens Literature* 21.1 (2002): 67-83. <http://dx.doi.org/10.2307/4149216>.

Kant, John. *Cormac McCarthy and the Myth of American Exceptionalism*. New York: Routledge, 2008.

Kauffman, Linda. "Special Delivery: Twenty-first Century Epistolary in *The Handmaid's Tale*." *Writing the Female Voice*. Ed. Elizabeth C. Goldsmith. Boston: Northeastern UP, 1989.

Kazin, Alfred. *F. Scott Fitzgerald: Man and His Work*. Cleveland: World Publishing, 1951.

Keane, Patrick J. *Coleridge's Submerged Politics*. Columbia: U of Missouri P, 1994.

Keats, John. *Complete Poems and Selected Letters of John Keats*. Ed. Edward Hirsch. New York: Random House, 2001.

Keats, John. *The Letters of John Keats*. Ed. Hyder Edward Rollins. Cambridge: Cambridge UP, 1958.

Kerber, Linda K. "Diversity and the Transformation of American Studies." *American Quarterly* 41.3 (1989): 415-31. <http://dx.doi.org/10.2307/2713148>.

Kim, Yoojin Grace. "'Then They All Move on Again': Knowledge and the Individual in Judge Holden's Doctrine of War." *Cormac McCarthy*. Ed. Harold Bloom. Philadelphia: Chelsea House, 2002. 169-82.

Kincaid, Jamaica. *Annie John*. 1983. New York: Farrar, Straus and Giroux, 1985.

Kincaid, Jamaica. *Lucy*. New York: Penguin, 1990.

Kinzer, Craig, Sandra Richards, Frank Galati, et al. "The Theater and the Barricades." 1995. *Tony Kushner in Conversation*. Ed. Robert Vorlicky. Ann Arbor: U of Michigan P, 1998. 188-216.

Kneale, J. Douglas. "Romantic Aversions: Apostrophe Reconsidered." *English Literary History* 58.1 (1991): 141-65. <http://dx.doi.org/10.2307/2873397>.

Kushner, Tony. *Angels in America: A Gay Fantasia on National Themes, Part 1: Millennium Approaches*. New York: TCG, 1992.

Kushner, Tony. *Angels in America: A Gay Fantasia on National Themes, Part 2: Perestroika*. New York: TCG, 1992.

Labbe, Jacqueline. *Romantic Visualities: Landscape, Gender and Romanticism*. New York: St. Martin's, 1998.

Lahr, John. "Earth Angels." *New Yorker* (13 December 1993): 133.

Ledent, Bénédicte. "Voyages into Otherness: Cambridge and Lucy." *Kunapipi* 14.2 (1992): 53-63.

Lee, Debbie. "Yellow Fever and the Slave Trade: Coleridge's *The Rime of the Ancient Mariner*." *English Literary History* 65.3 (1998): 675-700. <http://dx.doi.org/10.1353/elh.1998.0026>.

Levinson, Marjorie. *Keats's Life of Allegory: The Origins of a Style*. Oxford: Basil Blackwell, 1988.

"Lift To Experience." (2008): <http://www.bellaunion.com/artist.php?artcode=lifttoexperience>.

Limerick, Patricia Nelson. *The Legacy of Conquest: The Unbroken Past of the American West*. New York: Norton, 1987.

Lofaro, Michael A. *Daniel Boone: An American Life*. Lexington: UP of Kentucky, 2003.

Loftus, Margaret Frances. "John Keats in the Works of F. Scott Fitzgerald." *Kiyo: Studies in English Literature* 7 (1972): 17-26.

Lussier, Mark. "Blake Beyond Postmodernity." *Blake, Modernity and Popular Culture*. Ed. Steve Clark and Jason Whittaker. New York: Palgrave Macmillan, 2007. 151-62.

Lyons, Bonnie. "Using Other People's Dreadful Childhoods." 1987. *Margaret Atwood: Conversations*. Ed. Earl G. Ingersoll. Princeton: Ontario Review, 1990. 221-33.

Mackey, Eva. "'Death by Landscape': Race, Nature, and Gender in Canadian Nationalist Mythology." *Canadian Women's Studies* 20.2 (2000): 125-30.

Macovski, Michael. *Dialogue and Literature: Apostrophe. Auditors, and the Collapse of Romantic Discourse*. Oxford: Oxford UP, 1994.

Makdisi, Saree. *Romantic Imperialism: Universal Empire and the Culture of Modernity*. Cambridge: Cambridge UP, 1998. <http://dx.doi.org/10.1017/CBO9780511549779>.

Makdisi, Saree. *William Blake and the Impossible History of the 1790s*. Chicago: U of Chicago P, 2003.

Masters, Joshua J. "'Witness to the Uttermost Edge of the World': Judge Holden's Textual Enterprise in Cormac McCarty's *Blood Meridian*." *Critique* 40.1 (1998): 25-37.

McCabe, Terry. "'Angels' in Our Midst." *Chronicle of Higher Education* 50.15 (2003): B17-B19.

McCall, Dan. "'The Self-Same Song That Found a Path': Keats and *The Great Gatsby*." *American Literature* 42.4 (1971): 521-30. <http://dx.doi.org/10.2307/2924723>.

McCarthy, Cormac. *All the Pretty Horses*. 1992. New York: Vintage, 1993.

McCarthy, Cormac. *Blood Meridian, or, The Evening Redness in the West*. 1985. New York: Modern Library, 2001.

McCarthy, Cormac. *Cities of the Plain*. New York: Random House, 1998.

McCarthy, Cormac. *The Crossing*. New York: Random House, 1994.

McCarthy, Mary. "Breeders, Wives and Unwomen." Rev. of *The Handmaid's Tale*, by Margaret Atwood. *New York Times Book Review* 9 February 1986: 1.

McClintock, Anne. *Imperial Leather: Race, Gender and Sexuality in the Colonial Contest*. New York: Routledge, 1995.

McFarland, Thomas. *The Masks of Keats: The Endeavor of a Poet*. Oxford: Oxford UP, 2000. <http://dx.doi.org/10.1093/acprof:oso/9780198186458.001.0001>.

McGann, Jerome. "The Meaning of *The Ancient Mariner*." *Critical Inquiry* 8.1 (1981): 35-67. <http://dx.doi.org/10.1086/448139>.

McKusick, James. "Coleridge and the Economy of Nature." *Studies in Romanticism* 35.3 (1996): 375-92. <http://dx.doi.org/10.2307/25601180>.

McKusick, James. *Coleridge's Philosophy of Language*. New Haven: Yale UP, 1986.

McWatt, Mark. "The Madonna/Whore: Womb of Possibilities." *The Literate Imagination: Essays on the Novels of Wilson Harris*. Ed. Michael Gilkes. London: Macmillan, 1989. 31-44.

Mellor, Anne K. *English Romantic Irony*. Cambridge: Harvard UP, 1980.

Meredith, James H. "Fitzgerald and War." *A Historical Guide to F. Scott Fitzgerald*. Ed. Kirk Curnutt. Oxford: Oxford UP, 2004. 163-213.

Michael, Magali Cornier. "Freedom Reconsidered: Atwood's *The Handmaid's Tale.*" *Women in Literature: Reading Through the Lens of Gender*. Ed. Jerilyn Fisher and Ellen S. Silber. Westport: Greenwood, 2003. 134-36.

Middeke, Martin, and Werner Huber, eds. *Biofictions: The Rewriting of Romantic Lives in Contemporary Fiction and Drama*. Rochester: Camden House, 1999.

Miller, James E., Jr. "Boats Against the Current." *Twentieth-Century Interpretations of The Great Gatsby*. Ed. Ernest Lockridge. Englewood Cliffs: Prentice-Hall, 1968. 19-36.

Miller, Perry. *Errand into the Wilderness*. Cambridge: Harvard UP, 1956.

Miller, Perry. *Nature's Nation*. Cambridge: Harvard UP, 1967.

Minton, Gretchen E., and Ray Schultz. "*Angels in America*: Adapting to a New Medium in a New Millennium." *American Drama* 15.1 (2006): 17-42.

Mitchell, W. J. T. "Blake's Composite Art." *Blake's Visionary Forms Dramatic*. Ed. David V. Erdman and John E. Grant. Princeton: Princeton UP, 1970. 57-81.

Mitchell, W. J. T. "Dangerous Blake." *Studies in Romanticism* 21.3 (1982): 410-16. <http://dx.doi.org/10.2307/25600370>.

Mitchell, W. J. T. *Landscape and Power*. Chicago: U of Chicago P, 1994.

Mizener, Arthur. "Scott Fitzgerald in the 1920s." *F. Scott Fitzgerald*. Ed. Kenneth Eble. New York: McGraw-Hill, 1973. 99-111.

Mogen, David, Mark Busby, and Paul Bryant, eds. *The Frontier Experience and the American Dream*. College Station: Texas A&M UP, 1989.

Monk, Nick. "'An Impulse to Action, an Undefined Want': Modernity, Flight, and Crisis in the Border Trilogy and *Blood Meridian*." *Sacred Violence: Cormac McCarthy's Western Novels*. Ed. Wade Hall and Rick Wallach. El Paso: Texas Western UP, 2002. 83-104.

Monteiro, George. "James Gatz and John Keats." *Fitzgerald/Hemingway Annual* (1972): 291-94.

Morgan, Robert. *Boone: A Biography*. Chapel Hill: Algonquin Books, 2007.

Morrison, Toni. *Playing in the Dark: Whiteness and the Literary Imagination*. Cambridge: Harvard UP, 1992.

Morsberger, Robert E. "The Romantic Ancestry of *The Great Gatsby*." *Fitzgerald/ Hemingway Annual* (1973): 119-30.

Morton, Timothy. *The Poetics of Spice: Romantic Consumerism and the Exotic*. Cambridge: Cambridge UP, 2000.

Moyer, Kermit W. "*The Great Gatsby:* Fitzgerald's Meditation on American History." *Fitzgerald/Hemingway Annual* (1972): 43-58.

Moyer, Matthew. "Lift To Experience: *The Texas-Jerusalem Crossroads*." *Ink19* (November 2002): <http://www.ink19.com/issues/november2002/musicReviews/musicL/liftToExperience.html>.

Niesen de Abruna, Laura. "Family Connections: Mother and Mother Country in the Fiction of Jean Rhys and Jamaica Kincaid." *Jamaica Kincaid*. Ed. Harold Bloom. Philadelphia: Chelsea House, 1998. 13-36.

Nischik, Reingard M. "Margaret Atwood's Short Stories and Shorter Fictions." *The Cambridge Companion to Margaret Atwood*. Ed. Coral Ann Howells. New York: Cambridge UP, 2006. 145-60. <http://dx.doi.org/10.1017/ CCOL0521839661.011>.

O'Brian, John, and Peter White. Introduction. *Beyond Wilderness: The Group of Seven, Canadian Identity and Contemporary Art*. Ed. John O'Brian and Peter White. Montréal: McGill-Queen's UP, 2007. 3-10.

O'Callaghan, Evelyn. *Woman Version: Theoretical Approaches to West Indian Fiction by Women*. London: Macmillan, 1993.

Oczkowicz, Edyta. "Jamaica Kincaid's *Lucy*: Cultural 'Translation' As a Case of Creative Exploration of the Past." *MELUS: The Society for the Study of the Multi-Ethnic Literature of the United States* 21.3 (1996): 143-57.

Ornstein, Robert. "Scott Fitzgerald's Fable of East and West." *F. Scott Fitzgerald*. Ed. Kenneth Eble. New York: McGraw-Hill, 1973. 60-66.

Owens, Barcley. *Cormac McCarthy's Western Novels*. Tucson: U of Arizona P, 2000.

Page, Judith W. *Wordsworth and the Cultivation of Women*. Berkeley: U of California P, 1994.

Paravisini-Gerbert, Lizabeth. *Jamaica Kincaid: A Critical Companion*. Westport: Greenwood, 1999.

Parkes, Adam. "History, Bloodshed, and the Spectacle of American Identity in *Blood Meridian*." *Cormac McCarthy: New Directions*. Ed. James D. Lilley. Albuquerque: U of New Mexico P, 2002. 103-24.

Pearson, Josh T., Andy Young, and Josh Browning. "To Guard and To Guide You." *The Texas-Jerusalem Crossroads*. London: Bella Union, 2001.

Pease, Donald E., and Robyn Wiegman, eds. *The Futures of American Studies*. Durham: Duke UP, 2002.

Perry, Donna. "Interview with Jamaica Kincaid." *Reading Black, Reading Feminist: A Critical Anthology*. Ed. Henry Louis Gates, Jr. New York: Penguin Books, 1990. 492-509.

Pfau, Thomas. *Romantic Moods: Paranoia, Trauma, and Melancholy, 1790-1840*. Baltimore: Johns Hopkins UP, 2005.

Phillips, Larry W, ed. *F. Scott Fitzgerald on Writing*. New York: Scribner's, 1985.

Piper, Henry Dan. *F. Scott Fitzgerald: A Critical Portrait*. New York: Holt, Rinehart and Winston, 1965.

Posnock, Ross. "'A New World, Material Without Being Real': Fitzgerald's Critique of Capitalism in *The Great Gatsby*." *Critical Essays on F. Scott Fitzgerald's The Great Gatsby*. Ed. Scott Donaldson. New York: G. K. Hall, 1984. 201-13.

Prentice, Christine. "Out of the Pre-texts of Imperialism into 'a Future They Must Learn': Decolonizing the Allegorical Subject." *ARIEL: A Review of International English Literature* 31.1 (2000): 203-29.

Pyle, Forest. *The Ideology of Imagination: Subject and Society in the Discourse of Romanticism*. Stanford: Stanford UP, 1995.

Rajan, Tilottama. *Dark Interpreter: The Discourse of Romanticism*. Ithaca: Cornell UP, 1980.

*Red Dragon*. Dir. Brett Ratner. Universal City: Universal Studios, 2002.

Redfield, Marc. *The Politics of Aesthetics: Nationalism, Gender, Romanticism*. Stanford: Stanford UP, 2003.

"The Return of Lift To Experience Mainman Josh Pearson." (20 February 2008): <http://www.bellaunion.com/news.php?news_id=20051019185944934>.

Richardson, Alan, and Sonia Hofkosh, eds. *Romanticism, Race, and Imperial Culture, 1780-1834*. Bloomington: Indiana UP, 1996.

Richey, William. "'The Lion & Wolf Shall Cease': Blake's *America* as a Critique of Counter-Revolutionary Violence." *Blake, Politics, and History*. Ed. Jackie DiSalvo, G. A. Rosso, and Christopher Z. Hobson. New York: Garland, 1998. 196-211.

Robinson, Charles E. "The Influence of Byron's Death on America." *Byron Journal* 5.1 (1977): 50-63, 66. <http://dx.doi.org/10.3828/BJ.1977.6>.

Roe, Nicholas. *John Keats and the Culture of Dissent*. Oxford: Clarendon P, 1997. <http://dx.doi.org/10.1093/acprof:oso/9780198186298.001.0001>.

Rose, Charlie. "Tony, Tonys, and Television." 1993. *Tony Kushner in Conversation*. Ed. Robert Vorlicky. Ann Arbor: U of Michigan P, 1998. 44-50.

Rose, Gillian. *Feminism and Geography: The Limits of Geographical Knowledge*. Minneapolis: U of Minnesota P, 1981.

Ross, Marlon B. *The Contours of Masculine Desire: Romanticism and the Rise of Women's Poetry*. Oxford: Oxford UP, 1989.

Ross, Marlon B. "Naturalizing Gender: Woman's Place in Wordsworth's Ideological Landscape." *English Literary History* 53.2 (1986): 391-410. <http://dx.doi.org/10.2307/2873262>.

Roth, Verena Bühler. *Wilderness and the Natural Environment: Margaret Atwood's Recycling of a Canadian Theme*. Germany: Müller+Bass, 1998.

Rothstein, Mervyn. "No Balm for in Gilead for Margaret Atwood." *New York Times* (17 February 1986): C11.

Roulston, Robert. "Something Borrowed, Something New: A Discussion of Literary Influences on *The Great Gatsby*." *Critical Essays on F. Scott Fitzgerald's The Great Gatsby*. Ed. Scott Donaldson. New York: G. K. Hall, 1984. 54-66.

Roulston, Robert, and Helen H. Roulston. *The Winding Road to West Egg: The Artistic Development of F. Scott Fitzgerald*. Lewisburg: Bucknell UP, 1995.

Rowell, Charles H. "Interview with Wilson Harris." *Callaloo* 18.1 (1995): 192-200. <http://dx.doi.org/10.1353/cal.1995.0015>.

Rubenstein, Roberta. "Nature and Nurture in Dystopia: *The Handmaid's Tale*." *Margaret Atwood's* The Handmaid's Tale. Ed. Harold Bloom. Philadelphia: Chelsea House, 2001. 11-20.

Said, Edward W. *Culture and Imperialism*. New York: Vintage, 1993.

Salisbury, Neal. *Manitou and Providence: Indians, Europeans, and the Making of New England, 1500-1643*. Oxford: Oxford UP, 1982.

Salomon, Roger B. *Desperate Storytelling: Post-Romantic Elaborations of the Mock-Heroic Mode*. Athens: U of Georgia P, 1987.

Savran, David. "Ambivalence, Utopia, and a Queer Sort of Materialism: How *Angels in America* Reconstructs the Nation." *Theatre Journal* 47.2 (1995): 207-27. <http://dx.doi.org/10.2307/3208484>.

Scapp, Ron. "The Vehicle of Democracy: Fantasies toward a (Queer) Nation." *Approaching the Millennium: Essays on Angels in America*. Ed. Deborah R. Geis and Steven F. Kruger. Ann Arbor: U of Michigan P, 1997. 90-100.

Schaub, Danielle. "'I Am a Place': Internalised Landscape and Female Subjectivity in Margaret Atwood's *Surfacing*." *Mapping Canadian Cultural Space: Essays on Canadian Literature*. Ed. Danielle Schaub. Jerusalem: Hebrew UP, 2000. 83-103.

Scherr, Barry. "Lawrence, Keats and *Tender Is the Night*: Loss of Self and 'Love Battle' Motifs." *Recovering Literature* 14 (1986): 7-17.

Sepich, John. *Notes on* Blood Meridian. Louisville: Bellarmine College Press, 1993.

Shaviro, Steven. "'The Very Life of the Darkness': A Reading of *Blood Meridian*." *Perspectives on Cormac McCarthy*. Ed. Edwin T. Arnold and Dianne C. Luce. Jackson: U of Mississippi P, 2001.

Shaw, Gregory. "The Novelist as Shaman: Art and Dialectic in the Work of Wilson Harris." *The Literate Imagination: Essays on the Novels of Wilson Harris*. Ed. Michael Gilkes. London: Macmillan, 1989. 141-51.

Shaw, Gregory. "Wilson Harris's Metamorphoses: Animal and Vegetable Masks in *Palace of the Peacock*." *Callaloo* 18.1 (1995): 158-70. <http://dx.doi.org/10.1353/cal.1995.0017>.

Simmons, Diane. *Jamaica Kincaid*. New York: Twayne, 1994.

Slotkin, Richard. *The Fatal Environment: The Myth of the Frontier in the Age of Industrialization 1800-1890*. New York: Atheneum, 1985.

Slotkin, Richard. *Gunfighter Nation: The Myth of the Frontier in Twentieth-Century America. 1992*. Norman: U of Oklahoma P, 1998.

Slotkin, Richard. *Regeneration Through Violence: The Mythology of the American Frontier, 1600-1860*. 1973. New York: HarperCollins, 1996.

Smith, Henry Nash. *Virgin Land: The American West as Symbol and Myth*. 1950. Cambridge: Harvard UP, 1970.

Smith, Ian. "Misusing Canonical Intertexts: Jamaica Kincaid, Wordsworth and Colonialism's 'Absent Things.'" *Callaloo* 25.3 (2002): 801-20. <http://dx.doi.org/10.1353/cal.2002.0143>.

Spivak, Gayarti Chakravorty. "Sex and History in *The Prelude* (1805): Books Nine to Thirteen." *Texas Studies in Literature and Language* 23.3 (1981): 324-60.

Spivak, Gayarti Chakravorty. "Three Women's Texts and a Critique of Imperialism." *The Feminist Reader*. Ed. Catherine Belsey and Jane Moore. London: Macmillan, 1989. 148-63.

Stabb, Mark. "Canadian Authors Support Ontario Wetland Conservation." *Birdscapes* 3 (2003): <http://library.fws.gov/Birdscapes/win03/Partner.html>.

Staels, Hilde. "Margaret Atwood's *The Handmaid's Tale*: Resistance Through Narrating." *English Studies* 76.5 (1995): 455-67. <http://dx.doi.org/10.1080/00138389508598988>.

Stevenson, W. H. "The Shaping of Blake's 'America.'" *Modern Language Review* 55.4 (1960): 497-503. <http://dx.doi.org/10.2307/3721373>.

Stillinger, Jack. *Romantic Complexity: Keats, Coleridge, and Wordsworth*. Urbana: U of Illinois P, 2006.

Stoppard, Tom. *Arcadia*. London: Faber & Faber, 1993.

Stowe, Harriet Beecher. *Uncle Tom's Cabin*. 1852. Ed. Elizabeth Ammons. New York: Norton, 1993.

Sugg, Katherine. "'I Would Rather Be Dead': Nostalgia and Narrative in Jamaica Kincaid's *Lucy*." *Narrative* 10.2 (2002): 156-73. <http://dx.doi.org/10.1353/nar.2002.0015>.

Szentgyörgyi, Tom. "Look Back—and Forward—in Anger." 1991. *Tony Kushner in Conversation*. Ed. Robert Vorlicky. Ann Arbor: U of Michigan P, 1998. 11-17.

Tiffin, Chris, and Alan Lawson. "Introduction: The Textuality of Empire." *De-Scribing Empire: Post-Colonialism and Textuality*. New York: Routledge, 1994. 1-11. <http://dx.doi.org/10.4324/9780203203682>.

Tiffin, Helen. "Cold Hearts and (Foreign) Tongues: Recitation and the Reclamation of the Female Body in the Works of Erna Brodber and Jamaica Kincaid." *Callaloo* 16.4 (1993): 909-21. <http://dx.doi.org/10.2307/2932217>.

Tiffin, Helen. "'Flowers of Evil,' Flowers of Empire: Roses and Daffodils in the Works of Jamaica Kincaid, Olive Senior, and Lorna Goodison." *SPAN: Journal of the South-Pacific Association of Commonwealth Literature* 46 (1998): 58-71.

Toliver, Victoria. "Vodun Iconography in Wilson Harris's *Palace of the Peacock*." *Callaloo* 18.1 (1995): 173-90. <http://dx.doi.org/10.1353/cal.1995.0018>.

Torres-Saillant, Silvio. *Caribbean Poetics: Toward and Aesthetic of West Indian Literature*. Cambridge: Cambridge UP, 1997.

Tötösy de Zepetnek, Steven. "From Comparative Literature Today toward Comparative Cultural Studies." *Comparative Literature and Comparative Cultural Studies*. Ed. Steven Tötösy de Zepetnek. West Lafayette: Purdue UP, 2003. 235-67.

Trilling, Lionel. *Beyond Culture: Essays on Literature and Learning*. New York: Harcourt Brace Jovanovich, 1965.

Trilling, Lionel. *The Liberal Imagination: Essays on Literature and Society*. New York: Viking, 1950.

Turnbull, Andrew. *Scott Fitzgerald*. New York: Scribner's, 1962.

Vorlicky, Robert, ed. *Tony Kushner in Conversation*. Ann Arbor: U of Michigan P, 1998.

Wagner, Joseph B. "Gatsby and John Keats: Another Version." *Fitzgerald/ Hemingway Annual* (1979): 91-98.

Wallach, Rick. "Three Dreams: The Bizarre Epilogue of *Cities of the Plain*." *Proceedings of the First European Conference on Cormac McCarthy*. Ed. David Holloway. Miami: The Cormac McCarthy Society, 1999.

Watson, Richard. *An Apology for the Bible*. Boston: Manning & Loring, 1796.

West, James L. "F. Scott Fitzgerald, Professional Author." *A Historical Guide to F. Scott Fitzgerald*. Ed. Kirk Curnutt. Oxford: Oxford UP, 2004. 49-68.

Whitaker, Thomas R. *Mirrors of Our Playing: Paradigms and Presences in Modern Drama*. Ann Arbor: U of Michigan P, 1999.

White, Deborah Elise. *Romantic Returns: Superstition, Imagination, History*. Stanford: Stanford UP, 2000.

Wilentz, Gay. "English is a Foreign Anguish: Caribbean Writers and the Disruption of the Colonial Canon." *Decolonizing Tradition: New Views of Twentieth-Century "British" Literary Canons*. Ed. Karen R. Lawrence. Chicago: U of Illinois P, 1992. 261-78.

Williams, Mark. "Containing Continents: The Moralized Landscapes of Conrad, Greene, White, and Harris." *Kunapipi* 7.1 (1985): 35-44.

Wilson, Lanford. *5th of July*. 1978. New York: Farrar & Straus, 1990.

Woodward, Richard B. "Cormac McCarthy's Venomous Fiction." *New York Times Magazine* (19 April 1992): 29.

Woolf, Virginia. *A Room of One's Own*. 1929. New York: Harvest, 1989.

Wordsworth, William. *The Fourteen-Book Prelude*. Ed. W. J. B. Owen. Ithaca: Cornell UP, 1985.

Wordsworth, William. *Lyrical Ballads, and Other Poems, 1797-1800*. Ed. James Butler and Karen Green. Ithaca: Cornell UP, 1992.

Wordsworth, William. *Poems, in Two Volumes, and Other Poems 1800-1807*. Ed. Jared Curtis. Ithaca: Cornell UP, 1983.

Wu, Duncan. "Keats and the 'Cockney School.'" *The Cambridge Companion to Keats*. Ed. Susan J. Wolfson. Cambridge: Cambridge UP, 2001. 37-52. <http://dx.doi.org/10.1017/CCOL0521651263.003>.

Zheng, Yi. *From Burke and Wordsworth to the Modern Sublime in Chinese Literature*. West Lafayette: Purdue UP, 2011.

# Index